Contents

KU-610-559

Section 3 – Issues

Foreword by Lord Laming

Life can never be equally fair to everyone. That simply makes it all the more important that we go on searching for new ways to help each individual young person to fulfil their potential. That is what being a good parent means. Helping each young person to feel valued, respected and optimistic about their future is the challenge to us all.

When the record of local authorities is examined against what would generally be expected of a 'good parent' the picture which emerges is at best unsatisfactory at worst wholly unacceptable. The trend has been for young people to leave care as early as possible with neither a plan nor an agreed system of support. The reality is that we expect the most in survival skills from the young people who have been given the least. But it does not have to be this way. This book sets out in clear terms many examples of good practice. As a result many young people are having a much better experience and, because of the vision and skills of those around them, their life chances are enhanced.

As we know most families have an enduring commitment to their children which is expressed in life long support. Parents may well avoid any hint of interfering but they remain available when things go wrong or life gets tough. A word of encouragement, a loving cuddle, a good meal can go a long way in restoring morale. Young people leaving care can so very easily miss out on these things and find themselves alone in the world. At times it is a cheerless and frightening place to be. Even young people from the most favoured backgrounds will be familiar with such a description. We can all experience dark days.

Young people leaving care often face the reality that they have to cope on their own. Sometimes the odds are stacked high against them. Many will have been brought up in an atmosphere devoid of ambition for them. Just getting by was good enough. But the good news is that this book tells a different story.

I feel greatly honoured to have been invited to contribute this foreword to such a heartening record of achievement: the messages are encouraging, stimulating and inspiring. They demonstrate what can be achieved by both vision and learning from experience both good and bad. Highlighted, in particular are benefits which flow when able staff listen carefully and humbly to the young people. There are wonderful examples of support staff doing things 'with' a young person rather than 'for' a valued fellow human being. Travelling on the journey together overcoming together the obstacles on the way, is different from following a rigid route determined by someone else.

This book bristles with ideas and, more than that, it demonstrates what is being achieved today in many places. There is no reason why this good practice should not be available for every young person leaving care. For each young person there should be their own set of achievable goals. This is not a sterile plan on paper but a dynamic process which affords a sense of purpose and a confidence in their ability and value. Each can be helped to see themselves not only as being unique and worthwhile but as important contributors to the wellbeing of the community. We all have a part to play in this. This is a book for us all. It will give each of us the opportunity to think again and to be reminded of the great responsibility we have when society takes on the care of other people's children. It gives me pleasure to commend this book most warmly and to congratulate each of its many contributors.

Lord Laming, 2002

Acknowledgements

First, and most importantly, I would like to thank the young people who have contributed to this book.

I would also like to especially thank all the authors of the chapters who have given their time, effort and dedication in producing their pieces of work.

I would also like to thank Gabrielle and Nicho, for their work on the measurement tool.

Ena Fry receives a special mention and thanks for her work as critical reader and also for her advice and enthusiasm without which this book might not have been achieved.

As always I would like to thank my husband for his help, support and love.

Note:

About the contributors

Amanda Allard is a Public Policy Officer for NCH. Amanda is actively attempting to influence public policy in favour of young people. Her specialist fields are leaving care, youth homelessness and young people's education, employment and training issues. In her role as Policy Officer and as Chair of the Action on Aftercare Consortium she played a key role in the lobbying for, and on, the Children (Leaving Care) Act 2000.

Rebecca Berkley is a lecturer in music education in the Graduate School of Research and Education at the University of Southampton. Her interest in the education of care leavers stems from her work with the university's widening participation in summer schools.

Bob Broad is Professor of Children and Families Research, Children and Families Research Unit, De Montfort University, Leicester. He was previously lecturer in social work studies at the London School of Economics and Political Science. His book *Young People Leaving Care* was published by Jessica Kingsley, in 1998.

James Cathcart is Head of Target Groups – In and Leaving Care for The Prince's Trust where he set up a national network of mentoring projects. He has been a residential carer, social worker, juvenile justice worker and manager of leaving care services as well as developing *Preparation For Adulthood* (NCB 1996). He is a member of the Action on After Care Consortium and advisor to A National Voice.

Linda Daniel works for Hounslow's leaving care team in the Education and Employment Office. Linda has held posts in the commercial, national health and education sectors. Her passion is the value of education for young people and levelling the playing field for the disadvantaged.

Sue Daniel is a specialist nurse for looked after children in Southampton City. She has extensive experience in working in paediatric nursing both in the acute sector and community. She has a special interest in promoting the health of adolescents.

Mark Ellis has worked as a careers adviser and a teacher and is currently the education and employment adviser in the Leaving Care Team in the London Borough of Hackney.

Carol Florris spent 18 years in the care system, mainly in residential care, some time in foster care and at a boarding school. She attended Cardiff University, where she studied for a Sociology degree then a masters degree in Women's Studies. She worked for 2½ years for Voices from Care, developing the organisation. Following this she worked as an advocate with the Children's Society, before returning to Voices from Care as Advice and Support Manager.

Ena Fry is the Development Worker at the Young People's Project for Fostering Networks (previously NFCA). She has a background that includes 30 years experience as a social work practitioner, working mainly with young people in a range of settings, including local authority leaving care services.

Cathy Glazier is a qualified social worker and has worked in social care for over 20 years. She has experience in residential work with young people and in fostering and adoption. Cathy manages the Throughcare Service at the Caldecott Foundation where she has worked for the past four years.

Martin Hazlehurst is the Assistant Director of First Key (The National Leaving Care Advisory Service) where he develops and manages the training, consultancy and project work. Previously he worked on leaving care projects in the voluntary sector. He has written widely and in 1998 published *Partners in Care* (*A guide to good practice in partnership work with young people leaving care*).

Catherine Hill is a consultant community paediatrician and designated doctor for looked after children in the Southampton area. She is also Senior Lecturer in Community Child Health at the University of Southampton and her academic interests lie within the field of social paediatrics. She is a member of the British Agencies for Adoption and Fostering Medical Advisory Group and editor of the medical notes within the *Journal of Adoption and Fostering*.

Ann Heelas is a staff grade paediatrician and Adoption and Fostering Medical Advisor to Southampton City Council. She has extensive experience in community child health both in this country and from working in Hong Kong.

Ciaran Kelly is a consultant child and adolescent psychiatrist. He works in a unique multi-agency service in Southampton with children and young people who are the most challenging to society (The Behaviour Resource Service: NHS Beacon Site). Ciaran has a special interest in systemic therapy, children with extreme needs and the development of inter-agency collaborative working.

Selam Kidane is a refugee children project consultant for BAAF. Previously she has worked for family service units doing outreach work with refugee families affected by mental health difficulties, and for the NSPCC as a family therapist in a family support project. She came to the UK seeking asylum as an unaccompanied child in the 1980s.

Julie Harris (formerly Knowles) spent eight years working in community outreach support and later, in aftercare service development, before joining First Key in 1998. Julie was part of a research partnership with the Centre for Disability Studies at the University of Leeds, resulting in the *Whatever Next?* report. She is particularly committed to the involvement of service users in collaborative research. Julie also has a specific interest in quality assurance in the voluntary sector.

Kathy McAuley is Head of Coram Leaving Care Services (CLCS). She has 25 years experience of developing, delivering and managing a wide range of innovative services for young people in and leaving care within the youth, community and social work sectors.

Polnacha O'Mairthini has been a foster carer and also worked for Fostering Networks (NFCA) on a young people's participation project. He is now working in the Orkney Islands managing a fostering, adoption and residential children's unit in tandem with a community based preventative family support service. He is a board member of the International Foster Care Organisation with an active role on the International Development Committee and Young People's Participation Group.

Keir Parsons has worked in a variety of residential settings in the Stockport area. He completed his DipSW in 1998 and moved to Rochdale as an after care worker. He is currently on secondment in Oldham as Regional Development worker for the North West After Care Consortium.

John Pinkerton is Head of the School of Social Work in Queen's University Belfast. He was principal investigator on a major government funded project into leaving care in Northern Ireland in the early 1990s and is Chair of First Key (NI), an NGO promoting the interests of care leavers.

Mark Priestley is Senior ESRC Research Fellow in the Centre for Disability Studies at the University of Leeds (UK) and administrator of the international e-mail discussion group disability-research @jiscmail.ac.uk. Mark is currently involved in a three-year programme of research on disability, social policy and the life course, examining the generational aspects of disability associated with childhood, youth, adulthood and old age.

Parveneh Rabiee is Research Fellow in the Social Policy Research Unit at the University of York. She is currently working on a project identifying priorities and perceptions of disabled children and young people and their families regarding outcomes of social care. She was formerly in the Centre for Disability Studies at the University of Leeds, where she completed work on the Whatever Next? project.

Peter Sandiford has been involved in public care services for many years – as a baby living in it, as a member of staff working in it, as a trainer, lecturer and development manager. He is currently Principal of Caldecott College and Deputy Director of the Caldecott Foundation.

Omri Shalom is currently working for First Key. He has, also, worked with other organisations such as the CROA and the NSPCC to improve young people's life chances in the care system. Omri's aim is to become a Children's Rights Officer.

John Short is a freelance trainer and consultant, specialising in leaving care. He has extensive experience of the social care field and has developed and run leaving care projects in both the statutory and voluntary sectors. John also set up and ran the Centrepoint Leaving Care Project.

Sue Smith is a registered nurse with family planning and teaching qualifications. In her role with looked after children and young people she works on an outreach project which aims to engage young people in effective sexual health education.

Mike Stein is professor of Social Work and joint director of the Social Work Research and Development Unit at the University of York. For the past 22 years he has been researching the problems and challenges faced by young people leaving care and the way services respond.

Moira Walker (formerly Borland) is Senior Research Fellow (Children and Young People) in the Social Work Research Centre, University of Stirling. Her research has primarily focused on services for looked after children. Previously she worked as a social worker with children and families.

Ann Wheal is in the Department of Social Work Studies, University of Southampton. Ann was a teacher in multi-racial inner city schools and colleges before joining the University in 1990. She has published widely in the child care field.

Nicola Wyld works for Voice for the Child in Care as legal and policy officer. She also works as an advocate and mediator.

Introduction

Mark Ellis

These are exciting times for those of us who work with care leavers. Recently there has been a raft of new ideas, projects and real improvements to the life chances of the young people we work with, set in motion by the Government's focus on improving services to children through the Quality Protects initiative and, more specifically, the changes in the law set out in The Children (Leaving Care) Act 2000. In addition, the Government has encouraged inter-agency working for the benefit of care leavers throughout local authority and governmental departments, and the voluntary sector. This book offers a fascinating series of snap shots of this new landscape, whilst also pointing the way towards further developments.

My job as education and employment advisor in the leaving care team of the London Borough of Hackney was created and funded through Quality Protects, and I am intensely proud of the eight care leavers who I and my colleagues in the leaving care team have seen through to university this academic year, and who are, to date, all still going strong.

There is nothing intrinsically remarkable about a care leaver going to university. The only thing that care leavers have in common is their care status, and as a group they include individuals of all abilities. Yet until recently a care leaver who went to university was regarded as something of a maverick – if not a headache for the services concerned. A pervasive culture of low expectations deprived many young people of their right to have their hopes and dreams taken seriously.

Now however, The Children (Leaving Care) Act 2000 makes it a duty to consult young people on how they want to be supported, and it is incumbent on the local authority to provide that support. There has been a sea change in the involvement of care leavers in planning for their future.

It makes sense for practitioners, policy makers and planners alike to listen to what care leavers have to say. Care leavers know better than anyone else the impact the services they come into contact with have on their lives. For this reason, writers throughout the book refer frequently to the views and experiences of young people.

The bulk of the book is divided into three sections. The first section of the book explores the context within which all young people approach adulthood in the UK today. The first chapter is entitled 'Risk, Opportunity and Leaving Care' and sets out to explore the current social and policy context. It then considers the implications for the youth population as a whole and for looked after young people in particular. Chapter 2 then takes us through the legislative framework for leaving care and Chapter 3 details the latest research on the subject. The concluding chapter in this section looks at 'Developing an International Perspective on Leaving Care'.

The second section concerns practice. The first three chapters in this section are around participation, advocacy, empowerment and complaints told both from a professional and young person's perspective. Chapter 8 gives some examples of support groups and Chapter 9 explains what it is like to leave care from 'out of area' placements, and what is being done to help this group of care leavers. Chapter 10 describes good practice in preventative work for those involved with young parents. Chapters 11 and 12 give examples of accommodation options for care leavers and include details of supported lodging schemes. Chapter 13 in this section discusses the work of the Prince's Trust Volunteer Mentoring Scheme.

The third section looks at other issues that affect care leavers. Asylum seeking and refugee children, health, mental health, disability, education, training and employment matters are all covered here. This section concludes with a chapter explaining the role of the Connexions Service.

Finally, the editor draws on the themes of the chapters to develop a way forward for leaving care services.

To introduce some of the themes of the book from a young person's perspective, I gathered together Deresha, Mohammed, Elizabeth and Chantal, four Hackney care leavers, and asked them to tell me about their experience of leaving care. Deresha is 17, studying hairdressing and IT at college. Elizabeth is the mother of a three-year-old daughter. She's 19, working towards an NVQ 2 in business administration. Mohammed and Chantal have both just started university. They are 19 and 21 respectively. All four of them live in their own flats. Their experience of growing up in care includes the experience of a young person who has grown up in an inner city area with all the attendant difficulties of racism, poverty, failing schools and a strong youth culture which actively discourages engagement with conventional means of achievement.

They are well aware of most people's expectations of someone who has been in care:

When they see you in college or university, they're shocked because in the environment we live in, people outside look at people in care like negative – you're going to mess up, you're going to have a no good life, no good job, you're going to end up homeless.

Mohammed.

People think that the reason why you're in care is because either you've got in trouble with the police or you've done something bad – you've killed someone, you've been in prison. It had to be that you was this rude child that no one could handle which leads to you being locked up in this little room or something. They just have this weird stereotype and it's really disgusting the way that some people look at you when you say, 'Oh yeah, I'm in care' ... You have to choose your friends very carefully. People only want to be your friend because you get money every week and your own flat.

Deresha.

Unsurprisingly, they are grateful for the support they have received from social services:

It's given me great opportunities. Before, I didn't have a clue what I wanted to do. Now I know what direction I'm going in. At home my parents didn't care what I did.

Elizabeth.

I don't think I would have got to this stage if I wasn't in care.

Chantal.

There's a lot more support than at home. There's many different people that you can go to get support and help from when you're in care.

Deresha.

If your family is on benefits, the support you're going to get (with your education) *when you are in care you won't get it out there because* (there's) *going to be a lot of problems: books and materials. Probably you might end up giving up your education and working.*

Mohammed.

They value the encouragement they have received and have much admiration for those who have really taken an interest in them:

I've had Simon (caseworker) *pushing me and I've wanted to do something other than sitting around just following other people. I've done quite well for myself. If I was just listening to negative people all the time I'd be thinking what the hell am I going to do but I've got you lot* (the leaving care team) *telling me all the time.*

Deresha.

I had you lot (the leaving care team) *saying, 'What are you doing, are you just happy like that?' That really makes you sit up and think, 'What am I doing for those people to be putting me down?' and then when you see people that you was in school with, even if it's just one or two people out of your year, and you hear they left university, and you haven't even got onto a course at college, you're thinking, 'I don't deserve this' – it makes you want to go out there.*

Elizabeth.

In particular, what they appreciate is the way that social workers engage them in taking responsibility for their future:

If you're in care ... there is a lot of talking and support and help and discussing about your future, what you want to be. You end up being in education. If you're not in care you could say no you don't want to go and nobody would support you, talk to you and maybe change your mind.

Mohammed.

Having you lot telling me, 'This is what I think you should do, if you want to do it it's totally up to you,' and putting one into the situation where you have to make a choice is really good because if I wasn't in a position like that I wouldn't be doing nothing.

Deresha.

It's more nagging when it's your parents – you want to do the opposite.

Chantal.

They contrast this with the way that certain other professionals have dealt with them:

I was sixteen; (my foster carer) *kicked me out the house and told me, 'Don't come back till you've got a job.' She didn't have the proper training or advice given to her. It just made me a stronger person.*

Deresha.

In the (mothers and babies) *unit, they didn't help you with getting a job or anything. All they talked to you about was getting you onto income support. That was it.*

Elizabeth.

Criticism of social workers is mainly due to institutional factors. First of all, they aren't always available:

Sometimes you phone up and you can't get them on the phone. I get really paranoid. I think they're trying to avoid me.

Elizabeth.

They come and go and there aren't enough of them:

You see one and they're gone in two months – they're always reshuffling staff.

Chantal.

They need to get more staff. They don't have time to look into your files.

Mohammed.

Their caseloads are too large:

They need to make a lot more time for each individual person.

Deresha.

And they have a myriad of claims on their time:

You've got to do things out of the ordinary for them to notice that things are affecting you in a certain way ... if not they won't do it because they got so much things to do and you're like the last priority on their list, you're not important.

Deresha.

Finally, it is a big step for a young person to let go the attention they have received from their caseworkers. There is ambivalence towards caseworkers who have been very supportive of them at first but are now spending more time with younger care leavers:

(Chantal's caseworker) *has been my caseworker for five years and the longer I've known him the less I've seen him ... He might think I'm capable but he should still at least come to my house to check up on me.*

Chantal.

But there is also understanding:

I thought, 'Why is it they're spending all this time on that (other) *person?' and I realised that (it was) because I'm more independent. Because they trust me, and the more they trust me, it makes me want to prove to do good so that they will trust me more. Sometimes we have to blame the workers but sometime we have to understand, to support the workers.*

Mohammed.

Managing one's caseworker is an essential skill of an effective care leaver:

Instead of getting them to read everybody's file, we need to tell them our problems. Some problems you have you might feel bad or ashamed about and you'd expect them to know by reading the file but I've found that if you nag them constantly, phone them constantly, you get more done.

Elizabeth.

The case for effective pathway planning was cogently put:

You have to let the young people know ... You must tell them what kind of support you're going to give them ... Some people don't do well because they don't know what they're entitled to ... If they know there is support, that will encourage them.

Mohammed.

Having a say in when and where you move into your own accommodation is important. (In Hackney care leavers are entitled to a council property. A young person can say what areas they would not like to live in, but they only get one offer from the housing department).

If I could have chosen I doubt it would be now because I've just got myself back on my feet. Having a flat takes up a lot of time and is a lot of money as well. I really don't need the responsibility now because I'm still a child myself and anything can happen when you're living by yourself. You just think, 'Well, I can do whatever', and a whole load of things come behind like babies and boyfriends.

Deresha.

I wouldn't have picked my flat now. I would have liked to go and live in a hall of residence to get that experience ... I don't want to lose it and come back and live in a hostel ... the way I've decorated it and spent money on it.

Mohammed.

The leaving care grant was helpful for decorating the flat, but Elizabeth expresses some dissatisfaction with the fact that it is not means tested:

They should look at the person's flat and their situation before they decide how much money to give – they shouldn't just have a set amount to give to people. I had to pay £700 on carpets alone and I had to buy all the baby stuff too.

Elizabeth.

The immediate neighbourhood is significant to a young person who has been in care. Given their suspicion of other people, feeling safe is of paramount importance. With few family ties, neighbours are important as they may take on the kind of role that a family might have done in emergencies:

I'm so lucky with my neighbours; they are always asking how I am and looking out for me.

Elizabeth.

I didn't know the area, I didn't do my research. I felt pressured to have the flat now. My neighbours – I'm in fear of my safety. I wish that I'd refused it. Young people shouldn't be pushed into a flat.

Chantal.

However, despite their concerns, they agree that one of the best things about leaving care is getting your own place within which you feel safe and have total control:

I need to have my independence – (the flat) is mine and I don't want nobody to invade my space.

Elizabeth.

It's great, you don't have no one to tell you what to do, what time to get home, you can turn over the TV when you want, you can eat when you want to, you can have people sleep over, you can smoke as much as you like, you can have a party everyday!

Elizabeth et al.

Of course, along with the flat comes the responsibility for rent, council tax and paying the TV licence. There is unanimity on this being the most difficult aspect of living independently.

The young people make several references to having become stronger as a result of the difficulties they have experienced in care and since leaving it. The ability to turn negative experiences into life-enhancing ones is fundamental to personal development, and this ability can be learnt from those around you:

Surrounding yourself with positive people, I learnt that years ago. The more positive people you surround yourself with, the more you'll get up and get ahead.

Chantal.

The four young people are aware that they have bucked the trend and have a real sense of their own self-development:

I think I'm special because I tried and finished college.

Mohammed.

I'm making something from life, because there's a lot of people out there that's just sitting down and watching TV all day.

Deresha.

I want to be someone, I want to make something of my life, I don't want to be the statistic of a single mother on benefits who's going nowhere with her life.

Elizabeth.

I've got 2 GCSEs and a pass in my GNVQ, but I got into university ... I've kept myself busy with volunteer work ... it's kept me motivated and wanting to do better things, it makes you want to achieve more.

Chantal.

The sign of a young person's effective transition to independence is that the young person has taken control of the process for themselves. It is vital that this takes place, as the involvement of the leaving care team in a young person's life will eventually cease and subsequent personal development becomes the responsibility of the young person. The central tenet of our work must be to engender in the young people we work with the ability to manage their own development throughout their life.

The young people are concerned that if younger people do not start to manage their own transition to adulthood from an early age, they become trapped in negative relationships:

They need to teach you about relationships when you are young. It's much harder to change your friends when you get older, negative people bring you down and you need positive people around you to bring you up.

Mohammed.

They are keen to be able to pass on their expertise:

You know that you can talk to somebody if you've been through the same thing. (Young people) have probably been put in care because of what the adults have done to them. They're going to have it in for adults anyway, they're not going to trust them, so I would have thought that the smartest thing to

do was to try and get a (care leaver) *to speak to* (them).

Elizabeth.

They forget about the older young people who've been in care. They don't get in contact with them. They should try and get the older young people involved in what (the younger ones are) *doing.*

Mohammed.

Deresha makes the point that even as a 17-year-old, she has plenty to offer:

What they should do is place an older person with a younger person and try and share experience. Some younger people that are younger than me, they don't have the faintest idea where to go next. I do volunteer work and when I go out I get classed as an older person but I'm the youngest out of the whole volunteer group, and in fact you're experienced, the amount of things that you've been through. When you've got an older person there to guide you and to talk to you, you learn a lot more.

Deresha.

Deresha is talking from experience: she has a mentor who has had a big impact on her life, and she is keen for others to have the same experience:

They need to find them someone older that can give them good advice and treat them sometimes, someone who they think cares about them a lot, and it doesn't matter what the circumstances are, you can call them and express your feelings to them and have personal one-to-one with them.

Deresha.

Perhaps we could call them personal advisors.

Lastly, Chantal is concerned for those who don't manage their transition to independence as well or as smoothly as she has done. Her concern begs the question of whether the entitlement to a service that stops at 21 for everyone who is not in full time education is really good enough:

They'll get to like twenty-four and feel, 'What have I done with my life?' and come to (the) *leaving care* (service) *and it will be too late and that'd be awful.*

Chantal.

It is a tribute to the strength of the human spirit that a child who has endured great loss, abuse or neglect can successfully make the transition to adulthood. We are so familiar with the statistics that indicate that many care leavers struggle to achieve stability and a measure of fulfilment in their lives that we sometimes fail to sufficiently acknowledge those young people who have succeeded against all the odds.

I would like to acknowledge Deresha, Mohammed, Elizabeth and Chantal's achievements so far, and I look forward to what they are going to achieve in the future.

Section 1 – The Wider Context

1. Risk, Opportunity and Leaving Care

Moira Walker

Introduction

A quick survey of current UK social policy might give the impression that these were relatively propitious times for young people leaving foster or residential care in their late teens. Over the last decade legislation in each of the UK's jurisdictions has extended local authorities' duties towards young people who have been looked after, both in terms of scope and the age to which they are entitled to additional support. To this end a wide range of services and initiatives have been developed within the statutory and voluntary sectors. In addition, throughout the time they are accommodated, local authorities are required to focus on preparing young people for leaving. The introduction of the *Looking After Children* (LAC) materials constitutes a means through which appropriate plans can be developed and their effectiveness monitored. Particular attention has been paid to improving young people's educational performance, with joint guidance issued to departments of education and social work and minimum targets set for achievement at Standard Grade GCSE level. Their inclusion as a target group for the government's Social Exclusion Unit is further evidence that improving care leavers' life opportunities is now on the political agenda.

Yet, despite some excellent work within leaving care schemes, young people still face an uphill struggle to secure a job, decent housing and develop the relationships which will provide all important social support. Consequently they continue to be under represented among the prosperous and over-represented among young people on society's margins, for example those who are homeless or in prison (Broad, 1998; Stein, 2000). The impact of the Children (Leaving Care) Act, 2000 has yet to be tested.

The gap between policy objectives and young people's experiences can be attributed, at least in part, to insufficient funding for leaving care services (Broad, 1998; Stein, 2000). However, it is also acknowledged that the transition to adult life has become more of a challenge for all young people, as changes in economic conditions have made it more difficult to find secure employment and social welfare policies have reduced access to financial independence and housing. It has been argued that this creates new risks for young people, inevitably impacting more adversely on those with least social or financial support (Furlong and Cartmel, 1997; Jones, 2000).

This chapter sets out to explore the social and policy context in which young people approach adulthood in the UK today, then considers the implications both for the youth population as a whole and for those who have been looked after in residential or foster care. Risk is identified as a key concept which permeates young people's lives, welfare policy and current social work provision. Acknowledging that social work's key role in relation to looked after children is to minimise the effects of adversity and foster opportunity, the chapter concludes that this requires sustained, multi-faceted and skilled support which a predominantly risk focused social work system is not necessarily equipped to provide.

Risk

Whilst there is broad agreement that preoccupation with 'risk' has come to permeate modern life, the term itself can be understood in a variety of ways. Early uses of the word risk referred to the mathematically calculated likelihood of a positive or negative event occurring, but it is now generally unquantified and almost synonymous with the term 'danger'. Douglas argues that the term 'risk' has come to replace the concept of danger, partly because it sounds more 'scientific'. Its forensic resonance is well suited to a society which wishes to call to account the organisations and institutions blamed for creating dangers or at least being remiss in preventing them (Douglas, 1992). In everyday usage risk is assumed to be amenable to assessment, management and control.

While some academic perspectives accord with this view of risk as an objective reality waiting to be identified, other see it as a 'way of thinking' (Parton, 1996). Lupton identifies three positions: *realist*, *weak constructionist* and *strong constructionist* (Lupton, 1999). According to the *realist* definition, risk is indeed an objective hazard which may be distorted or biased through social and cultural frameworks of interpretation, but nevertheless exists independently. A *weak constructionist* understanding also views risk as an objective hazard but considers it cannot be known or understood outwith the context of social and cultural processes which define it. The *strong constructionist* perspective is that nothing is a risk in itself. Rather what is understood as risk is a product of historically, socially and politically contingent ways of thinking.

Drawing on the work of Bhaskar and *critical realism*, Houston proposes a middle way which, he claims, combines elements of these objectivist and subjectivist positions. This approach relies on identifying underlying causal mechanisms which exist independently but are activated in particular ways in individual situations. Thus to understand the nature of risk, it is necessary to take into account not only the structural or personal factors which present a danger but the *meaning* of these to the individuals concerned. Houston argues this is a sound basis on which to assess risk in child welfare (Bhaskar, 1989; Houston, 2001). Its focus on the interaction between social structures and individual agency also make it a useful framework within which to consider the implications of modern life for young people.

The 'Risk' Society

It scarcely needs saying that we live in a rapidly changing world where many of the old certainties no longer apply. Beck has coined the term 'risk society' to describe the uncertain and fragmented nature of current social life. Contrary to earlier expectations, developments in the natural and social sciences have not resulted in untrammeled progress but have had negative as well as positive effects (Beck, 1992).

The risks are many and varied. At a global level, technological developments have resulted in fears that the future of the planet itself might be jeopardised through pollution and nuclear war. Following the 11th September attrocity, anxiety about threats from terrorism and war has become even more pervasive and intense. More locally, the industrial base has been eroded resulting in the demise of traditional occupations and associated way of life in many, predominantly working class, areas. Consequently, communities which grew up around particular industries have become impoverished and fragmented (Holman, 1998; Charlesworth, 2000). Decisions about job losses are often taken at the other side of the world, so that people have little sense of being able to influence them. Individuals can no longer expect a job for life, but rather live with the expectation of periods of unemployment, part-time work and retraining. Alongside this, traditional forms of family life have been replaced by a range of more fluid and diverse arrangements. Thus job insecurity, poverty and social isolation have become predominant risks in modern life. They are also well documented as the key problems which face young people leaving care (Biehal, Clayden et al., 1995; Stein, 1997; Marsh, 1999).

Though making life more precarious, it has also been argued that the loosening of traditional structures and expectations opens up unprecedented opportunities, for example through increased access to further education and life style choice. While acknowledging that class and gender still constrain individual options, Beck argues that there is more scope for social mobility as individuals are no longer expected to travel life along a predefined path. Beck claims that, through a process of *individuation*, people are able, indeed required, to 'create their own biographies'. This, he argues is a calculative process in which individuals assess options, taking into account the potential risks and opportunities (Beck, 1992) . This notion of a life based on personal choice finds resonance in an increasingly individualistic ethos within government social policy.

Risk and Opportunity in Social Policy

With fewer families fitting the traditional model of two parent family with a male earner, the early welfare state's principles of universal welfare provision and pooling risk have been replaced by an ethos which emphasises individual responsibility. In the UK the policies of the Thatcher government marked a shift towards an ideology based on individualism rather than collectivist notions of the common good. Increasingly, individuals were held responsible for their own or their children's welfare, the withdrawal of benefits to 16–18-year-olds being but one example of this trend. At the same time individual service users were in principle given more power and choice, as services were increasingly provided by a range of voluntary and private providers and market principles of competition were introduced to the public sector. State action to manage and distribute risk was weakened, instead relying on the calculating choices of individuals (Parton, 1996). Freeing individual enterprise was considered both morally superior and the best means of generating wealth. That risks and opportunities would be unequally distributed was not in itself considered a problem (Holman, 1998).

On coming to power in 1997, the Labour government highlighted that the previous administration's lack of action had allowed risks to accumulate in certain communities which had become characterised by high levels of poverty and unemployment, poor social amenities and social problems such as crime and drug use. Tackling social exclusion has been high on the government's agenda, with a predominant focus on getting people back into work or training and community regeneration (Social Exclusion Unit, 1999; Social Exclusion Unit, 2001). Some of the results have been impressive, notably a 70 per cent reduction in

youth unemployment over three years through the New Deal. The prime minister talks of providing '*ladders of opportunity for those from all backgrounds, no more ceilings that prevent people from achieving the success they merit*' (Blair, 1999).

However, the government's approach to social exclusion does not represent a return to the welfarism of the past. Instead they claim to be following a 'third way' which emphasises individual *rights* to employment and opportunity alongside *responsibilities* to be as self-sufficient as possible and contribute to the community. In most respects the individualistic and market led approach of the previous administration has been retained. For example in education, central plank of the social exclusion programme, a plethora of initiatives have been introduced to improve attendance and attainment among disadvantaged pupils. However, the trend towards marketisation, privatisation and competition continues unabated in ways which, it has been argued, potentially undermine inclusion and the possibility of achieving better opportunities for all (Power, 1999; Blyth, 2001). The government's approach is essentially to provide additional support for those most at risk within the system, but not to change the system itself. The goal is to produce equality of opportunity, not equality of outcome (Jordan, 2001).

Reviewing the key discourses in social exclusion policy, Williams identifies the Labour government's approach as focusing on individual behaviours and reintegration into normative society, rather than tackling unequal distribution of social and economic power. This, she claims, is associated with fears about an excluded 'underclass' which threatens society's values and safety (Williams, 1998). Within present UK policy the key aims are to reduce welfare dependency, mainly through paid work, to strengthen the family and to tackle social problems such as crime and drug misuse. Services are provided to help people back into mainstream society, but these are offered alongside harsher penalties for those who remain on the margins, for example withdrawal of benefit if offers of training or employment are refused and stricter controls on anti-social behaviour. These measures impact predominantly on young people who are particularly feared as a developing 'underclass', are required to take up work or training and, in the name of 'crime prevention', can be subject to a wide range of monitoring and controls (MacDonald, 1997; Social Exclusion Unit, 1999; Muncie, 2002).

Implications for Social Work

The impact on social work of the social and policy changes described above have been immense in terms of redefining the social work task, the organisational ethos and the nature of relationships between social workers and those who are offered a service.

Assessing and managing risk have become central social work tasks, at least within the statutory sector. In the last 30 years child protection has come to dominate child welfare services, creating a climate in which resources are allocated on the basis of risk, sometimes under the cloak of 'in need'. Inevitably this has resulted in fewer resources being available for supporting those children and families who have extensive needs but are not in immediate danger (Parton, 1997; Tunstill, 1996; Gibbons, Conroy et al., 1995). Jordan notes a tendency within New Labour discourse to associate social work almost exclusively with social control functions in relation to child protection, criminal justice and mental health. On the other hand, roles associated with creating opportunities, for example within the Connexions service, are undertaken by people other than social workers, even though they work in a similar way (Jordan, 2001). Even within the social work field, Jones argues the voluntary sector is increasingly undertaking the more supportive and enabling work, thus further restricting statutory social work to assessing and managing risk (Jones, 2001).

In common with other public services, social work is now run in accordance with a managerial rather than professional ethos, so that service development is guided by considerations of cost effectiveness and organisational efficiency. Hence several local authorities have concentrated social workers in centrally based teams covering a wide geographical area, a policy which promotes

organisational effectiveness but makes staff remote from the individuals and communities they serve. At the same time social work has become increasingly subject to regulation and guidance. On the positive side this is intended to improve standards. However, it can also reduce the scope for professional discretion and result in services being provided on the basis of organisational expectations and procedures, rather than working out with an individual client what would be most helpful in a specific situation (Gilligan, 2000; Jones, 2001).

The social policy emphasis on individual autonomy has inevitably impacted on the relationship between social workers and the people to whom they offer a service. Service users are now constituted as 'consumers', freely and rationally entering into a contract with social work agencies. In this context many social workers have become care managers, co-ordinating a range of services but without engaging with clients in an enabling or personally meaningful way (Jones, 2001).

Howe associates these and similar developments with the development of 'surface' social work, concerned with *what* people do and achieving observable results, and contrasts this with 'depth' social work which is concerned with *why* people behave in certain ways and *how* individuals can be helped to cope and even grow in certain situations. He argues that to carry out 'surface' social work practitioners need only be competent technicians, whereas depth social work also requires knowledge, understanding and considerable interpersonal skills (Howe, 1996). Gilligan expresses concern that whereas looked after children require the latter, present training and service provision has resulted in many social workers being able to offer only 'surface' support (Gilligan, 2000). Correspondingly, experienced social workers interviewed by Jones reported that increasing administrative burden, pressure of work and focus on assessment meant they were seldom able to establish more than a superficial relationship with individual clients (Jones, 2001).

The implications of these developments for care leavers are explored further later in the chapter.

Implications for Young People and Care Leavers

Opportunities and risks

Inevitably the social and policy changes outlined above have had a profound impact on how all young people manage the transition to adulthood, with care leavers also crucially affected by developments in the social work services. Yet understanding the impact of the changes is not straightforward. An optimistic perspective would view young people's lives as characterised by increased opportunity, freed from the expectation to move into traditional occupations and family roles. At the same time, in the context of a social exclusion programme geared to breaking down the barriers to opportunity, more disadvantaged young people have increased access to training and employment (Social Exclusion Unit, 1999). However, these opportunities are provided in a context of insecure employment and community fragmentation which arguably pose a whole new set of risks, while also undermining the aforementioned opportunities for choice and progress (Furlong and Cartmel, 1997; Cole, 2000).

The implications for young people are therefore contradictory and inevitably vary depending on class, gender, race and disability as well as the circumstances of individual young people. Williams makes the point that the impact of social policies can no longer simply be assessed in terms of the distribution of risks. In addition it is essential to understanding the *meaning* individuals attach to the policies and the problems or risks they are intended to alleviate. These, she claims, reflect personal perspectives but also social positioning and structures of power:

> *Whilst quantitative studies can indicate the distribution of risks (for example from the casualisation of labour, forms of discrimination, homelessness, economic and welfare restructuring, including the marketisation of welfare, as well as environmental hazards and crime and violence), in depth qualitative research can explore people's own perceptions or meanings, of the risks to which they are exposed, as well as the opportunities and resources available to protect themselves. Again whilst these aspects refer to individual perceptions and actions they are underpinned by existing personal, institutional and social relations of power.*
>
> Williams, 1998, p23.

As Williams explains, this perspective involves rethinking the links between structure and agency, and emphasising people's capacity to be 'creative, reflexive human agents of their lives, experiencing, acting upon and reconstituting the outcomes of welfare policies'. It is from this perspective that some of the implications for young people are assessed.

Delayed transition to adulthood

Attaining adult status is widely described as a series of three interlinked transitions: from school to work; from families of origin to families of destination and from living with family members to living independently (Coles, 1995). One of the consequences of the economic and policy context described above is that each of these transitions has become more diverse and for many, more difficult, protracted and uncertain (Jones, 1992; Cole, 2000). Very few young people now move from school directly into work. Instead they remain in education or training, intended to enhance their future prospects but on allowances which do not afford financial independence. In addition, entitlements to a range of financial supports including housing benefit and income support have been reduced to encourage young people to remain within the family home (Jones, 2000). Inevitably the adverse effects are more serious for those who cannot rely on family support.

Policies which reduce state support in order to encourage reliance on parents present something of a paradox for young people who are looked after, since the state in the form of the local authority has some parental duties for their welfare. They should in principle look to public services for the support others can expect from the family, yet these are being curtailed to reduce welfare dependency and costs. Under the Children (Leaving Care) Act, 2000, personal advisors are to support young people leaving care until they reach age 21.

This should go some way towards ensuring they receive a better deal, though considerable resourcing would be required to replicate the flexible, reliable and enduring support parents are expected to provide. It is still likely that many care leavers will find themselves setting up home long before most of their peers are able to consider this option.

Choice and social mobility?

For Furlong and Cartmel, restrictions which delay the gaining of adult status undermine claims that the more fragmented 'risk society' offers young people more lifestyle choices. Instead, they argue, diversity of options gives an illusion of choice, which in reality can only be exercised within the confines determined by social and economic policies. In practice, they claim, young people have very little control over their lives (Furlong and Cartmel, 1997).

Based on a detailed study of the experience of young people from one estate, Johnston and colleagues demonstrated the complexity and diversity of individual transitions. Work status varied over time, for example through youth training, part or full time employment, involvement in the informal economy or the New Deal, with each change highly unpredictable and contingent on both young people's previous experience and local job availability. Young people were aware that their choices were limited but tried to make the best of what was on offer (Johnston, 2000).

Furlong and Cartmel (1997) also demonstrate that quite distinctive routes to adult life can still be predicted on the basis of class, gender, race and disability. Though the diversity of routes available obscures the social processes which perpetuate advantage, these none the less remain powerful. The social processes they refer to include both an economic and welfare system which favours powerful sections of the community and the myriad of daily interactions through which more advantaged children benefit from social and cultural capital, while others have their inferior status confirmed (Charlesworth, 2000). Consequently, the risks associated with modern life still fall most heavily on more disadvantaged members of the population, who may find themselves blamed

for not overcoming obstacles which are not immediately obvious and are outwith their control.

The conclusion of Furlong and Cartmel's study is that opportunities for choice and mobility have been overstated, adding to young people's stress as they are told they have unbounded opportunity, yet in practice experience little control over their own lives.

This research raises a number of implications for looked after young people for whom achieving better outcomes is a key service aim. First there is the question of whether, while in residential or foster care, looked after children have opportunities to develop the educational, cultural and social capital so critical to progress. For some the effects of early trauma continue to present serious obstacles to progress, so that skilled therapeutic help is required before they can benefit from school or informal learning (Cairns, 2000). Since risks accumulate in certain communities, one might also question whether an individual based approach is likely to offer much protection, should the young person return to live in a socially disadvantaged area. With these concerns in mind, some critics of the Looking After Children Assessment and Action Records have suggested that their use encourages an oversimplified view of what achieving better outcomes entails for disadvantaged children (Knight, 1998). A potential danger is that young people feel a sense of personal failure when they do less well than they had hoped. However, more positively, Johnston and colleagues reported that future life chances could be contingent on quite specific aspects of previous experience, so that even small achievements could potentially open the door to wider opportunities (Johnston, 2000).

Identity and purpose

Leaving care studies have repeatedly reported that social isolation, identity confusion and lack of self-esteem are the most intransigent problems for care leavers, often undermining the effectiveness of other work, for example on self-care skills and budgeting (Biehal, Clayden et al., 1995; Stein, 1997; Broad, 1998; Emond, 2000). A coherent sense of identity and how the young person came to be looked after is generally associated with better self-esteem and ability to form relationships. This is evidently a difficult area for young people who have been separated from their family and may have had painful experiences amidst frequent moves. Help to make sense of their lives has to be on going throughout the time they are looked after and, if necessary beyond (Fahlberg, 1994).

Quite apart from the effects of dislocation and trauma, there are indications that some aspects of modern life make it difficult for all young people to develop a sense of identity. This is in part attributed to the delay in achieving adult roles and responsibilities, leaving young people in limbo and with no clear sense of purpose and meaning in their lives (Jones, 1992; Furlong and Cartmel, 1997). Indeed it has been argued that this contributes to the increase in psychological problems among young people such as depression, suicidal behaviours and eating disorders (West, 1996).

Giddens' account of identity formation in the modern world supports the view that developing a coherent sense of identity constitutes an on going personal challenge. He argues that the diversity and flux which characterise the risk society means that individuals can no longer base their identity on stable membership of a particular occupational group, family or community. Instead, people have to constantly recreate a sense of who they are, drawing together somewhat disparate elements of their past life and 'reflexively' making sense of their present situation. For the well supported and resourced, this may open up opportunities for personal development, but it also creates a fundamental insecurity about the point of existence itself (Giddens, 1991).

As creative agents in their own lives, young people set about finding meaningful roles for themselves. Miles suggests that young people's preoccupation with consumption and lifestyle can be understood as an attempt to find an arena in which they can establish a sense of identity and some degree of control over their lives (Miles, 2000). Others with less purchasing power may turn to less socially acceptable activities. For example, Taylor describes how the companionship, routines and skills associated with illegal drug use provides young women with a sense of purpose and outlet for

their talents (Taylor, 1993), while some of the young people in the study by Johnston and colleagues described their criminal activities as work (Johnston, 2000). It has also been suggested that some young women may choose motherhood as one of the few socially valued roles available to them (Wallace, 1987).

Young people as a threat

Drug use, crime and teenage pregnancy are all problems targeted by social exclusion policies, highlighting the relevance of Williams' point that, to be effective, policies have to take into account the meaning of the behaviours to individuals concerned, not just how services are delivered (Williams, 1998).

Evidently some of these options involve considerable personal risk to young people. In addition behaviours such as drug use, crime and teenage pregnancy are also seen as constituting a threat to society, so that young people find themselves stigmatised and subject to increasingly harsh controls (Muncie, 2002). Some will also come within the criminal justice system where sentencing policy is increasingly based on assessing the 'risk' of future offending. Since unemployment, homelessness, chaotic drug use and lack of social support are taken as indicators of 'risk', young people with the least resources may find themselves further disadvantaged within the criminal justice system (Goldson, 2000). The implications for more damaged and needy care leavers is clear.

Maximising Opportunities and Reducing Risks

It seems fair to conclude that life for young people today presents diverse and exciting opportunities, but also new risks and uncertainties. How these are distributed continues to reflect gender, social position and power, so that the risks outweigh the opportunities for disadvantaged young people. Insecure employment, isolation in a more fragmented society and lack of a clear sense of identity or purpose have been identified as the main hazards in the transition to adult life.

Many young people leaving care are ill equipped to cope with these risks in that their educational attainment is lower than the average (Borland, Pearson et al., 1998; Scottish Executive, 2001), they lack family and community support (Marsh, 1999), and have had more disruption and trauma to cope with than most of their peers. Of course this does not apply to all young people leaving care. Some have had successful school careers, have a good sense of who they are and how they came to be looked after and are able to rely on continuing support from foster carers or members of their own family. However, many more have far fewer resources to protect them from the adversities that life has in store.

Recognition of care leavers' vulnerability and their entitlement to a better deal has resulted in a much sharper focus on improving outcomes for looked after children. Targets have been set to improve educational attainment, while education and social work services are required to co-operate more fully in order to reduce exclusions and ensure appropriate schooling is provided (Scottish Executive, 2001). In addition young people receive support to access the range of employment and training schemes now on offer (Social Exclusion Unit, 1999). The importance of fostering family and community links is now identified and there are some indications that placements with the extended family are being developed (Aldgate, 2001). However, there is cause for concern that they continue to receive insufficient support to tackle the deep seated and complex difficulties which characterise most looked after children's lives. While systems are set up to identify, review and manage these, it is less clear that the skills and knowledge are available to help children overcome them (Gilligan, 2000).

Ironically, it might be argued that social work's preoccupation with risk is resulting in a situation where looked after children, highly 'at risk' in the long term, are receiving insufficient help. Resources channelled into child protection means fewer are available to support children and carers. At the same time social workers who have become accustomed to risk assessment and short term work may find it difficult to offer the sustained and personally challenging support looked after children need. Gilligan argues that three interlinking strategies are needed to rise to the challenge of serving

the needs of children in care in the coming decades:

- Enveloping the skill and knowledge base of social workers.
- Engaging more fully with informal resources in the child's network.
- More realistic public investment and support for social work with children in state care.

Gilligan, 2000.

These elements very much fit with an appreciation of the challenges young people will face on leaving care. The key message is that support should be sustained, while also based on detailed understanding of the young person's perspective, needs and daily life.

In terms of increasing the likelihood of employment, the research by Johnston and colleagues showed that job opportunities were highly contingent on young people's previous experience, stretching back to the early teens. For example an early gap in secondary schooling might reduce opportunities, while joining a club or learning a skill might increase them (Johnston, 2000). This indicates that the accumulation of work related capital is about much more than obtaining formal qualifications, even if these remain key collateral. Thus support in small every day and apparently insignificant activities can be crucial to future opportunities.

However, it might also be argued that critical importance of encouragement in the every day detail of life is to build a sense of worth and self-efficacy. Feeling valued is essential to building a coherent sense of self, a particular challenge for young people in the modern world. For young people who are looked after this would include receiving help to understand why they are separated from their family and acknowledge the pain and grief associated with this. Arguably this is the most challenging and crucial work social workers are asked to take on, while some young people will also require appropriate specialist services (Walker, 2002 forthcoming). There is clear evidence that young people who have not been helped in this way find it very difficult to move on emotionally and establish supportive relationships (Emond, 2000).

Valuing young people also means that their needs and perspective are at the centre of service planning and delivery. Williams' point that the effectiveness of social policies has to be assessed in terms of how they are received and impact on people's lives also applies to social work services. For example, practice to improve how a young person performs at school will have more chance of success if based on an understanding of what they expect from formal schooling and what matters to them in the course of the school day. In addition young people would need to be given information about their rights and encouraged to pursue these. This would include explicitly identifying obstacles to progress in an attempt to prevent young people feeling personally responsible for factors beyond their control.

Community support and links to natural networks are important both in terms of giving young people a sense of belonging and affording access to social capital which can be critical in terms of employment opportunities and personal well-being (Jack and Jordan, 1999). Again these have to be fostered throughout the time young people are looked after. During the teenage years it is particularly crucial that young people are able to build up contacts with local people and institutions which will continue to offer support when they leave care (Marsh, 1999; Walker et al., 2002).

It is hardly novel to draw attention to these elements, all of which are key to fostering resilience (Gilligan, 1997; 1999). However it is by no means clear that the present statutory service is able to provide them (Howe, 1996; Gilligan, 2000; Jones, 2001). Evidently residential and foster carers are key to providing sensitive and skilled day-to-day care (Walker and Maguire, 2001; Walker et al., 2002). However, as Gilligan argues, the field social worker also has a potentially key role in direct work with young people, supporting carers and generating and fostering links with informal networks (Gilligan, 2000). Some accommodated children and young people interviewed about a proposed advocacy service said it would be good to have someone who:

- Got to know you really well.
- Stuck by you through difficult times.
- Took you out sometimes.
- Understood and helped you understand what it was like to be in foster or residential care.

- Knew how to help sort out problems.
- Would stick up for you and your rights when necessary.

> Walker and Maguire, 2001.

It was hard to avoid the conclusion that they were asking for an effective social worker. However, in practice they found most of the social workers they knew were unreliable and overworked:

> *It wouldn't really matter how good the social worker was, it's just the name that puts you off ... they never have time to see you or do anything.*
>
> Boy in foster care, quoted in Walker and Maguire, 2001.

As this boy recognised, individual social workers cannot be expected to improve the service they offer, unless the situation in which they are working facilitates this.

Despite many promising developments to support them, young people leaving residential and foster care continue to face significant risks. Equipping them to cope with these has implications for how they are cared for and supported throughout the time they are accommodated. Yet it would be unfortunate if their entitlement to skilled care and support were justified predominantly in terms of risk. A more positive alternative would be to appreciate children and young people's right to develop their present and future potential, while also acknowledging that, in the longer term, this constitutes the best protection against adversity.

References

Aldgate, J. S. (2001) *The Children Act Now: Messages from Research*. London, The Stationery Office.

Beck, U. (1992) *Risk Society: Towards a New Modernity*. London, Sage.

Bhaskar, R. (1989) *The Possibility of Naturalism*. Hemel Hempstead, Harvester Wheatsheaf.

Biehal, N., Clayden, J. et al. (1995) *Moving on: Young People and Leaving Care Schemes*. London, HMSO.

Blair, A. (1999) *Speech to the Institute for Public Policy Research*, London.

Blyth, E. (2001) The Impact of the First Term of the New Labour Government on Social Work in Britain: The Interface between Education Policy and Social Work. *British Journal of Social Work* 31(4): 563–78.

Borland, M., Pearson, C. et al. (1998) *Education and Care Away from Home A Review of Research, Policy and Practice*. Edinburgh, Scottish Council for Research in Education.

Broad, B. (1998) *Young People Leaving Care Life After the Children Act 1989*. London, Jessica Kingsley.

Cairns, K. (2000) The Effects of Trauma on Childhood Learning. in Jackson, S. *Nobody Ever Told us School Mattered: Raising The Educational Attainments of Children in Care*. London, BAAF.

Charlesworth, S. (2000) Bourdieu, Social Suffering and Working Class Life. in Fowler, B. *Reading Bourdieu on Society and Culture*. Oxford, Blackwell, The Sociological Review.

Cole, J. (2000) Young People in Britain at the Beginning of a New Century. *Children and Society* 14: 230–42.

Coles, B. (1995) *Youth and Social Policy*. London, UCL Press.

Douglas, M. (1992) *Risk and Blame: Essays in Cultural Theory*. London, Routledge.

Emond, R. (2000) '*I Thought it Would be a Bed of Roses*' *An Exploration into the Difference Between the Perception and Reality of Leaving Residential Care*. Glasgow, Scottish Institute for Residential Child Care.

Fahlberg, V. (1994) *A Child's Journey Through Placement*. London, BAAF.

Furlong, A. and Cartmel, F. (1997) *Young People and Social Change*. Buckingham, Open University Press.

Gibbons, J., Conroy, S. et al. (1995) *Operating the Child Protection System*. London, HMSO.

Giddens, A. (1991) *Modernity and Self-identity Self and Society in the Late Modern Age*. Cambridge, Polity Press.

Gilligan, R. (1997) Beyond Permanence? The Importance of Resilience in Child Placement Practice and Planning. *Adoption and Fostering* 21: 12–20.

Gilligan, R. (1999) Enhancing the Resilience of Children and Young People in Public Care by Mentoring Their Talents and Interests. *Child and Family Social Work* 4(3): 187–96.

Gilligan, R. (2000) The Key Role of Social Workers in Promoting the Well-being of Children in State Care: A Neglected Dimension of Reforming Policies. *Children and Society* 14: 267–76.

Goldson, B. (2000) *The New Youth Justice*. Lyme Regis, Russell House Publishing.

Holman, B. (1998) Neighbourhoods and Exclusion. in Barry, M. and Hallet, C. *Social Exclusion and Social Work*. Lyme Regis, Russell House Publishing.

Houston, S. (2001) Transcending the Fissure in Risk Theory. *Child and Family Social Work* 6(3): 219–28.

Howe, D. (1996) Surface and Depth in Social Work Practice. in Parton, N. *Social Theory, Social Change and Social Work*. London, Routledge.

Jack, G. and Jordan, B. (1999) Social Capital and Child Welfare. *Children and Society* 13: 242–56.

Johnston, L. M. R., Mason, P., Ridley, L. and Webster, C. (2000) *Snakes and Ladders Young People, Transitions and Social Exclusion*. Bristol, Policy Press.

Jones, C. (2001) Voices from the Front Line: State Social Workers and new Labour. *British Journal of Social Work* 31(4): 547–62.

Jones, G. (2000) Youth Homelessness and the 'Underclass'. in MacDonald, R. *Youth the 'Underclass' and Social Exclusion*. London, Routledge.

Jones, G., Wallace, C. (1992) *Youth, Family and Citizenship*. Buckingham, OUP.

Jordan, B. (2001) Tough Love: Social Exclusion, Social Work and the Third Way. *British Journal of Social Work* 31(4): 527–46.

Knight, T., Caveney, S. (1998) Assessment and Action Records: Will they Promote Good Parenting? *British Journal of Social Work* 28: 29–43.

Lupton, D. (1999) *Risk*, Routledge.

MacDonald, R. (1997) Dangerous Youth and the Dangerous Class. in MacDonald, R. *Youth, the 'Underclass' and Social Exclusion*. London, Routledge.

Marsh, P. (1999) *Leaving Care in Partnership: Family Involvement with Care Leavers*. London, The Stationery Office.

Miles, S. (2000) *Youth Lifestyles in a Changing World*. Buckingham, Open University Press.

Muncie, J. (2002) A New Deal for Youth? Early Intervention and Correctionalism. in Hughes, G. McLaughlin, E. and Muncie, R. *Crime Prevention and Community Safety New Directions*. London, Open University Press.

Parton, N. (1996) Social Work, Risk and the Blaming System. in Parton, N. *Social Theory, Social Change and Social Work*. London, Routledge.

Parton, N. (1997) Child Protection and Family Support: Current Debates and Future Prospects. in Parton, N. *Child Protection and Family Support*. London, Routledge: 1–24.

Power, S. W. G. (1999) New Labour's Education Policy: First, Second or Third Way? *Journal of Education Policy* 14(5)

Scottish Executive (2001) *Learning with Care The Education of Children Looked After Away from Home by Local Authorities*. Edinburgh, HM Inspectors of Schools & Social Work Services Inspectorate.

Social Exclusion Unit (1999) *Bridging the Gap: New Opportunities for 16–18 Year Olds not in Education, Employment or Training*. Parliamentary Report.

Social Exclusion Unit (2001) *A New Commitment to Neighbourhood Renewal: National Strategy Action Plan*. London, Cabinet Office.

Stein, M. (1997) *What Works in Leaving Care?* Ilford, Barnardo's.

Stein, M. Pinkerton, J. and Kelleher, P. (2000) Young People Leaving Care in England, Northern Ireland and Ireland. *European Journal of Social Work* 3(3): 235–46.

Taylor, A. (1993) *Women and Drug Use. An Ethnography of a Female Injecting Community*. Oxford, Clarendon Press.

Tunstill, J. (1996) Implementing the Family Support Clauses of The 1989 Children Act. Legislative, Professional and Organisational Obstacles. in Parton, N. *Child Protection and Family Support. Tensions, Contradictions and Possibilities*. London, Routledge.

Walker, M., Hill, M. and Triseliotis, J. (2002 forthcoming) *Testing the Limits of Foster Care*. London, BAAF.

Walker, M., Maguire, R. (2001) *Advocacy Consultation: Accommodated Children and Young People's Views on Advocacy Services*. Centre for the Child and Society, University of Glasgow.

Wallace, C. (1987) *Between the Family and the State: Young People in Transition. The Social World of the Young Unemployed*. London, Policy Studies Institute.

West, P. and Sweeting, H. (1996) Nae Job, Nae Future: Young People and Health in a Context of Unemployment. *Health and Social Care in the Community* 4: 50–62.

Williams, F. (1998) Agency and Structure Revisited. in Barry, M. and Hallet, C. (Eds.) *Social Exclusion and Social Work*. Lyme Regis, Russell House Publishing.

2. The Legislative Framework for Leaving Care

Amanda Allard

The Children (Leaving Care) Act 2000 is the third legislative attempt in recent history, to better the support and outcomes for young people leaving care. It builds on both the Child Care Act 1980 and the Children Act 1989. Arguably it addresses the main concerns regarding these two pieces of legislation; that the predominance of powers rather than duties led to a geographical lottery for young people.

Similar legislation to The Children (Leaving Care) Act 2000 has been passed in Wales but with minor differences. Revised Leaving Care Legislation in Scotland and Northern Ireland is currently in the planning and discussion stage.

The financial arrangements are the same throughout the UK.

The Child Care Act 1980

The Child Care Act 1980 set the following legal framework for leaving care:

- Section 27 allowed local authorities the discretion to make contributions for accommodation and maintenance to assist with education or work, to young people leaving care, aged between 17 and 21.
- Section 28 bestowed a duty on local authorities to advise and befriend any young person aged between 16 and 18 who was in voluntary care unless the authority was satisfied that that was not required.
- Section 29 allowed the local authority to offer advice and assistance (including financial help) to anyone formerly in care (either statutory or voluntary) after their seventeenth birthday up to the age of 21.
- Section 69 bestowed a duty on local authorities to advise and befriend any young person who was in the care of a voluntary organisation, unless the authority was satisfied that this was not required or they had arranged for the voluntary organisation to offer after care.
- Section 72 allowed local authorities to house anyone under 21 in a community home if it is

provided solely for children who are over compulsory school age.

The legislation could be said to have allowed local authorities to provide a comprehensive aftercare service, and indeed some did by exercising their powers to their fullest extent. However, because there was a large element of discretion generous interpretation was by no means general. A number of organisations highlighted this problem. A survey conducted by The National Association of Young People in Care (NAYPIC) found considerable variation in both support and financial assistance provided by local authorities in different parts of the country (Stein and Maynard,1985). The Children's Legal Centre highlighted the particular problems of the discretionary nature of Section 27 of the Child Care Act 1980, with young people not being given adequate financial help to pursue further education. At the same time research was highlighting the poor outcomes disproportionately experienced by care leavers such as homelessness. (Randall, 1984).

There was also official concern with the Short Report identifying a number of shortcomings with the legislation:

The main cause for concern is the considerable variation in the sort of assistance which can be expected, which is at present unacceptably dependent on geographical happenstance. This wide variation in turn arises from the weak and confused state of the law in this respect ... present legislation on continuing care for young people leaving local authority care is diffuse and misleading, and is by nature discretionary rather than obligatory.
Second Report from the Social Service Committee, Children in Care, 1984, V1, Para 302–3.

The recommendations of the Short Report were amended and included in the 1987 White Paper

The Law on Child Care and Family Services, which formed the basis of the relevant sections of the Children Act 1989.

In the 1980s, in addition to concern about the inefficacy of legislation concerning aftercare provision, the links between care leaving and homelessness also led to calls for care leavers to be added to the priority categories specified in the Housing (Homeless Persons) Act 1977. The Government resisted these calls in *Children in Care, Government Response* arguing that it should be left to the discretion of the local authority to decide whether young people leaving care should be treated under the 'vulnerable' category of the existing legislation.

Another area of considerable concern was the impact of social security changes on young people leaving care. The Supplementary Benefit (Amendments) Miscellaneous Provisions Regulations were introduced in April 1985. They restricted claims by those under the age of 26 living in lodgings, hostels and bed and breakfast accommodation. There was an exemption for young people who had left care within the previous 12 months but a failure to ensure awareness and therefore implementation of that exemption (*Guardian*, 20 Jul 1985). For those care leavers out of care for 12 months and a day the impact of the change was to drastically reduce benefit by cutting board and lodging payments. This forced many young people to move. For those local authorities who had used board and lodgings payments to fund transitional accommodation for care leavers it significantly reduced the pool of safe accommodation options they could offer to young people leaving care.

The Social Security Act 1986 introduced lower rates of benefit for those under 25. The Social Security Act 1988 then withdrew benefit entitlement from the majority of 16 and 17-year-olds. It was replaced with the 'guarantee' of a suitable Youth Training Scheme (YTS) place and the possibility of short-term payments of Income Support for those who could 'prove' that they would otherwise be in danger of 'severe hardship'.

The reduction in benefit rate was justified both on the basis that it related benefit levels to earning levels, young people should expect to get lower wages, and therefore lower benefits,

and on the grounds that most under 25-year-olds lived 'at home'. The Government stressed its belief that single young people aged 16 and 17 should remain in the parental home unless there were 'good reasons' for them not to do so, and that the benefit system should provide disincentives for them to leave home. This caused problems for young people who had good reasons not to remain at home. It also caused problems for young people who had left 'home' when they left care. Care leavers found themselves in the position of living on reduced benefit entitlement and living alone usually by definition without financial subsidy from their families and often without financial subsidy from their local authority parents.

The Children Act 1989

The leaving care provisions contained in the Children Act 1989 were designed to respond to the concerns outlined in the Short Report. During the passage of the Bill attempts were made to add further duties. David Hinchliffe MP proposed an amendment which would have placed a duty on local authorities to make six monthly contact with care leavers up until they were 21, in order to ensure that they were receiving necessary advice and assistance. He and other MPs saw the changes to social security as significantly adding to the vulnerability of care leavers and therefore wanted to extend the local authority safety net. The government was unwilling to cede on this point although further powers were given to local authorities, for instance in relation to providing financial assistance with education, training and employment.

When it was finalised, the Children Act 1989 set the following legal framework for leaving care:

- S24(1) conferred a duty on local authorities to advise and befriend a 'looked after' young person with a view to promoting their welfare after leaving care, up until the age of 21.
- S24(6), (7), (8) and (9) stated that local authorities could also assist those they were required to advise and befriend and that that assistance could be in kind or in exceptional circumstances in cash. Financial assistance could be given to assist with expenses

concerned with undertaking employment or training. This assistance might extend beyond a young person's 21st year if they were completing a course of education or training.

- S24(11) and (12) stated that local authorities had a duty to inform a recipient local authority when a young person they had been advising and befriending moved to that area. Also that anyone who had been caring for a young person had a duty to inform the local authority when a young person over 16 left their accommodation.
- S24(14) required every local authority to establish a procedure for considering any representation or complaint a young person might wish to make with regard to their preparation for leaving care or after care services.

In terms of the local authority's duty to provide assistance with aftercare accommodation:

- S20(3) stated that the local authority had a duty to provide accommodation for any child in need who had reached 16 and whose welfare would otherwise be likely to be seriously prejudiced.
- S20(5) gave local authorities the power to accommodate young people 16 to under 21 in a community home.
- S27(1) and (2) addressed the issue of 'corporate parenting' and stated that local authorities had the power to request the help of other authorities, including housing authorities, to enable them to comply with their duties to provide accommodation, and that if so requested the housing authority had a duty to assist so far as was compatible with their own statutory duties.

The duties and powers contained in the Children Act 1989 were, again, generally seen as providing an excellent framework for comprehensive aftercare provision. However, there were concerns that the money provided by central government to local authorities to fund the Children Act were insufficient, and that therefore the large element of discretion allowed local authorities would be unlikely to deal with the problem of variation referred to in the Short Report:

Whilst the duty to advise, 'assist and befriend' is sufficiently broad to allow local authorities to cater for the individual and varying needs of their care leavers it could also lead to even more variation in the quantity and quality of provision ... The impression we gained from our discussions ... with social workers and their managers was of a service already stretched to its limits. Imposing new duties without a parallel increase in resources is therefore unlikely to improve the situation of young people leaving care.

Garnett, 1992.

Studies carried out by First Key (1992) and the Royal Philanthropic Society (Broad, 1994) in the first years after the Children Act 1989's implementation showed that these fears had indeed been well founded and that regional and local variations in the level of services available to young people had persisted. In 1996 the Action on Aftercare Consortium published *Too Much Too Young*. The report was published shortly after campaigners had again failed to persuade the government to add care leavers to the priority categories specified in the Housing Act 1996. The report catalogued the difficulties faced by care leavers in relation to housing, education, training, employment and welfare benefits. It made clear that in the experience of Consortium, member agencies comprehensive and integrated services which could help care leavers negotiate these myriad problems were far from typical and were increasingly vulnerable to cuts in budget.

During this time the issue of welfare benefits and care leavers was once again on the agenda. Housing Benefit and Council Tax Benefit circular AX95 had reminded local authorities that young people 'under a care order or where a social services department is providing accommodation under Section 20' would not normally be entitled to housing benefit. There was considerable concern that this would increase early discharge from care as local authorities sought to minimise financial responsibilities (Barnardo's, 1995).

In addition, the development of supported housing ground to a halt and some supply was lost as a result of the Housing Benefit and Council Tax Benefit circular A36/95. Up until this time providers had been using Housing Benefit to pay for the counselling and support necessary to enable vulnerable tenants, including care leavers, to maintain independent or semi-independent accommodation. The circular stated that only those services which were concerned with the 'fabric of the dwelling' were eligible for payment. As a result payment to providers wholly reliant on Housing Benefit dropped. In April 1996 draft amendment regulations were introduced which were intended to confirm in statute the intentions of the circular. However, in response to widespread concern from many organisations the Secretary of State announced the withdrawal of the draft amendment and an urgent inter-departmental review of the arrangements for funding supported accommodation (DSS, 1996). However, in the meantime only support charges for existing projects was guaranteed.

In July 1995 new guidelines were introduced tightening up the assessment process for 16 and 17-year-olds living away from home and claiming severe hardship payments as a result of estrangement. Care leavers found themselves asked to prove estrangement from the local authority. In addition they were being pushed from pillar to post in respect of setting up home grants. Many local authorities insisted that young people make a claim for a community care grant before they would consider bestowing a leaving care grant, and basically only did so if young people were unsuccessful.

On the 13th June 1996 the Prime Minister announced the setting up of the Children's Safeguards Review. Chaired by Sir William Utting it was charged with assessing whether the safeguards introduced in the Children Act 1989 were sufficient to protect children living away from home. When it reported in July 1997 the Review argued that:

No responsible parent turns a child away at 16 – or even 19 – unsupported financially and emotionally, without hope of succour in distress. We were particularly concerned about the volume of anecdotal information about young people ceasing to be looked after at the age of 16, which suggested that some authorities operated informal policies of encouraging premature 'independence'.

And concluded by recommending that:

Section 24 of the Children Act should be amended to extend the duty of local authorities to give assistance to young people they have looked after, including helping foster carers to continue providing support.

In the meantime young people leaving care were the subject of an additional tussle between local authorities arguing about who would pay for their after care support. In a case involving Lambeth and Kent in which Lambeth had placed a young man in foster care in Kent the judge held that it was the responsibility of Kent County Council to provide continuing advice and assistance under the Children Act Sections 24(4) and (5). This was contrary to general understanding, practice and Department of Health guidance (R v Lambeth London Borough Council ex parte Caddell (1998)1 FLR 253).

However, in November 1998 the Government responded to the Children's Safeguards Review and announced that, amongst other things:

Council's duty of care [would be extended] from the age of 16 to the age of 18, with better support and services for young people leaving care.

Hot on the heels of this announcement, *Me Survive Out There?* was published in July 1999. The key elements of the new legislation were contained in the consultation paper, although the provisions suggested were less exacting than those finally contained in the Act. Local authorities were to be given a duty to assess and meet the needs of 16 and 17-year-olds in and leaving care. The power to assist with education and training was to be extended up to the age of 24 no matter when the course was started. Local authorities were to be made responsible for the personal and financial support of 16 and 17-year-old care leavers. Every young person was to have a pathway plan clearly setting out how the support and assistance the young person had been assessed as needing would be provided. Each young person would be allocated a personal advisor. The local authority that looked after the young person was to retain the responsibility for continuing support when they left care, no matter where they lived. The provisions were designed to address key concerns regarding care leaving services, such as the perceived perverse incentives for local authorities to discharge young people from care early so that they could claim benefits and no longer be the financial responsibility of the authority.

Energetic lobbying proceeded the publication of the Consultation paper and also the first draft of the Bill. Action on Aftercare held a meeting at the House of Commons prior to the second reading of the Bill in order to raise their concerns about its limitations.

The two key issues that the voluntary sector were calling for, was an extension of the duty to assess and meet need up to the age of 21, and the conversion of the power to assist with education, training and employment into a duty. Although sympathetic the government refused to extend local authorities' duties ahead of the Comprehensive Spending Review. Fortunately they didn't need to. The Bill was still in passage when the Review reported favourably and local authority duties were duly extended.

The Provisions of the Children (Leaving Care) Act 2000

The main aims of the Children (Leaving Care) Act 2000 are:

- To delay young people's discharge from care until they are prepared and ready to leave.
- To improve the assessment, preparation and planning for leaving care,
- To provide better personal support for young people after leaving care.
- To improve financial arrangements for care leavers.

In order to meet these aims, the Children Act 1989 has been amended by the Children (Leaving Care) Act 2000. The Children (Leaving Care) Act makes it clear that the **responsible authority** is the council which last looked after the child or young person. The Act also creates new categories of care leavers.

Eligibility

In order to qualify for the provisions contained in the Act young people need to have been looked after by the local authority for a period of 13 weeks since the age of 14, and have been

looked after at some time while 16 or 17. The regulations are worded so as to exclude children who experience respite care from eligibility. Thus children who have been placed in a pre-planned series of short-term placements, none of which individually exceeds four weeks will not be eligible. However, it is the nature not the length of the placement that is critical and a child or young person who has not experienced respite care but has had a series of unplanned emergency placements none of which lasted four weeks but did aggregate to more than 13 weeks would be eligible. It is also important to note that the young person does not have to start being looked after before their sixteenth birthday to achieve eligiblity.

Those young people who meet these requirements and remain looked after are **eligible children**.

Those young people who meet these requirements and have left care are **relevant children**.

If a young person is eligible but on leaving care is successfully returned home for a period of six months then they lose their relevant status.

There are two additional groups of relevant children:

- Those who would have been relevant children but for the fact that on their 16th birthday they were detained through the criminal justice system or in hospital.
- Those who have been successfully returned home but the return has broken down.

Once an eligible or relevant child reaches the age of 18 they become **former relevant children**. This status continues until the young person is 21. However, if at the age of 21 the young person is still being helped by the responsible authority with education or training, he or she remains a former relevant child until the end of the agreed programme of education or training even if that takes him or her past the age of 21.

Those young people who left care before October 1st, or who leave care subsequent to October 1st but do not qualify as eligible children are **qualifying children and young people over 16**. This status continues until the young person reaches 21, or 24 if in education or training.

The direct impact of the legislation on young people leaving care depends on their status.

Eligible children retain the benefits of all the provisions of the looked-after system. In addition the local authority must appoint them a personal advisor and carry out an assessment of their needs. They must then prepare a pathway plan setting out clearly how these needs are to be met.

Relevant children

Again the local authority must appoint a personal advisor, carry out a needs assessment and prepare a pathway plan, if it has not already done so. The authority must also safeguard and promote the young person's welfare by maintaining him and providing him with or maintaining him in suitable accommodation, and providing any additional support set out in the pathway plan, unless they are satisfied that his welfare does not require it. If the local authority loses touch with a relevant child they must take reasonable steps to re-establish contact and continue to take such steps whilst the young person remains a relevant child.

Former relevant children

The authority must continue the appointment of a personal advisor and keep the pathway plan under regular review. The authority must provide the young person with assistance generally. Specifically they must provide assistance by contributing to expenses incurred by them in living near their place of employment, education or training, or by making a grant to enable them to meet expenses connected with education or training. This assistance is to be provided to the extent that the young person's welfare requires it. The local authority must again keep in touch and re-establish contact if they lose touch. Authorities must also provide former relevant children with vacation accommodation for higher education or residential further education if this is needed.

All of these duties are extended if the young person is completing a programme of education or training which takes them beyond their 21st birthday. The extension is for the period of the education or training programme.

Qualifying children and young people over 16

The authority should provide the assistance set out in the 1989 Children Act, before amendment. The 1989 Act has been amended in respect of qualifying children who were looked after by the local authority so that the local authority must in addition keep in contact with the young person to the extent that is necessary to provide him or her with advice and assistance; and provide vacation accommodation for higher education courses or residential further education courses if necessary. They may also provide assistance with education and training up to the age of 24.

The new provisions apply regardless of any other special status a young person may have. So unaccompanied asylum-seeking children and children who are looked after under section 20 of the Children Act 1989 are also covered by these provisions.

What do the new provisions mean in practice?

Responsible authority

In terms of responsibility for relevant and former relevant young people the new provisions mean that where ever that young person lives in England or Wales the authority which last looked after them is responsible for funding their after care. Where a young person chooses to move into a second authority, and does so precipitously then both authorities will need to act quickly to ensure that the young person is provided with support services whilst new arrangements are being made and where necessary funds transferred. This is likely to mean that the second authority has to initially fund subsistence payments and other support.

Needs assessment and pathway plans

The responsible authority has to carry out a needs assessment for each eligible child and also for any relevant children for whom one has not already been done. The assessment needs to determine what advice, assistance and support they should provide both while they are looking after them and when they have ceased to look after them. It should be based on the needs assessment carried out when the young person's care plan was formulated.

Each local authority has to produce a written statement setting out how it will be assessing the needs of eligible and relevant children. They must make sure that all those involved in the assessment process, including the young person, have access to this statement and have had it explained to them. Regulations state that the responsible authority should take all reasonable steps to involve the young person in their needs assessment and the development of their pathway plan. The assessment has to be completed within three months of an eligible child becoming 16. In the case of children who become eligible after the age of 16 or relevant children who do not already have a pathway plan then the assessment must be completed within three months of them becoming an eligible or relevant child. Regulations set out the factors which should be considered in carrying out the assessment, including needs for care, support and accommodation, financial, education, training and employment needs, and possible support available from family and other relationships.

The pathway plan must be completed, in writing, as soon as possible after the assessment has been completed. The responsible authority must keep a copy and provide one to the young person in a form which is accessible to them. If another agency or person is identified as playing a role in the pathway plan then they should have a copy of the part which relates to their input.

The plan must set out how the needs identified in the assessment are to be met. The level of support to be provided, including financial support, the accommodation the young person is to occupy and what contingencies are in place should the plan prove to be insufficient to meet the assessed need.

There is considerable detail on the kind of issues which should be addressed in the assessment and pathway planning process and the ways in which they should be addressed.

The pathway plan should be reviewed at least every six months or when the young person or their personal advisor requests a review.

Personal advisor

The personal advisor's role is to provide advice and support to the young person, to participate in the assessment and preparation of the pathway plan and any reviews. To liaise with the responsible authority over its implementation and to help co-ordinate provision of services. The guidance views the role as requiring high levels of knowledge and skill. The guidance also states that young people should have a choice about who their personal advisor is, and that the local authority should seriously consider a request from a young person that, for instance, their foster carer or residential key worker becomes their personal advisor. However, the authority also needs to be satisfied that the person suggested has the requisite skills and the necessary availability, and are part of a structure which enables care to continue to be provided to the young person should the personal advisor be absent because of leave or illness.

Provision of accommodation

The accommodation identified for the young person in their pathway plan has to meet a number of criteria. It has to be suitable in the light of the young person's identified needs, including health needs. The local authority has to be satisfied as to the character and suitability of the landlord. The local authority needs to have taken into account the young person's wishes and feelings and practical considerations relating to the education, training and employment needs.

Whilst regulations do not prohibit the use of certain types of accommodation the guidance does make it clear that it would not generally be sensible for 16 and 17-year-olds to live independently and to carry the responsibility of their own tenancy without support. Similarly, that bed and breakfast accommodation would not normally be regarded as suitable although it may occasionally be justified as a short-term emergency measure.

Keeping in touch

Normally it will be the personal advisor who will fulfil the local authority's duty to keep in touch with the young person. The guidance states that the advisor should respect the young person's wishes with regard to their attempts to maintain contact, whilst ensuring that they convey an interest in the young person's well being. For relevant young people the guidance suggests that the frequency should be dictated by the personal advisor's knowledge of the young person and their circumstances. For former relevant young people it suggests contact should occur at least on a six monthly basis in order to review the pathway plan – the very amendment which David Hinchcliffe MP tried to make to the Children Bill when it was being debated. For contact to qualify as 'keeping in touch' the council must receive some response from the young person. So, for instance, calling round and finding the young person out would not constitute keeping in touch.

Financial arrangements

The majority of relevant young people can no longer claim benefit and the responsible authority will now be their primary income safety net. The guidance is clear that no young person should receive a package of support for their accommodation and maintenance which comes to less than they would have received if they had been entitled to claim Income Support or Jobseeker's Allowance and Housing Benefit. It also makes it clear that a relevant child has an absolute right to accommodation and support so long as their welfare requires it and this right is not qualified by any requirements.

This is not to say that there is no flexibility about financial support packages. Local authorities are encouraged to take the young person's skills and needs into account in deciding on how financial support is to be delivered. Therefore for young people coping well with independent living and budgeting the entirety of their subsistence allowance may be paid into their bank account fortnightly. Others may have payments made weekly or even twice weekly and for some young people authorities may initially handle all significant expenses for them.

In addition to their subsistence allowance the young person's pathway plan may identify the need for further financial support. The guidance states that local authorities should produce a written schedule of the areas where they would normally provide funding and suggests that

priorities for consideration would include expenses associated with education, childcare, contact with family and counselling and therapeutic needs. Although the local authority cannot sanction a young person they can cease incentive payments if for instance those additional payments are linked to attendance at college and the young person then fails to undertake the course.

Relevant young people who are also lone parents or sick and disabled are still eligible to claim Income Support or Jobseeker's Allowance, but not Housing Benefit. The responsible authority is additionally still responsible for providing the additional support identified in the pathway plan which is disregarded for the purposes of their benefit entitlement.

Where young people have funds of their own such as legacies or income through employment then the responsible authority should treat these funds according to the Department for Work and Pensions (DWP) regulations governing Income Support. However, where a young person has been awarded money in compensation for criminal injury then the council should disregard the capital entirely in the case of a relevant child.

Although most relevant young people will no longer be benefit claimants they will still be entitled to help with health costs and will be fast-tracked to help through the NHS Low Income Scheme.

Where a relevant or eligible child turns up in another authority's area and needs help then the second authority should provide short-term assistance under section 17 of the Children Act 1989.

Representations and complaints

There is a new duty on local authorities with regard to complaints from young people. If a relevant, former relevant or qualifying young person makes a complaint the responsible authority must put it into writing and submit it to their complaints officer. They must then try to reach an acceptable solution with the young person and have 14 days to do so. If they fail they must then move to the full complaints system as set out in the Representations Procedure (Children) Regulations 1991.

Associated developments

Housing

The Government is amending the Housing Act 1996 to extend the priority need categories for homeless people in order to include former relevant children. The Code of Guidance has already been amended to state that 16 and 17-year-olds and care leavers should be treated as vulnerable in most cases.

The Transitional Housing Benefit Scheme which has been in operation since 1999 has allowed the development of supported accommodation funded by Housing Benefit. The Department for Transport, Local Government and the Regions is using the Transitional scheme to separate out support costs from rent costs and in 2003 support costs will be transferred into a separate funding stream, allocated to local authorities on the basis of spend prior to 2003.

Connexions

The Connexions service (see Chapter 20) will be providing personal advisors to all 13–19-year-olds. In order to avoid a proliferation of advisors the Children (Leaving Care) Act guidance states that the leaving care personal advisor will normally also act as the young person's Connexions advisor. However, there may be instances in which eligible and relevant young people have built up a relationship with their Connexions personal advisor and wish them to take on the role of the Children (Leaving Care) Act personal advisor as well. A decision will then have to be made as to whether the Connexions advisor has the requisite skills. Because of their involvement from 13 the Connexions advisor will clearly have an important role to play in the assessment and pathway planning process.

Will the changes make a difference

The Children (Leaving Care) Act has already, and will continue to have, a huge impact on leaving care services, and the experiences of young people leaving care. Along with the associated changes to housing and benefits legislation the Act should end the majority of instances of young people being pushed from pillar to post by making it clear who is responsible. It removes the perverse incentives to discharge young people from care early. By increasing the number of duties as opposed to powers which local authorities have towards care leavers it will even up geographical disparities in provision.

Local authorities have however, expressed considerable concern about the amount of money which they have been allocated to fund the new provisions. It is true that in some areas their allocation is lower than they were spending on leaving care services prior to the implementation of the Act. It is also true that the oft mentioned geographical disparity in pre 2001 provision means that local authorities are starting from very different base lines in their efforts to fulfil the vision of the new Act. It is likely that these different starting points, and the limited funding may, especially in the early years, lead to very differing interpretations of the duties contained in the legislation.

For instance, there is likely to be a significant gap between current provision of accommodation available in local authorities and that required to meet the definitions laid down in the Act. Those with mature, well resourced existing leaving care services are more likely to have had the time and resources to tackle this gap. Others may find that they continue to overuse bed and breakfast accommodation because it is the least worst option.

Another concern from the past which the new legislation is unlikely to address is the difference in the rates of personal allowances for those under 25, which are unjustifiable for those having to live independently. The additional financial support which it is in the gift of local authorities to bestow may make a considerable difference to those aged 21 and under, but again funding may limit this difference since it is the under 25s rate of benefit which has been transferred across to local authorities from the DWP.

It is too soon yet to know what impact the legislation will have. Many areas are still struggling with implementation and there are bound to be a plethora of teething problems. What is different this time around is that once the fog of implementation has cleared, those councils who are not delivering on their services to relevant and former relevant young people can be brought to book as never before.

References

Action on Aftercare Consortium (1996). *Too Much Too Young: The Failure of Social Policy in Meeting the Needs of Care Leavers*, Essex, Barnardo's.

Broad, B. (1994). *Leaving Care in the 1990s*, Westerham, Royal Philanthropic Society.

DSS (1996). *Peter Lilley Announces Government Review of Social Security Provision for Service Charges in Supported Accommodation*, press release No. 96/140, Jul. DSS.

First Key (1992). *A Survey of Local Authority Provisions for Young People Leaving Care*, Leeds, First Key.

First Key (2001). *The Children (Leaving Care) Act 2000, Department of Health Implementation Seminars, Workshop Notes*, Leeds, First Key.

Garnett, L. (1992). *Leaving Care and After*, NCB.

Guardian (1985). letters to the editor, 20 Jul.

House of Commons (1984). *Second Report from the Social Services Committee, Session 1983–84, Children in Care*, V 1, Para 302-3.

Randall, G. (1988). *No Way Home*, Centrepoint.

Stein, M. and Maynard, C. (1985). *I've Never Been So Lonely*, National Association of Young People in Care, NAYPIC.

Utting, W. (1997). *People Like Us: The Report of the Review of the Safeguards for Children Living Away from Home*, London, The Stationary Office.

3. Young People Leaving Care: A Research Perspective

Mike Stein

Introduction

This chapter reviews the research evidence and official data from England, Northern Ireland, Scotland and Wales in relation to young people, aged 16–18, who leave the care of local authorities in these jurisdictions. It draws on and further develops the author's earlier and ongoing collaborative work in this area (Stein and Carey, 1986; Biehal et al., 1995; Stein, 1997; Stein and Wade, 2000; Stein et al., 2000, Dixon and Stein, 2002).

Numbers and Characteristics of Young People who Leave Care

In the year ending 31st March 2000 (the latest year for comparable data for all four jurisdictions), 6800 young people, aged 16 and over, left care in England, 1057 left care in Scotland, 106 left care in Wales aged 18 (no data on 16 and 17-year-olds, and 178 left care in Northern Ireland. In England and Scotland most of these young people left at 16 and 17, only in Northern Ireland did over half leave at 18. Data based on England and Scotland reveals a greater percentage of young men than young women, aged 16–18, who left care.

There is no official data available on the numbers of black (Black Afro-Caribbean, Asian, Mixed Heritage) young people leaving care within the four jurisdictions. Research evidence indicates that children of mixed heritage are more likely to enter care than white children and are the largest sub-group of black children being looked after and leaving care, aged 16–18 (Bebbington and Miles,1989; Biehal et al., 1995; Garnett, 1992; Rowe et al., 1989).

In England, between 1993/4–1998/9, the proportion of care leavers (of all 16–18-year-olds and over) aged 16 and 17 rose from 51% to 67% but in 1999/2000 fell back to 59%.

Research evidence from Northern Ireland and England would indicate that between 50 and 66% respectively, of young people aged 16–18, leave care to live independently of their families (Biehal et al., 1995; Pinkerton and McCrea, 1999).

Care leavers, aged 16–18, represent approximately 0.5 to 1% of all 16–18-year-olds within the four UK jurisdictions.

Being in care

Children and young people become 'looked after' by local authorities because their parents are unable to care for them for a variety of reasons – parental problems, abuse or neglect – or because they experience difficulties as they grow up. And some young people become looked after when they arrive in the UK without their parents, seeking refuge from war or oppression in their home country.

From the mid-1970s research studies have made connections between young people's care and after care experiences. These studies have highlighted the diversity of looked after young people and their care histories. Care may have been valued by young people but it often contributed to further problems: disruption through placement movement; a weakening of links with family and community; low educational attainment and participation; poor self-esteem and confusion about their identity, often amplified for black young people brought up in a predominantly 'white' care system; stigma and misunderstanding about care from the general public; and often poor preparation for adulthood with a focus on practical rather than psycho-social skills (see Stein, 1997 for a discussion of these studies).

Leaving home, leaving care and homelessness

Young people leave care to live independently at a much earlier age than other young people leave home. An English survey of 183 young people showed that two thirds of young people left care before they were eighteen and just under a third did so at just sixteen. This contrasts starkly with 87% of 16–18-year-olds who were still living at home (Biehal et al., 1992)). In a Scottish survey of 107 young people, nearly three quarters of those who legally left care did so at 15 (21%) or 16 (52%) years of age in contrast to a modal age of 22 for males and 20 for females (Dixon and Stein, 2002).

Care leavers are over-represented among the young homeless population. A two year follow up study of young people leaving care suggests that over half of the young people will make two or more moves and just over 20% will become homeless at some stage (Biehal et al., 1995). Comparative research drawing on data from England, Northern Ireland and Ireland showed that 15% of young people in England, 20% in Northern Ireland and 16% in Ireland, experience homelessness at some point within six months after leaving care (Stein et al., 2000). In the Scottish survey of 107 young people, 61% of young people had moved 3 or more times, and 40% reported having been homeless since leaving care (Dixon and Stein, 2002). Estimates based upon young homeless people living in hostels suggest between 30%–59% have been in care at some time in their lives (Randall, 1988;1989).

Education

Educational disadvantage casts a long shadow. Young people leaving care have lower levels of educational attainment and participation rates than young people in the general population. In the English survey of 183 young people, two thirds had no qualifications at all, only 15% had a GCSE (A–C grade) or its equivalent, and 0.5% an A level pass. For the equivalent year, nationally, 38%, and locally, 30%, attained five or more GCSE passes at A–C grade. As regards A level, 25% of boys and 29% of girls attained at least one pass (Biehal et al., 1992). In the Scottish survey almost two thirds of young people had no standard grade qualifications compared to the national average of 7 standard grades, and most had experience of truancy (83%) and exclusion (71%) (Dixon and Stein, 2002).

Analysis of data from the UK wide National Child Development Study, comparing 12,128 young people who had never been in care with 372 who had experienced care, revealed that of the 23-year-olds who had been in care, 43% had no qualifications compared with only 16% of their peers who had never been in care (Cheung and Heath, 1994).

Employment and careers

Care leavers are more likely to be unemployed than other young people, aged 16–19, in the population at large. In a recent survey and follow up study 36.5% and 50% respectively were unemployed compared to a mean of 19% for other young people (Biehal et al., 1995). Nearly two thirds of young people surveyed in the Scottish research had poor employment outcomes (Dixon and Stein, 2002).

Analysis of the National Child Development Study UK data revealed that young people who had been in care were much more likely to be unemployed or be in unskilled or semi-skilled manual work, and were less likely to be in managerial work than their peers who had never been in care (Cheung and Heath, 1994). Analysis of the same data also revealed that unqualified young people who had been in care were also more disadvantaged in employment opportunities than unqualified young people who had never been in care.

A survey of leaving care projects working with 2,905 young people showed that just 11% of the total sample were working full time, 27.5% were participating in youth training, further or higher education, 4% were in part-time work and 51% were unemployed – two and a half times the unemployment rate for young people in this age range (Broad, 1998).

Comparative research showed that 66% of care leavers in England and 50% in Northern Ireland and Ireland left school with no qualifications at all. Most of those young people who had qualifications had low achievement levels and left school at the minimum school leaving age in their respective areas (Stein et al., 2000).

Poverty

The impact of poor educational and employment outcomes leaves many care leavers ill prepared for an increasingly competitive youth labour market. The pattern for many of these young people was periods of unemployment punctuated by training schemes and short-term unemployment. A consistent finding from the UK studies completed since the mid 1970s has been that the vast majority of care leavers live at or near the poverty line (see Stein, 1997; Broad, 1999; Dixon and Stein, 2002; Pinkerton and McCrea, 2000).

Young parenthood

Two English research studies reveal that young women leaving care between 16–18 are more likely to be young mothers than other young women of that age group. They show that between 25%–50% of young women, aged 16–19, were young parents compared to 5% in the same age population. Also, just over half of the young parents reported that their pregnancies were unplanned (Garnett, 1992; Biehal et al., 1992;1995). For young parents who are supported, parenthood may also bring some benefits – a renewal of family links and improved relationships as well as furthering an adult 'non care' status (Hutson, 1997).

Differences between black and white young people

There are very few studies which have been able to make significant comparisons between black and white young people, or are solely of black young people leaving care. The largest group of black young people being 'looked after' and leaving care are young people of mixed heritage (Rowe at al., 1987). As a group black young people enter care earlier and stay longer than white young people. Research has also highlighted identity problems derived from a lack of contact with family and community as well as direct and indirect discrimination upon their lives after leaving care (Ince, 1998).

After leaving care black young people had similar employment and housing careers, but were slightly more likely to make better educational progress than white young people. Most black young people had experienced racist harassment and abuse and some mixed heritage young people felt they were not accepted by black or white people (Barn, 1993; Barn et al., 1997; Biehal et al., 1995).

Young disabled people and young people with mental health problems

There has been very little research into the experiences of young disabled people leaving care (Rabiee et al., 2001). Data on 131 young disabled people showed that there was a lack of planning, inadequate information and poor consultation with them. Their transitions from care could be abrupt or delayed by restricted housing and employment options and inadequate support after leaving care (Rabiee et al., 2001).

Research studies show that approximately 13% of young people leaving care have special needs including emotional and behavioural problems, learning difficulties, a physical disability or mental health problems. Compared to other young people leaving care this group of young people have fewer educational qualifications, are more likely to be unemployed and be homeless (Biehal et al., 1995).

Analysis of UK data from the National Child Development Study, comparing the mental health of care leavers with other young adults, indicates the higher risk of depression at age 23 and 33, the higher incidence of psychiatric and personality disorders and greater levels of emotional and behavioural problems (Cheung and Buchanan, 1997).

In a study of care leavers, 17% had long term mental illnesses including depression, eating disorders and phobias, females being greatly over-represented. In the same study just over a third had deliberately self harmed, two thirds had thought about taking their own lives and 40% had tried to between the age of 15–18, at the time of leaving care (Saunders and Broad, 1997).

Offending, drug and alcohol abuse

Popular perceptions connect being in care with crime, alcohol and substance abuse – although the very limited research in this area indicates care leavers are similar to their peers. In one study over half of care leavers never had any involvement with the police and a further quarter had relatively minor problems prior to or during their time in care – a similar pattern to non-care young people. Young people interviewed at the time of leaving care reported a similar pattern of drug use to young people in the general population, nearly one half having never used drugs (Biehal et al., 1995).

Estimates based on adult and young prisoners who at some time in their lives have been in care suggests 23% and 38% respectively (Prison Reform Trust, 1991). However, we need to take into account that these estimates include a prison population of all ages who at sometime in their lives – any time from a week upwards, at any age, from birth onwards, have been in care. Care may have literally been a week of their lives when they were three weeks old! Many other factors may have influenced their lives.

Leaving Care Services

From the mid-1980s, partly in response to the problems documented by the research cited above, some voluntary organisations and local authorities began to develop specialist leaving care projects and schemes. These aimed to provide a focused response to the core needs of care leavers – for help with accommodation, personal support, assistance with finance and help with careers.

In the literature, specialist schemes have been classified in different ways. In 1986, Stein and Carey made the distinction between independence and inter-dependence models and linked programme content, the former training young people to manage on their own at sixteen years of age – domestic combat courses, the latter focusing on inter-personal skills, developing self-esteem and providing ongoing support after leaving care (Stein and Carey, 1986).

In 1995, Biehal et al. proposed a three dimensional classification based upon:

- Approaches to service delivery in terms of perspective, methods of working and the extent to which their work is young person demand-led or social work planned.
- The nature of the providing agency.
- The contribution schemes make to leaving care policy within their local areas.

Biehal et al., 1995.

In 1998, Broad made the distinction between three models of leaving care work: a social justice model aimed at empowerment, a social welfare model aimed at improvement and a technical assistance model aimed at independence (Broad, 1998).

In 2000, Stein and Wade described four main models of local authority wide provision based upon a survey of best practice: a non-specialist service – where responsibility for delivering service rests primarily with field workers; a centrally organised specialist service – comprising of a centrally organised team of workers providing an authority wide service; a dispersed specialist service – in which individual specialist leaving care workers are attached to area based teams; and a centrally organised integrated service – providing a service to a wider range of vulnerable young people 'in need' including homeless young people, young offenders and young disabled people (Stein and Wade, 2000).

Research studies in the four jurisdictions have also highlighted the variation in the quality, range and resourcing of leaving care and aftercare services (Broad, 1998; Stein et al., 2000; Dixon and Stein, 2002). In England and Wales the permissive nature of the leaving care provisions contained within the Children Act 1989 and the complex, inconsistent and discouraging social policy framework, identified by research, have contributed to a strengthening of the law through the introduction of the Children (Leaving Care) Act 2000.

The Outcomes of Leaving Care Services

How effective are leaving care services? This is not an easy question to answer as there have been very few studies which have compared the outcomes for care leavers receiving specialist services with the outcomes for other groups of care leavers. The only English study to make such comparisons pointed to two ways of answering this question (Biehal et al., 1995).

First, leaving care schemes can make a positive contribution to specific outcomes for care leavers in respect of accommodation and life skills, including budgeting, negotiating and self-care skills. They were less able to compensate young people who had poor social networks and relationship skills, nor were they able to improve the career paths of young people, an area in which poor outcomes were the norm for both samples of care leavers.

Second, the study was able to identify other factors which contributed to positive outcomes. Successful educational outcomes were closely linked to placement stability, more often achieved in foster care placements, combined with a supportive and encouraging environment for study. Without such stability and encouragement, post-16 employment and career outcomes were likely to be very poor. Success in social networks, personal relationships and in having a positive self-image, although assisted by specialist schemes, was also closely connected with young people having positive, supportive relationships with family members or former carers. There is also evidence that those young people who leave care later do better than those who leave at 16 or 17 years of age.

The main findings from this English study are supported by research carried out in Northern Ireland, particularly in relation to the positive contribution made by schemes in assisting young people with their accommodation and self-care skills. Those young people who made successful transitions from health board care were likely to have experienced more stability and continuity, have more educational qualifications, experience planned transitions from care, and leave care at an older age, than less successful care leavers (Pinkerton and McCrea, 1999). Research in to the outcomes of leaving care services in Scotland has demonstrated the positive contribution made by stability to educational attainment, as well as throughcare planning, and personal and professional support to assisting young people after care (Dixon and Stein, 2002).

Conclusion

Most young people, whether they are living with their own family or in foster care or a children's home, experience some problems during their journey to adulthood. Care leavers share a lot in common with other young people but the research evidence points to some significant differences.

In comparison to their peers in the general population, too many young people leaving care have to cope with the challenges and responsibilities of major changes in their lives – in leaving care and setting up home, in leaving school and entering the world of work, or more likely being unemployed, and in being parents – at a far younger age than other young people. Too many of these young people have both compressed and accelerated transitions to adulthood.

Young disabled people may experience abrupt and delayed transitions and black young people may face additional problems due to their isolation from their families as well as racism.

Specialist leaving care services may assist these young people. But they must build upon good quality substitute care. Providing placement stability, continuity of caring, family and carer links, encouragement with education, and planned transitions – young people leaving care at an age when they are prepared and ready – are the essential foundations of providing effective after-care services.

References

Barn, R. (1993) *Black Children in the Public Care System*, London, Batsford.

Barn, R., Sinclair, R. and Ferdinand, D. (1997) *Acting on Principal: An Examination of Race and Ethnicity in Social Services Provision to Children and Families*, London, BAAF.

Bebbington, A. and Miles, J. (1989) The Background of Children Who Enter Local Authority Care, *British Journal of Social Work* **19**: 5, 349–36.

Biehal, N., Clayden, J., Stein, M. and Wade, J. (1992) *Prepared for Living? A Survey of Young People Leaving the Care of Three Local Authorities*, London, National Children's Bureau.

Biehal, N., Clayden, J., Stein, M. and Wade, J. (1995) *Moving on: Young People and Leaving Care Schemes*, London, HMSO.

Broad, B. (1998) *Young People Leaving Care, Life after the Children Act 1989*, London, Jessica Kingsley.

Cheung, Y. and Heath, A. (1994) After Care: The Education and Occupation of Adults Who Have Been in Care, *Oxford Review of Education* 20: 3, 361–37.

Cheung, Y. and Buchanan, A. (1997) Malaise Score in Adulthood of Children and Young People Who Have Been in Care, *Journal of Child Psychology and Psychiatry* 38: 5, 575–80.

Dixon, J. and Stein, M. (2002) *Still a Bairn? A Study of Throughcare and Aftercare Service in Scotland*, Edinburgh, Scottish Executive.

First Key (1987) *A Study of Black Young People Leaving Care*, Leeds, First Key.

Garnett, L. (1992) *Leaving Care and After*, London, National Children's Bureau.

Hutson, S. (1997) *Supported Housing: The Experience of Care Leavers*, Ilford, Barnardo's.

Ince, L. (1998) *Making it Alone: A Study of the Care Experiences of Young Black People*, London, BAAF.

Pinkerton, J. and McCrea, R. (1999) *Meeting the Challenge? Young People Leaving Care in Northern Ireland*, Aldershot, Ashgate.

Prison Reform Trust (1991) *The Identikit Prisoner*, London, PRT.

Rabiee, P., Priestley, and Knowles, J. (2001) *Whatever Next? Young Disabled People Leaving Care*, First Key, Leeds.

Randall, G. (1988) *No Way Home*, London, Centrepoint.

Randall, G. (1989) *Homeless and Hungry*, London, Centrepoint.

Rowe, J., Hundleby, M. and Garnett, L. (1989) *Child Care Now*, London, Batsford BAAF.

Saunders, L., and Broad, B. (1997) *The Health Needs of Young People Leaving Care*, Leicester, De Montfort University.

Stein, M. and Corey, K. (1986) *Leaving Care*, Oxford, Basil/Blackwell.

Stein, M. (1997) *What Works in Leaving Care?* Barkingside, Barnardo's.

Stein, M., Pinkerton, J. and Kelleher, P. (2000) Young People Leaving Care in England, Northern Ireland and Ireland, *European Journal of Social Work* 3: 3, 235–46.

Stein, M. and Wade, J. (2000) Helping Care Leavers: Problems and Strategic Responses, London, DoH.

4. Developing an International Perspective on Leaving Care

John Pinkerton

Leaving care is more firmly on the child care agenda in the UK than it has ever been before and attention to it is growing. Long term campaigning by a wide range of concerned individuals and organisations within both the voluntary and statutory sector, the research community and by young care leavers themselves at last seems to be getting results. There is well founded cause for optimism that legislation, policy and services are going to come together to ensure care leavers with the opportunities they need and deserve to achieve their potential and have satisfying and successful lives. Given that achievement it seems an opportune moment for everyone involved within the leaving care field to take some time for reflection. This chapter will argue that such reflection must include locating the progress that has been made in the UK within an inter-country and global context. It will also suggest that this is not easy to do because whilst a start has been made on developing an international perspective on leaving care there is still much to be done before there is even a sound foundation in place.

Developing an international perspective has to be accepted as yet another area of work to add to the immediate challenges of drafting legislation, developing policy, putting operational management systems in place, delivering support and services, researching and evaluating. The potential benefits for all those involved in care leaving, especially the young people themselves, fully justifies the effort. Developing an international perspective is one of the ways, and an increasingly important one, through which to build up the commitment, understanding and networks of the support that are crucial to ensuring that the present advances being made for care leavers in the UK are secured and become part of a global resource.

Why an International Perspective is Useful

The idea of 'globalisation' has become a part of the everyday vocabulary of culture, politics and economics. Even so there is considerable debate about the term: what exactly does it mean; is it a recent phenomena or centuries old; should it be understood as a process or a stage of social development; should it be viewed as positive or negative (Clarke, 2000; Khan and Dominneli, 2000; Mann, 2001). Whatever the answers to those questions, the ascendant position of the term clearly registers the extent to which it is now recognised that there is a world wide interconnectedness and interdependence that both characterises and is driving social change. Recognising and understanding the characteristics and process of change through globalisation is necessary if it is to be managed – particularly if it is to be managed in the interests of groups who find themselves pushed into the margins of society. Young people leaving care are just such a socially excluded group. As with all their peers (Coleman and Hendry, 1999) their transition to adulthood requires that they 'negotiate a set of risks which were largely unknown to their parents' and contend with a pace of change that creates 'increased uncertainty (that) can be seen as a source of stress and vulnerability' (Furlong and Cartmel, 1997, p1). Their particular vulnerability is evidenced in the litany of poor life chance indicators associated with care leaving: educational underachievement, early parenthood, homelessness, poor employment prospects and poverty. Such outcomes are known only too well to care leavers themselves and to those working with them, as well as being demonstrated repeatedly by research (Atherton and Williams, 2000). To take an international perspective is to recognise that the success or failure of the serious attempt being made in the UK to address the risk and vulnerability of care leaving will be linked to world wide social, economic and political developments.

It is increasingly acknowledged that developments in any single country cannot be explained without setting them in the context of wider – global – changes. Yet there is a danger that the new orthodoxy may make it rather easy to espouse a comparative approach without being quite clear why or what questions can be most helpfully illuminated through comparison.

Cochrane, 1993, p1.

That caution is a useful one, especially at the start of developing an international perspective on care leaving. To be clear about why and what questions to ask requires firstly recognising that there are a number of ways of thinking internationally. One is to look for concepts that have a global relevance. Are there key ideas that would allow anyone anywhere in the world to ask useful questions about leaving care in their own country and in other countries? If there are such concepts, how might they inform a review of the present situation in the UK? Do they reframe our experience in a way that extends our understanding? Do they give cause for optimism or caution?

A second approach to thinking internationally is to try to locate within different national contexts what appear to be similar types of need and the associated services. In other countries are there young people making the transition to adulthood from state care? What legal, policy and service provision is made to prepare them for leaving and to support them once they have left care? Where such young people exist does the way in which their needs are understood add anything to how care leavers needs are thought about in the UK? Within the provision that is made for these young people in other countries are there ways of doing things which could be transposed and adapted to improve our legislation, policy and practice?

Both these approaches provide the means for cross national transfer of knowledge and

information which can provide the basis for global benchmarking. This is a two way process providing opportunities for the UK experiences to inform developments in other countries as well as learn from them – 'the model is not one of enslavement, borrowing or copying but creative transformation' (Hetherington et al., 1997, p187). Such international sharing of knowledge and information in pursuit of the creative transformation of practice requires comparison and explanation at three levels or 'domains' – the macro, the mezzo and the micro:

The macro domain refers to large scale international social processes directly affecting nation states and indirectly effecting local ... practices within them ... The mezzo domain can be viewed as the site where relationships between the nation-state, welfare regimes and social professions are played out ... Whilst the macro and mezzo domains tend to focus more on the role of wider social structures and institutional prerogatives, the micro domain alludes to the specific activity of everyday ... practice.

Houston and Campbel, 2001, p68.

Difficulties with Cross Country Comparison

As more attention is given to international comparison there is growing recognition of the difficulties involved in achieving it (May, 1998). One difficulty lies with gathering the necessary information. There are a huge number of potential sources of information – international instruments, national laws, statutory guidance and regulations, government statistics, academic research and accounts of practice reported in books, journals, pamphlets and conference proceedings. Whilst access to these through systematic literature review has been made much easier by the developments in information technology many practical difficulties continue to exist (Higgins and Pinkerton, 1998). There is the very real constraint of not knowing more than one language; a particular problem within countries where English is the first language. The dominance of British imperialism in the past and America in the present, means that whilst on the one hand many different countries experiences can be accessed through English, on the other hand the stunted language proficiency of many English speakers closes off other potentially rich sources. There is also the difficulty of finding data which is really comparable. National information gathering systems are generally geared to meeting the requirements of their own administrative structures. These take many different forms reflecting the varied cultural norms, economic strength and political choices found across the world. As a result even where reliable data sets exist they may not lend themselves to meaningful cross country comparison.

Even the most cursory attempt at a search of the international literature on leaving care will demonstrate the types of practical problems mentioned above, but there is also a more deep seated difficulty. The experience of attempting an international literature review of leaving care prompts the same sense of 'after care – afterthought' that was so characteristic of the field in the past in the UK. An earlier book in this series, focused on foster care, included a chapter that provided an international perspective (Sellick, 1999). Whilst it noted the 'enormous difficulties in constructing definitions, comparisons or frameworks for shaping foster care on a world stage' (p33), it was at least able to draw on 'a considerable amount of recent literature (which) has sought to achieve a world view of foster care policy and practice' (p33). At present such a resource does not exist for leaving care. It seems that in the international child welfare literature leaving care has yet to be recognised as an area of shared global concern. This both reflects and is reflected by the underdeveloped state of international networks linking those responsible for providing leaving care services, the young people experiencing them or researchers with an interest in the area.

It is also worth noting that in general international comparison of social care needs and services suffer from the degree to which they are culturally and system specific. This is perhaps a particular difficulty for leaving care which is in essence about the move from a state system of child care to the world of adulthood within civil society. Both the state

and the civil society sides of that transition are heavily marked by national circumstances. Just consider the difficulties in trying to meaningfully compare the leaving care practice of a newly established voluntary organisation in Romania with a local authority project in England. Both the nature of the state and of civil society are so different in the two countries. Increasingly that question may also have relevance within the UK itself, as New Labour's constitutional reforms allow England, Scotland, Wales and Northern Ireland to develop services specifically tailored to their national contexts. It is already the case that in primary children's legislation leaving care is dealt with differently in Scotland from the other jurisdictions (Tisdall, Lavery and McCrystal, 1998). There are efforts being made to ensure that additional legislation anticipated in Northern Ireland following the Leaving Care Act 2000 for England and Wales is grounded in local experience that is being increasingly more confidently articulated (First Key NI, 2001).

That said, research to date across the whole of the UK is depressingly similar in the picture it paints of care leaving as a challenge to young people who are not ready, well prepared or supported in their struggle to meet it (Stein, 1997). Greater confidence can be placed in research findings when a similar approach used in different contexts produce consistent results. For that reason it is interesting to note a set of three linked research projects which surveyed the experience of leaving care not only in two different jurisdictions in the UK, England and Northern Ireland, but also in the Republic of Ireland (Biehel et al., 1992; Pinkerton and McCrea, 1999; Kelleher et al., 2000). Methodology for surveying care leavers developed by researchers in Leeds in the early 1990s was adapted for use in Northern Ireland in the mid 1990s and that in turn was used as the basis for a study in the late 1990s in the Republic of Ireland. In this way comparable data was generated for each jurisdiction. However, even in these closely linked studies there were differences; including the exact definition of what constituted leaving care. In Ireland, in addition to welfare care leavers, young people were surveyed who had left training schools in the North and special schools and probation hostels in the South.

When the survey results for the welfare care leavers within the Irish and the two UK jurisdictions were compared a great deal of similarity was reported about care careers and outcomes (Stein, Pinkerton and Kelleher, 2000). In all three jurisdictions around three in five of the young people had entered care aged over 11 years old, four out of five had been in care for more than a year, significant proportions had experienced multiple placements and for two out of five the last placement was residential care. Despite differences in the timing of care leaving and the type, source and extent of support provided in each jurisdiction, all three surveys found that significant proportions of the young people experienced difficulties in achieving stable accommodation, underachieved in education, and failed to find employment. Whilst acknowledging that the projects had been undertaken in three closely linked European jurisdictions, comparison of the findings did seem to suggest that there were shared themes and issues which could 'provide a starting point for comparative work with other European countries ... (which would) ... contribute to a greater understanding of the determinants of social inclusion and the achievement of citizenship status of this highly vulnerable group of young people' (Stein, Pinkerton and Kelleher, 2000, p245).

European Comparisons

A very useful start to considering the position of care leavers more broadly within Europe has been made by the Centre for Europe's Children (CEC), a partnership between Glasgow University, the Council of Europe, the National Society for the Prevention of Cruelty to Children, Save the Children Fund – UK and the United Nations Children's Fund (http://eurochild.gla.ac.uk). From a Scottish starting point the CEC attempted to review what comparative information was available on through care and aftercare across the European Union (Bilson et al., 2001). From what has been said earlier it could be predicted that this was not going to be easy. A study carried out for the European Commission looking more generally at young people and youth policy in Europe found that: 'The majority of young

people continue to be bound to their local contexts and their national perspectives, cultural habits and lifestyles' (IARD, 2001, p11). However the CEC took the view that:

Although there are problems in carrying out comparative research, cross national comparison is not a fruitless exercise. However it should be noted that there is a need to undertake it with a full appreciation of its complexity and to recognise that, even where similar terms are used these may have substantial differences in meaning and be applied within very different contexts. The benefit of considering these different approaches is that they can highlight hidden assumptions in our own thinking; offer evidence of different approaches to problems; and can help to appreciate the developing thinking behind the social policies of the European Union.

Bilson et al., 2001, p7.

The CEC review points out that the countries of the European Union (EU) have a shared legal and policy context for leaving care based on two European institutions, both the EU itself and the Council of Europe, and on the United Nations as a global institution. The latter has set an international agenda for children through the Convention on the Rights of the Child (UNCRC) which all European countries are signed up to; as is every other country in the world with the exception of Somalia and, to its shame, the United States of America. The UNCRC recognises both 'that children have civil and political rights, in addition to the more generally accepted rights to protection and provision', and that 'children's lack of an effective voice in the political, judicial and administrative systems that impinge on their lives, renders them particularly vulnerable to exploitation, abuse and neglect' (Children's Rights Development Unit, 1994, p3). This double recognition is important for young people leaving care in that it links that transition to the evolving capacity of all children for taking on the rights and responsibilities of citizenship. This allows for 'challenging the construction of marginalised groups as passive victims while keeping sight of the discriminatory and oppressive political, economic and social institutions that still deny them full citizenship' (Lister, 1998, p6). It also makes it clear that the importance of challenging the social exclusion of care leavers, as with any other marginalized group, 'lies not only in what it can achieve in terms of practical outcomes ... but also in the process of involving them in working for change and the impact that both the outcomes and the involvement can have on those individual's capacity to act as citizens.' (Lister, 1998, p6).

The EU framework for national laws provided by the Maastricht and Amsterdam Treaties falls far short of the aspirations of the UNCRC. The CEC review concluded that 'the overall lack of focus on children within the treaties is particularly true for policies relating to state care' (Bilson et al., 2001, p3). That assessment is in line with the assessment of EURONET, a coalition of networks and organisations campaigning for the interests and rights of children (http://europeanchildrensnetwork.gla. ac.uk). It has not only drawn attention to the restricted and unintegrated approach to children's issues by the EU but has also suggested that 'aspects of EU legislation and policy can have unintended but highly damaging consequences for children' (Ruxton, 1999, p2). That said particularly because for care leavers who are engaged in the youth transition from childhood to adulthood there is a range of European law and conventions that are relevant (Bilson et al., 2001, Appendix 1). These relate to both general issues such as citizenship, social exclusion, and discrimination and more specific areas such as prostitution, youth unemployment, education and training.

Further evidence of the lack of attention to children within European social policy is that Eurostat, the EU's statistical service, provides very little information on children and none on care leavers. Faced with that gap, CEC looked for information on care leaving in the most recent national reports submitted by EU countries to the United Nations Committee on the Rights of the Child (under Article 44, State parties to the UNCRC have to make a report within two years of becoming a signatory and thereafter every five). The results were limited. 'The issue of rehabilitation to the child's family is addressed within reports, but the

notion that some young people may commence the transition to adulthood from a care environment rather than a family environment is rarely acknowledged.' (Bilson et al., 2001, p9). That said, references to after care provision were found in the reports submitted by Austria, Belgium, Denmark, France, Germany, Italy, the Netherlands and Spain. However, none of those countries included in their reports specific mention of care leaving and neither did the UK report, despite its considerable attention to issues relating to looked after children.

The report for Sweden, where aftercare is obligatory, identified the task of 'following up and helping children placed in public care' as a major responsibility but did not outline the type of arrangements involved. The report from Norway referred to the fact that care measures which are implemented before the child attains the age of 18 can continue up until the age of 20 with the consent of the young person. The report from Finland noted the obligation of municipalities to 'support the child with after care in the form of non institutional measures e.g. a voluntary placement with a family or an institution'. The report from Ireland referred to Section 45 of their Child Care Act which empowers Health Boards to provide assistance to care leavers until they are twenty one years old or until they complete full time education. Such assistance can include contributing towards maintenance to help with the completion of a young person's education, placement in a suitable trade, and co-operation with housing authorities in planning accommodation:

What the reports of the various countries reveal is a difference in the age limits and approaches to state support for young people. For example education is compulsory until 18 years old in the Flemish community in Belgium, and in Austria a vocational training allowance is payable to young people until age 27. In Finland young people subject to child welfare measures are entitled to special housing as a welfare measure ... the importance of agency networking (is emphasised) in the report from the Netherlands and (in) Finland's on research and monitoring to ensure that policy and legislation are achieving their goals.

Bilson et al., 2001, p9.

In addition to scanning the UN Committee national reports the CEC focused on statistics, legislation, policy and practice in Scotland, England and Wales, Finland, Germany and the Netherlands. Even though they only focused on that small number of jurisdictions, two of which are within the UK, they found that 'comparative analysis of throughcare and aftercare in the five countries is difficult to achieve due to the paucity of systematic data and the differences in definitions' (Bilson et al., 2001, p4). Despite these difficulties the review of the five jurisdictions (summarised in Table 1) does provide some basic information and a sense of the different ways in which leaving care is approached. It suggests that there is an area of law, policy and practice found across Europe which has as its focus a set of needs and associated services which can be loosely characterised by the term leaving care. However, it is also clearly an area in which there are significant national differences reflecting cultural expectations, law, policy, institutional arrangements and practice traditions.

International Similarities and Suppositions

Looking further afield, a similar description to that applied to Europe can be made in relation to Australia and North America. In a literature review of leaving care undertaken for government in the UK (Stein and Wade, 1999) attention was drawn to an important American study which undertook a systematic comparison of young people leaving 'foster care' (the term used by Americans to cover any form of out of home placement) to one peer group in the general population and to another living below the poverty level:

In general, the status of discharged foster care is only adequate at best. With respect to education, early parenthood, and the use of public assistance, discharged foster care youth more closely resembled those 18–24 year olds living below the poverty level than they did the 18–24 population.

Cook quoted Stein and Wade, 2000, p9.

Poor outcomes have also been clearly identified as a feature of care leaving in Canada (Meston, 1988, Raychaba, 1989). At the same time as noting the over representation of care leavers in the homeless population, in the justice system and in the mental health system, two Canadian researchers drew attention to the lack of systematically gathered data on after care provision, termed post wardship support, by baldly stating that: 'We do know how many young people flounder and fail after they leave care'. In Australia too both research and practice experience show that compared to their peers care leavers are 'more likely to experience homelessness, unemployment, early parenthood, loneliness and despair' (Maunders et al., 1999, pvii). Research there into the experience of leaving care, or wardship to use the term they share with the Canadians, has also shown that, as in Europe, both care and aftercare encompass a wide variety of experiences (Cashmore and Paxman, 1996).

The variation in experience in part reflects the complex and varied nature of need, including that of indigenous peoples, but it also reflects the complicated levels of administrative structures that follow from the federated nature of the United States, Canada and Australia. Central government is limited in its legislative capacity generally having to encourage child welfare and youth policy development through standard setting and funding. The mixed economy of welfare, particularly in its heavily privatised form in the US, further works against a single model of provision. Depending on circumstances of place as much as of need, any one of a wide variety of 'emancipation' services and activities may be offered to care leavers in the US (Nollan, 1996). They may receive help to achieve a high school diploma or take part in vocational training. They may be provided with training in daily living skills such as budgeting, locating and maintaining housing and career planning. Individual and group counselling is also offered. One review of US services (Stein, 1997) divided them into two main types. Categorical Independent Living Services focus on the 'hard skills' that are required to meet the practical demands of independent living. The Integrated Services model by contrast has case work at its core,

Table 1. Some European Comparisons (based on Bilson et al., 2001)

Country	Legislation	General approach	Service example
England and Wales	Children Act 1989	Growth in specialist local authority teams backed by specific policy.	In response to very high rates of unemployment a London project focused on providing vocational guidance, career profiling, help with writing applications and doing interviews, computer training and support, access to training materials, business and enterprise advice and access to administrative support.*
Finland	Child Welfare Act 1983	Provision, which in some municipalities includes specialist throughcare and aftercare projects, depends on local finance and practice traditions.	The YMCA run Spinnaker Project uses a social pedagogic approach to providing training and support for 17–25-year-olds who have been in care, received other forms of child welfare, or are involved in employment support projects
Germany	Children and Youth Assistance Law 1990	Focus is on vocational and educational support with some attention to housing.	Pestalozzi-Frobel-Haus offers therapeutic supervised housing to support adolescents over the age of 14 to come to terms with serious social and psychological problems and learn to shape their lives through vocational guidance and finding appropriate housing
Netherlands	Child and Youth Assistance Law	Provincial and municipal government are responsible for different aspects of financing and providing the extensive and varied network of services	Stichting Jeugdzorg provides not only independence training for young people leaving residential care but also an information and advice project, youth work with young parents, intensive support with schooling and training, support for homeless young people and young refugees and crisis intervention for runaways
Scotland	Children (Scotland) Act 1995	Growth in specialist local authority teams with the Scottish Throughcare and Aftercare Forum providing a national focus	Types of services include individual counselling, group work, drop in advice centres, specialist worker for young people with mental health problems, a 24 hour on-call paging service

*This service example was taken from Broad, 1999, p85.

and emphasises 'soft skills' with self-esteem and emotional well being as the core goals. The review notes that evaluations that have been done of the two approaches highlight the importance of individual assessment in tailoring services and suggest that Categorical programmes tend to miss important areas such as managing birth and foster family relationships. By contrast the Integrated programmes were able to promote both emotional and the practical readiness.

Similarly in Australia it is recognised that many young people leaving care require assistance and support in developing both hard and soft skills (Cashmore and Paxman, 1996). The National Baseline Standards for Out of Home Care requires that 'each child or young person leaves the out of home care placement in a planned and supported manner to enable a successful and sustainable transition' (quoted Maunders et al., 1999, pviii). This requires that young people are directly involved in decision making about their care leaving, have a detailed post placement support plan and leave with relevant documentation, possessions and life records. The reality however is that the policy and procedural manuals guiding much of the day to day practice 'outline broad case-planning principles but pay scant attention to preparing young people for life after care and to ensuring options for ongoing support and assistance' (Maunders et al., 1999, pviii). Despite all the States and Territories having endorsed the National Baseline Standards, research suggests that many young people are discharged in an unplanned fashion, at the age of 15 and 16, before they are ready to cope. However there are examples of innovative practice such as that focused on meeting the needs of aboriginal young people – an expression of cultural sensitivity from which UK practice could learn (Ince, 1999).

It may well be that anywhere in the world where there is a system of out of home care a similar picture of care leaving exists to the one that is emerging from the countries reviewed above. Globally leaving care may be characterised by the vulnerability of the young people involved and the inadequacy of the preparation and support made available to them. However, without the comparative data available that can only be a supposition. It is also important to be open to the possibility of differences that go beyond just national variations on the characteristics that have been identified here. For example it may be that the scale of need in certain countries requires a very different way of thinking about services. In central and eastern Europe the massive economic and social dislocation that has accompanied the political collapse of the Soviet Union and its allied states has led to a situation of somewhere in the region of a million children, that is one in a hundred, being in care. The negative aspects of that are compounded by a tradition of heavy reliance on large scale institutional care. What does leaving care mean in that context?

A monitoring report on central and eastern Europe by the United Nations Children's Fund, (UNICEF, 1997) notes that lack of information is a major problem and that 'many countries provide no data on exits from care' (p17). Data from Russia, the country that contains over half the children in public care in the region, shows that 'between 1989 and 1995 the number of new registrations of children left without parental care jumped by 130 per cent – up from 49,100 to 113,2962' (p17) and that some 80,000 children and young people left care in the mid 1990s. Such rapid and unplanned care leaving for thousands of young people has led to a situation where it has been reported that one in three care leavers become homeless and one in ten attempts suicide (Bilson et al., p5). Discussion of the benefits of individual young people attaining either hard or soft skills seems almost irrelevant in that context. Similarly, can the experience of North America or Europe really hold good in countries where, as a UN End of Decade Review follow up to the 1990 World Summit for Children notes: 'the issue is not excessive reliance on institutionisation ... (but) ... over-reliance on informal or traditional forms of adoption or fostering, or on private child care institutions or international adoption networks, which frequently operate in a legal vacuum with little or no supervision, often as a result of the weakness of the public sector.' (United Nations, 2001, p114). What are the leaving care issues likely to be in that context?

Towards an International Perspective

It is clear that there is a long way to go before there is anything close to an adequately informed and coherent international picture of leaving care. However, even in the review above there is enough to suggest the direction that needs to be taken if the questions posed at the start of this chapter and the end of the last section are to be answered. Just as it has now been recognised within the UK that it is networks of support which are required to deliver the necessary joined up solutions required by care leavers (Broad, 1999) so too making progress on developing an international perspective will depend on effective networking. In this context network can be usefully defined as 'an international association, union, federation or grouping of organisations, experts or individuals to share information and (devise) a common course of action on a problem or issue' (Harvey quoted in Lyons, 1999, p46). There are already a number of existing networks that could share information and agree a common course of action on issues of leaving care. There are ones concerned with general child care issues such as EURONET and Childwatch International (http://www.childwatch.uio.no). Childwatch is a non-profit, non-governmental network of institutions involved in research for children. It aims to initiate and co-ordinate research and information projects on children's living conditions and the implementation on children's rights as expressed in the UN Convention on the Rights of the Child. It is the sort of network that could ensure the pooling of the national research and information that exists and provide the basis for cross national research based on a shared, but flexible methodology. A systematic review of recent national reports to the UN Committee on the Rights of the Child would also be a useful exercise for such a network.

Other networks based on more specific areas of child care such as the International Foster Care Organisation (www.internationalfostering.org) and the European Association for Residential and Youth Care (www.euroarc.net/) would clearly have an interest in promoting exchange around issues of care leaving. Of particular importance is the forging of relations between the various national organisations of young people in care themselves. There is also great scope for cross national coalitions around specific short term projects. For example the Umbrella Programme is a European funded three year project involving partner organisations in Scotland, Finland, Germany, Sweden and the Netherlands. The aim of the project is to address issues relating to socially excluded youth with an emphasis on education and training and a particular focus on young people leaving care. The intention is to produce collaboratively new practice materials for through care and after care and also study modules for higher education and initial vocational training (Bilson et al., p19–20).

In consolidating these networks there are a number of key ideas that are worth exploring for their potential to ask useful questions about leaving care in different countries and as a global issue. At the level of the macro domain there needs to be work done on whether and in what way the concept of globalisation helps in characterising and explaining the large scale international social processes underpinning the social exclusion experienced by so many young people leaving care. At the mezzo level citizenship, understood as 'a force for social inclusion' (Lister, 1998, p5) and linked with the idea of youth transition, would help to identify the similarities and differences in the way in which nation-states, welfare regimes and social professions respond to care leavers. At the micro level the idea of care career, with its focus on the components of time periods and key decisions, would provide structure to help in the production of comparable, detailed descriptions of practice. Such descriptions could be usefully considered against criteria based on global best practice principles such as:

- Managed process of assessment, planning, implementation and review.
- Engagement sought from the relevant informal and formal support networks.
- Full range of material and psycho social needs addressed.
- Young person actively involved and consulted throughout.

Leaving care is fundamentally about the state shouldering its responsibility to young people leaving its care and so inter-governmental co-operation is crucial to advancing an international perspective. This is not easy to achieve. The UN End of Decade Review noted:

What is striking about the follow up process in the aftermath of the World Summit for Children is the time it took – and still takes – for political consensus on children to be translated into effective action. For many reasons we do not always quickly apply what we know.

United Nations, 2001, p132.

The same document stresses the importance of setting targets if effective action is to be taken. The UN Children's Rights Committee (UNCRC) has held a number of Days of General Discussion where a subject, for example violence in the family and schools, was chosen for attention. A UNCRC Day of General Discussion on children in state care which could give leaving care the attention it warrants would be a major boost to developing political and professional consensus around an international perspective on leaving care.

References

Atherton, C. and Williams, M. (Eds.) (2000) *Transitions to Adulthood: Services for Care Leavers*, Dartington, Research in Practice.

Barry, M. (2001) *A Sense of Purpose: Care Leavers' Views and Experiences of Growing Up*, Edinburgh, Save the Children.

Biehel, N., Clayden, J., Stein, M. and Wade, J. (1992) *Prepared for Living*, London, National Childrens Bureau.

Bilson, A., Buist, M., Caulfield-Dow, A. and Lindsey, M. (2001) *A Safe Launch: Scottish Throughcare and Aftercare in a European Context*, Glasgow, Centre for Europe's Children.

Broad, B. (1999) Young People Leaving Care: Moving Towards 'Joined Up' Solutions? *Children and Society* **13**, 81–93.

Cashmore, J. and Paxman, M. (1996) *Longitudinal Study of Wards Leaving Care*, New South Wales, Department of Community Services.

Children's Rights Development Unit. (1994) *UK Agenda for Children*, London, CRDU.

Clarke, J. (2000) A World of Difference? Globalization and the Study of Social Policy in Lewis, G., Gewirtz, and Clarke, J. (Eds.) *Rethinking Social Policy*, London, Sage.

Cochrane, A. (1993) Comparative Approaches and Social Policy in Cochrane, A. and Clarke, J. (Eds.) *Comparing Welfare States*, London, Sage.

Coleman, J. and Hendry, L. (1999) The Nature of Adolescence (3rd edn) London, Routledge.

First Key NI. (2001) *Submission to the Department of Health, Social Services and Public Safety on Proposals for a Children Leaving Care Bill*, Belfast, First Key (NI).

Furlong, A. and Cartmel, F. (1997) *Young People and Social Change*, Buckingham, Open University Press.

Hetherington, R., Cooper, A., Smith, P. and Wilford, G. (1997) *Protecting Children: Messages from Europe*, Lyme Regis, Russell House Publishing.

Higgins, K. and Pinkerton, J. (1998) Literature Reviewing: Towards a More Rigorous Approach, in Iwaniec, D. and Pinkerton, J. (Eds.) *Making Research Work*, Chichester, Wiley.

Houston and Campbel. (2001) Using Critical Social Theory to Develop a Conceptual Framework for Comparative Social Work, *International Social Welfare*, 10, 66–73.

IARD. (2001) *Study on the State of Young People and Youth Policy in Europe – Executive Summary*, Milan, IARD – Instituto di Ricerca S.C.R.L.

Ince, L. (1999) Preparing Young Black People for Leaving Care, in Barn, R. (Ed.) *Working with Black Children and Adolescents in Need*, London, British Agencies for Adoption and Fostering.

Kelleher, P., Kelleher, C. and Corbett, M. (2000) *Left out on Their Own: Young People Leaving Care in Ireland*, Dublin, Oak Tree Press.

Khan, P. and Dominneli, L. (2000) The Impact of Globalization on Social Work in the UK, *European Journal of Social Work* **3**:2, 95–108.

Lister, R. (1998) Citizenship on the Margins: Citizenship, Social Work and Social Action, *European Journal of Social Work* **1**:1, 5–18.

Mann, M. (2001) Globalization and September 11, *New left Review*, 12 (Second Series), 51–72.

Martin, F. R. and Palmer, T. (1997) Transitions to Adulthood: A Child Welfare Youth Perspective, *Community Alternatives* 9:2, 29–59.

Meston, J. (1988) Preparing Young People in Canada for Emancipation from Child Welfare Care, *Child Welfare* LXVII:6, 625–34.

May, M. (1998) The Role of Comparative Study in Alcock, P., Erskine, A. and May, M. (Eds.) *The Student's Companion to Social Policy*, London, Blackwell.

Maunders, D., Liddell, M. and Green, S. (1999) *Young People Leaving Care and Protection*, Hobart, Australian Clearinghouse for Youth Studies.

Nollan, K. A. (1996) *Self Sufficiency Skills Among Youth in Long Term Foster Care*, PhD Dissertation University of Washington, USA.

Pinkerton, J. (1999) Leaving Care and Fostering Issues, in Kelly, G. and Gilligan, R. (Eds.) *Foster Care, Policy, Practice and Research*, London, Jessica Kingsley.

Pinkerton, J. and McCrea, R. (1999) *Meeting the Challenge? Young People Leaving State Care in Northern Ireland*, Aldershot, Ashgate.

Raychaba, B. (1989) Canadian Youth in Care: Leaving Care to be on our own with no Direction from Home, *Children and Youth Services Review* 11: 61–73.

Ruxton, S. (1999) *A Children's Policy for 21st Century Europe: First Steps – Executive Summary*, Glasgow, Euronet.

Sellick, C. (1999) The International Perspective of Foster Care, in Wheal, A. (Ed.) *The RHP Companion to Foster Care*, Lyme Regis, Russell House Publishing.

Stein, M. (1997) *What Works in Leaving Care?*, Essex, Barnardo's.

Stein, M., Pinkerton, J. and Kelleher, P. (2000) Young People Leaving Care in England, Northern Ireland and Ireland, *European Journal of Social Work* 3:3, 235–46.

Stein, M. and Wade, J. (2000) *Helping Care Leavers: Problems and Strategic Responses*, London, Department of Health.

Tisdall, K., Lavery, R. and McCrystal, P. (1998) *Child Care Law: A Comparative Review of New Legislation in Northern Ireland and Scotland*, Belfast, Centre for Child Care Research.

United Nations (2001) *We the Children: End-decade Review of the Follow-up to the World Summit for Children*, New York, United Nations.

UNICEF (1997) *Children at Risk in Central and Eastern Europe: Perils and Promises*, Florence, UNICEF.

5. Involving Young People: A Help or a Hindrance?

Martin Hazlehurst and Omri Shalom

In this chapter we will attempt to make sense of what involvement is, discuss the seeming tension between the involvement and children's rights agenda and the role of the local authority as a good parent and examine practical workable examples of good practice in work with care leavers. From the start let us make ourselves clear. We believe involvement is a help not a hindrance. How it can be achieved is the question we will seek to answer.

What is Involvement?

Before proceeding to a definition of involvement we must identify the parameters of what we are talking about. First and foremost young people want to be treated well, to be shown care and respect, to be safe and to have stability and continuity in their lives. Involvement in decision making, whether it be about the decisions relating to their own lives or wider policy and service development, is a crucial and integral part of this. Young people want two different but related and interdependent things. Firstly, to be involved in their individual care planning and the day-to-day decisions which influence their lives. Secondly, many want to be involved in designing the very services to which they have access. This distinction between the individual and strategic is a difference of focus and method. The principles are not different. The operation of a culture which enables one will facilitate the other. Experience tells us that if a social services department wishes to involve young people on a strategic level this will only succeed if young people already feel involved at an individual level. This chapter will focus

specifically on the involvement of young people in the service development. The principles of empowerment relate equally to young peoples feelings of involvement in their care planning and pathway planning.

Next we must clarify the terms we are using. You will notice that so far we have used the term involvement – not consultation. The two, we believe are very different. Consultation is a process of investigation and information collection, involvement is an interactive process requiring control of the process, outputs and outcomes to be a partnership with young people. Very often the term participation is used. We regard this as virtually synonymous with involvement. This distinction is highlighted in the work of Croft and Beresford, pioneers of Community Action. They identified two approaches that they called Consumerist and Empowerment.

Similar issues have been approached in a different way in the Ladder of Participation produced by UNICEF and adapted to work with children and young people (See Figure 2, p47). This provides a clear description of both the differences between consultation and involvement and a methodology for reviewing current practice and planning future strategies.

Successful involvement requires the application of both these theoretical frameworks to real situations and projects. In *First Key* this is represented by a set of criteria to be used in making decisions as to whether a project meets the aim of facilitating genuine involvement. These are:

- Young people must control the agenda of the project.

- The project must aim to establish structures for ongoing involvement.
- The project must seek to develop young peoples' skills and self esteem.

An answer in the affirmative to each of these questions will go a long way to ensuring that involvement not consultation is the purpose of the project and provide one of the benchmarks against which the success of projects can be measured. They are, however, only a starting point to guide and determine the processes to be used.

The policy context

In recent years the question of why and how young people can be involved and influence the shape of their own individual support and care and change the wider environment of the care system itself has become a major issue for social services departments. We do not have to look very far for the reasons for this. The list of statutory, regulatory and international provisions requiring those with responsibility for young people to listen to, and involve them, grows by the year:

- **Children Act 1989 S22(4)**: Before making any decision with respect to a child whom they are looking after, or proposing to look after, a local authority shall, so far as is reasonably practicable, ascertain the wishes and feelings of the child.
- **UN Convention on the Rights of the Child Article 12**: Article 12 1. States: Parties shall assure to the child who is capable of forming his or her own views the right to express those views freely in all matters affecting the child, the views of the child being given due weight in accordance with the age and maturity of the child.
- **Quality Protects Objective 8**: To actively involve users and carers in planning services and in tailoring individual packages of care; and to ensure effective mechanisms are in place to handle them.

Further, a central feature of the Best Value Agenda for public services is the views of consumers of these services.

Of these the current profile given to the need to enable care leavers, and other young people, to participate in the planning, delivery and review of services has been prompted by the Quality Protects Initiative. In their annual Management Action Plans (MAPS) local authorities have to demonstrate the action they have taken towards satisfying Objective 8. In a thematic review of participation in both service planning and delivery and individual care planning in 1999–2000 MAPS some of the conclusions were:

- There was little evidence of overall strategies.
- Some groups of young people, including care leavers, were being consulted more than others.
- There was little evidence of identification of outcomes of participation.
- There was little evidence that a result of activities were structured to ensure regular, ongoing feedback to elected members.

The third of these points requires emphasis. The reading of local authorities' MAPs reveals a great deal of activity to facilitate young peoples' participation but hardly anything which tells us what changed as a result. Concentration on outputs not outcomes will ultimately lead to disillusionment and short-term interest by young people. The fundamental question asked by young people is 'What will change as a result of this'. An inability to answer this will jeopardise the whole process.

In the following year the Department of Health Overview of MAPs for 2000–2001 could say:

Virtually every one of these elements (involvement in individual care planning, involvement in strategic policy development and review and an effective complaints process) have shown significant improvements in the MAPs this year ... The most fundamental improvement of all is in the development of strategic frameworks for involvement.

We are, if this is to be believed, in a period when we no longer have to advocate for the involvement of young people. We can focus on the how not the why.

These measures do not exist in isolation from wider societal changes. Slowly, sometimes very slowly, young people are being given more influence over their own lives. Most parents of teenagers will tell you that the relationships they

FULL PARTICIPATION

8 Child-initiated, shared decisions with adults

Children have the ideas, set up the project and come to adults for advice, discussion and support. The adults do not direct but offer their expertise for the children to consider.

7 Child-initiated and directed

Children have the initial idea and decide how the project is to be carried out. Adults are available but do not take charge.

6 Adult-initiated, shared decisions with children

Adults have the initial idea but children are involved in every step of the planningand implementation. Not only are their views considered, but they are also involved in taking the decisions.

5 Consulted and informed

The project is designed and run by adults but children are consulted. They have a full understanding of the process and their opinions are taken seriously.

4 Assigned but informed

Adults decide on the project and children volunteer for it. The children understand the project, and know who decided why they should be involved and why. Adults respect their views.

3 Tokenism

Children are asked to say what they think about an issue but have little or no choice about the way they express those views or the scope of the ideas they can express.

2 Decoration

Children take part in an event, e.g. by singing, dancing or wearing 'T' shirts with logos on, but they do not really understand the issues.

1 Manipulation

Children do or say what adults suggest they do, but have no real understanding of the issues OR children are asked what they think, adults use some of the ideas but do not tell them what influence they have had on the final decision.

NON PARTICIPATION

Figure 2. The Ladder of Participation

have with their children are very different to those they had with their parents only a generation ago. There is more openness, honesty and a willingness to involve young people in important decisions affecting the family. The Victorian mantra of "children should be seen and not heard" has been left a long way behind us. Young people, also, have far more economic power than in previous generations. They can shape or be shaped by, depending on your point of view, the environment they live in and the goods they consume. For looked after young people the days of local orders and snakes of children being taken to the shoe shop are hopefully long gone.

What do Young People Want?

At the centre of the debate about involvement is the concern that involvement undermines the role of the parent in the transition of young people from childhood to adulthood. In the case of young people leaving care the local authority is carrying out this parenting role. It is often said that social workers, leaving care workers and other representatives of the local authority should act in the manner of a 'good parent'. How this role impacts on the day-to-day care and support of young people depends on a variety of internal and external forces, including the personal culture and beliefs of the individual worker, the culture and policies of the local authority, the services available and the determination of the young person to kick against boundaries set.

Whether we are concerned with decisions about the lives of, and plans for, an individual young person or involvement in the development of policy and services there is a frequently held belief that young people want everything – and now. This view assumes that young people do not see either the individual or institutional context in which decisions are made. This is rarely true.

Omri Shalom is 18 and has recently left care and now works to improve the care system for other young people. He provides his own explanation of what young people want.

Why should social services want to consult or involve young people?

... because young people have first hand experience of being looked after and social services need to remember they are the service users. To improve services for young people social services need to involve them. How are we supposed to provide a better service without consulting the service users? Also social services should want to consult young people so they (social workers) feel they are trying to improve the service with the help of the service providers. Young people are living in the care system today; they have extensive knowledge of the system and how it can be improved.

Do young people want to be involved? Surely they have better things to do?

Young people (in my opinion) would want to be involved so they can improve the service they receive for themselves and others. We don't like decisions being made about ourselves, wouldn't we prefer to be consulted in the day to day living of our own lives? Young people would prefer to improve the way they receive services from the local authority. They would want to be involved in something which was going to affect them.

What is the difference between being consulted and being involved?

A young person can be told what is going to happen in their life i.e. in care; this is done by being consulted in what will happen. Its important that social services involve young people in making decisions which will affect their daily life so they have some say in what is happening or will be happening to them. Also being consulted can be informing a young person of something and then not seeing them again, whereas being involved is a continuous matter. The local authority needs to realise the importance of young people's involvement.

When the chance to be involved is given why do so few young people take up the offer?

Young people have tried to get their social services to listen to them for ages but instead social services hear what young people say but do they listen? One without the other is like fish without water, pointless! Young people have been involved before but when it was important for them to be involved they were only consulted, this being a waste of time because it defeats the object. Social services need to build trust with young people. At the moment young people will assume that they wont be listened to so they prefer not to waste their time.

It is said that those that do get involved are those who want to moan, not those who have anything positive or helpful to say?

Young people moan because they don't get listened to. If you went into a shop and paid for a telly which didn't work, would you moan? I think you would. Young people don't get listened to enough so moaning is a way of getting it off your chest. It's frustrating talking and being ignored, so instead young people can sometimes moan instead. If we took the time to listen we would probably find that young people have a lot of suggestions to improving and providing a better service. It's hard for young people when they have been ignored for such a long period of time, to automatically trust social services.

Shouldn't social workers do what they think is best for young people rather than always ask them what they want?

How would you feel if someone else ran your life? You had no control in where you lived, what you did and so on. We don't like other people running our lives. You're probably thinking 'OK, but do young people know what's best for them?' so lets compromise. Involve young people, let them have their say, don't lead their lives, guide them. Once again we need to remember that young people are the service users and they are the most important people. No two young people are going to have exactly the same circumstances so their needs will be different and need to be met to their individual case.

Don't adults know best?

About what? Quantum physics ... probably! But its unfair to say adults know better about how young people should lead their lives, when adults are not young people. I'm not saying there is no need for social services. Together we can work as a team. Separately we'll collapse. I'm not saying don't let adults

make any decisions about young people's lives because the local authority is responsible for the young person's welfare, but involve young people. Communicate, discuss, explain, negotiate. Will an adult know better about the care system at the moment when at the end of the day they go home. Young people are in the care system 24/7 (twenty-four hours a day, 7 days a week) and this needs to be remembered.

What difference would it make if social workers did not ask young people what they want?

... they would not be providing a good or adequate service. Are young people not important? You wouldn't go into a restaurant if the waiter didn't give you a choice in what you ate, but this is different. Most young people who are in care don't have a choice; they need to be in care for safety reasons and many others. However we should try and keep a young person's life as stable as possible. To accomplish this we need to involve them. If you're not going to ask them what they want, why are you doing your job?

It has been said that spending valuable time involving young people, takes away valuable time and resources which could be better spent improving services. What do you think about this?

Every person is different, regardless if they are a young person or an adult. Consult every young person as an individual, because we're all individuals. Assuming you know what a young person wants could be wrong for that person. It's not hard to ask them and it makes a difference. We wouldn't like it if people started assuming what we were thinking would we? Why should a young person be different?

How are you going to sort out young people's problems if you don't know what they are? It's good to work with individuals and groups of young people to get a wider picture. This way you can start to make a change for the better. Put the time in and you'll have something to work with. Start making changes to young people's problems, generally you'll find they'll be more comfortable in a focus group for example, and will share their concerns with you. Don't put a price on a young person.

Does anything change as a result of young people being involved?

> *Of course things change. We can find out what's wrong in the care system from young people. Will the staff tell you what is wrong? Considering most of them go home regularly, back to their lives they view things differently. Young people are in the system day in, day out. They don't have somewhere to escape to, because it's their home. The system can be changed for the better, but doing this without the involvement of young people will make it impossible.*

The Barriers to Involvement

In the era of *Quality Protects*, *Best Value* and *Performance Management* it would be dangerous to assert that a local authority would actively discourage the involvement of its care leavers either in their individual Pathway Planning or in Service Development and Review. As we have seen, the MAPS for 1999/2000 show that every local authority has taken some steps to consult and involve care leavers and other looked after children. There are, however still problems. Local authorities or more accurately perhaps, social services departments, still seek assistance and reassurance. The ambition and scope of their activities are limited and the outcomes uncertain or unknown. The enthusiastic response to the Department of Health sponsored Training Pack – Total Respect (CROA, 2000) highlights the demand for solutions and help with a process which should be integrated into everything a department does with its care leavers and other young people.

What then is preventing the development of effective involvement strategies? We can identify a number of barriers that relate to the culture, needs, resources, and expertise of many local authorities. They are generalisations and the success that some authorities have had in overcoming these barriers can provide the impetus for others to do likewise.

Organisational culture

Social services departments have grown and developed as agencies that are separate from both the communities they serve and the community of those who use their service. They are designed and expected to respond to an individual's or family's problems and difficulties. They do not find it easy to take account of wider group interests whether they are concerns of a community or looked after children and care leavers.

In relation to care leavers this means that the alienation many young people feel from the local authority, who are acting as their parent, stems from the concentration on solving their problems rather than supporting them through what is primarily a process of growing up. Those leaving care teams having the most success in engaging with young people and involving them in designing the support they get are those who have merged styles of working closer to youth and community work with the need for individual case work and statutory accountability.

Organisational need versus young people's concerns

A social services department needs data that can be used for statistical reporting and monitoring. Often this is very specific to meet the requirements of Performance Assessment Framework Indicators or Best Value. The request from members or senior managers is likely to be to find out what young people think about, for example, foster care, not to find out what it is young people are worried about.

Consultation and research maintains power in the hands of the organisation and the individuals directing the process. It is designed to meet organisational need not the concerns of young people who are passive recipients of the process.

Practice example – involvement of disabled young people

> *First Key* was commissioned by one local authority to consult with disabled young people using respite care. A small group of disabled young adults helped design the research and interviewed other young people. Their priorities for the consultation was not to ask about the quality of the service offered but to ask about how young people

felt about having friends and deciding when they use respite care. The resulting findings were that the most important issue for young people was whether they went to the respite unit when their friends were there. This was not an issue considered in the project specification and one that challenged the whole basis of respite care as a break for parents and carers not young people themselves.

This principle applies equally to the way that young people feel excluded from their own individual care planning and review. The response to identified failings in planning and review has been to impose adult designed Looked After Children Systems and Assessment Frameworks that can seek to ensure that assessments and reviews are comprehensive and able to be defended if challenged but pay little regard to what young people themselves want to get out of their planning and statutory reviews.

Ownership

Involvement is often the responsibility of an individual social services department officer or group. This person or group is charged with the task of improving involvement in isolation from operational considerations and without the active support of those responsible for strategic development. It is not uncommon for interest in changing the practice and approach of service providers to be restricted to those areas where there are managers with a particular interest.

During *First Key's* work to help young people organise events to 'kick-start' involvement it has frequently been the case that whilst leaving care teams, foster carers and residential units have been actively involved there has been no representation from field work teams who carry a large part of the responsibility for working with care leavers. Experience has shown that for a fundamental change in culture and approach to be achieved the impetus needs to come from the highest levels of the department. The involvement and active interest of the director and elected members not only gives a lead throughout the department but convinces young people that what they have to say is being heard and taken seriously by those people who can make a difference.

This needs to be associated with department wide publicity about the process which is happening and a debate about current practice and the changes that might result from greater involvement of young people. It should include training for staff as a way of reflecting on the benefits and implications of a change in approach. This has been recognised by the Department of Health through the publication of the Total Respect Pack to be used in staff training.

Resources

Social services departments face competing demands on their limited resources. Unfortunately, developing involvement and more young people centred styles of working can be seen as a luxury that cannot compete with other more immediate demands on resources. In recent years, specific grants have made funding available but it is still likely that the cost of a process seeking genuine involvement will be greater than anticipated in both money and staff time.

Good Practice in Involvement

This section will discuss different ways of involving young people and examine the practice issues involved in putting them into practice.

Omri Shalom has his top 10 tips for good involvement; they are in reverse order:

10. Don't talk to young people as if they are kids; talk to them like you ... would talk to a friend.
9. Make the time to see young people. Don't restrict yourself to a limit, be flexible.
8. Hear what young people say, don't just listen.
7. Be prepared to act on things when a young person tells you of something that is wrong and should not be happening.
6. Remember each and every young person is an individual. Every young person will have different views.
5. Remember why you are involving young people in the first place.
4. Remember young people have expertise of the looked after care system.

3. Show young people you want to make a change.
2. Don't keep looking at your watch in front of young people.
1. Don't consult young people, involve them.

Then most importantly, young people want high quality care which meets all their needs including the need to be involved.

Local authorities have sought to use many different models to involve young people. These take different forms and require different levels of commitment and resources. Their effectiveness as instruments for change and their ability to comply with the ground rules for genuine involvement used by *First Key* (see above) vary both in relation to the model and the style and method of implementation.

Strategic Issues

Before we examine each of these models there are issues of good practice identified from *First Keys* fieldwork. These issues need to be addressed as part of any programme of involvement.

No right way

Firstly, there is no one right way to involve young people. Young people have different levels of interest, motivation and ability. A successful strategy will provide a number of different approaches and opportunities for young people to contribute. Young people should be offered as many avenues as possible to be involved. No assumptions should be made that the view of the young person who helps organise events, chairs their own review and edits a newsletter are any more important than those of the young person who wants nothing to do with it all except to say that she or he is not getting what they want.

Timing

Frequently we have heard social services managers say that they are committed to involving young people more in service development and review but now is not the right time – there is a restructuring going on, a sensitive investigation is diverting time and energies, a joint review is imminent – are just

some of the reasons which have been given for delay. Our advice to those advocating for an immediate start is to ask 'When will be a good time?' – waiting for a social services department not to be in a process of change or crisis could be a very long wait. The advice is always not to wait. Delay will be seen by young people as another betrayal.

High level support

Too often the impetus for involvement comes from champions who, whilst committed and enthusiastic, do not have the seniority or authority to carry through a process which will lead to change taking place as a result of young people being listened to. It is common for the drive for involvement and the management of the process to be lodged with individuals without the ability to force changes in strategic thinking. These are usually children's rights officers, leaving care teams or independent reviewing officers.

Involvement in decision making at a leaving care team level may result in increased responsiveness or young people focused services. At that level it will not create the strategic changes young people are seeking. They do not compartmentalise services in the way organisations do. The care system for them is a whole, not a series of discreet service areas. Being asked for views on leaving care is almost certain to include comments on foster care, residential care or the statutory review system.

One of the first tasks is to engage with senior managers and if possible elected members. Their support and commitment will both ensure that other less enthusiastic sections of the department or agency will have to engage with the process and the outcome is much more likely to be positive change.

Young people's agenda

The role of professionals managing involvement is not to pursue their own agenda for change. Their role is of facilitator and supporter of the process. Of course young people and their adult supporters will often share a common agenda. The faults in any system will be apparent to those who both receive it and have to implement it. However, the methods and approaches young people want to use will not always be the most convenient for their supporters.

Practice example – young peoples conference

- *First Key* were commissioned to broker a dialogue between looked after young people and managers and members. One of the methods was to be a consultative conference. When planning the event the young people insisted that they were not going to use this as an opportunity for managers to hear what they thought of the care system. They planned the programme around a series of questions to which they wanted answers. The Director of Social Services disapproved of this approach and wanted to cancel the event. Officers supporting the young people and *First Key* had to stand firm and advocate strongly for the young peoples' approach to be respected. The event went ahead as planned, the result was a strong group of young people who felt empowered by the process and who went on to create a group which was active for a year afterwards. (In our experience a long time for young people to stay together)

Publicity throughout the agency

It is easy for some sections of a department or agency to ignore the messages coming from young people or the changes in approach or culture being sought. It has become an unfortunate commonplace in *First Key's* work with young people and local authorities that very few field social workers engage with the process or attend events and meetings. It is the responsibility of managers to ensure that everyone within the agency is aware of what is happening and that there is an expectation that they get involved – even if this involves working on one Saturday afternoon. It is impossible to put too much effort into publicity and remarkable how the reluctant and suspicious can claim ignorance of what is going on.

Support for young people

Promoting empowerment does not mean that young people should be left to carry out every task themselves. Adult support is vital to them

achieving their aims. This may be in the form of administrative help or training in interview skills, meeting skills or public speaking. In our professional lives we rely on the back up of a whole range of support staff and functions to work effectively and efficiently. Young people are no different.

One of the first jobs of the adult supporter to young people is to identify those areas where young people will need assistance. It is not empowering to expect young people to, for example, layout and format a newsletter when someone else acting on the instructions of young people can do it in a fraction of the time with a more professional result. In time it may be the aim to train young people to be able to take this on themselves but to expect it without training will lead to frustration and an inferior product.

Constant renewal

It hardly needs to be said that a requirement of a young person led involvement strategy is a pool of young people prepared to give their time and energy to the process. Although a small group of activists does not constitute genuine involvement their availability is essential to an ongoing initiative. Very often strategies collapse when young people lose interest or their life circumstances change and they are no longer able to devote the time they once could.

There needs to be an awareness that most young peoples' involvement will be time limited and the recruitment of new activists should never stop. It is our experience that this is not best left to young people themselves. In one group supported by *First Key* the recruitment of new members to it was an item on every agenda, but it never happened. When confronted the young people revealed that they felt embarrassed talking to other young people about the group because they felt the reaction would be hostile and open them to ridicule for being 'stooges' of the department.

We should, also, be aware that introducing new members to a core group might be seen as threatening the position of influence and power the existing young people have built for themselves. Renewal is essential but needs to be handled sensitively and respectfully.

Independent brokerage

The role of the broker is to bring together parties who have a similar aim but come from different perspectives. It follows that it is difficult for this role to be performed by someone employed by, and accountable to, one of the parties. It can be done, and many leaving care team managers or children's rights officers have successfully managed it. However, for it to succeed requires a high level of understanding from the department, political skill from the individual and trust from the young people which is not always easy to achieve but easy to lose.

Commissioning an individual or agency from outside provides a level of impartiality and even-handedness not easy for the employee to achieve. In the example above of the young peoples' conference the situation was only able to be resolved because *First Key* were able to confront the director of social services in a way that officers of the department felt unable to. Whilst these serious conflict situations arise infrequently most initiatives have a series of small potential points of tension. The independent broker is more likely to be able to ensure that the balance of power in the process between the department and young people is more equal.

Payment of young people

First Key receive more enquiries about whether, how and how much young people should be paid to be involved in a participation process. Payment does two things: it recognises the contribution young people are making as 'consultants' to the local authority or organisation and there is no doubt that money is a great incentive to young people whose help is needed. On the other hand there has to be limits to what is paid. Where does it end, attending a consultative meeting or taking part in a survey are legitimate occasions when a financial incentive is justified but payment for attending a statutory or pathway plan review would obviously not be appropriate, despite the fact that both are crucial to a department fulfilling its responsibility to involve.

There are, also, legal implications. A young person in receipt of social security benefits can earn only a small amount before it affects their benefits. Payment of small amounts of money in gift vouchers or to cover expenses will be allowed if they are a 'one-off' or very irregular gift. Similarly payments made under S24 of the Children Act are disregarded for benefits purposes but should only be used as payment for providing a service on a limited basis.

It is important to clarify from the start what is available and what it is for. A failure to do this can sour relationships with young people and jeopardise their future involvement. Any payments should be paid promptly, especially when they are to cover expenses or child care.

Models of Involvement

We have identified four common models for involvement processes. Although in practice there are variations of them in use, most initiatives will fall generally into one of these. Of course, some use a combination of all four and the aim of one is often to kick-start a further more empowering process.

The four models we will examine are:

1. one-off events or conferences
2. group work
3. research or surveys
4. newsletters

One-off events and conferences

For those social services departments or other agencies nervous about embarking on a journey to a more inclusive and involving culture there are great attractions in the one-off consultative event or conference. These events happen on a wide range of scale and in many different formats and are probably still the most common means of consulting with young people.

There are many advantages in this method of involving young people. Conferences are manageable – visible demonstrations of a commitment to listening to young people. They are relatively cheap although if done properly they can be expensive in staff time. For managers and members seeking information of immediate use in designing services they are an effective way of gathering this.

However, on their own they do not constitute an involvement strategy and have many limitations. They can be tokenistic and the prospect of either participating in the organisation or attending conferences usually appeals only to a minority of young people. The high profile nature of the conference format makes it difficult for the local authority to accept the loss of control necessary for the event to genuinely reflect the concerns of young people and unpalatable views may be marginalised in favour of upbeat positive messages. This is particularly true if elected members are to be invited. There is inevitably some element of 'news management' involved in the design and content of the event.

As a one-off event the conference cannot satisfy the need for continuing dialogue and involvement with young people. It is difficult to ensure that information gathered is acted upon in its entirety. It is tempting to hear and act upon the less difficult messages leaving more contentious conclusions untouched.

First Key is often asked to facilitate young peoples' conferences and consultative events. Through these some conclusions have been reached which seek to address the limitations of the model

- The event should be the part of a strategy of involvement not the involvement itself. It should either be the culmination of a much longer process or have the specific aim, not of receiving feedback from young people on the quality of services but how in future young people are going to be involved.
- Young people should be given control of the content of the agenda for the event without interference from social services staff. The role of the adult organiser is of facilitator and administrator. They should give advice on how to effectively communicate information, not on what the information should be.
- Young peoples' involvement should not end with the event. They should also be charged with the job of reporting the event and its conclusions.
- No effort should be made to limit the audience to particular groups of staff. Further, the role of managers is to ensure that the whole range of providers of children's services should be represented.
- The event should be held at a time and at a venue of young people's choice. They often

want events at weekends, not only because this is more convenient for many young people but also because staff devoting what would be their free time is a symbolic demonstration of their commitment to listening to young people. Young people have often preferred conferences to be held in the formal surroundings of 'County Hall' rather than more apparently 'young people friendly' surroundings. They want the status that the formality brings and find an assumption that they will be intimidated by this patronising. Let young people decide where they meet.

Group work

Successful ongoing, almost permanent in-care or after-care groups which can campaign on issues important to young people and have a direct influence on service planning and review are quite possibly creatures more of mythology than reality. I can hear colleagues already rising up to claim great things achieved by small self-selected groups of young people acting independently or as a by-product of an advocacy, services, children's rights services or leaving care team. The true reality is somewhat different. Groups of this type were fashionable and every children's rights service had to have one. Their achievements were questionable and too often existed for the benefit of professionals rather than young people themselves.

Group work with young people has many difficulties. Groups are difficult to maintain over long periods. Managing the process of keeping young people together can become the task rather than the focus being on what it is trying to achieve. If it is intended to last longer than the completion of a specific task, issues of renewal become important. Bizarrely, in the past, many people have had mixed feelings about young people getting jobs or moving on positively because of the impact on the group in which they had invested much time and energy. It is easy to underestimate the expense of maintaining relatively small groups of young people.

This is not to say that group work with young people as one method of involving young people does not have a place and is going on in many local authorities. It can achieve significant outcomes for young people and can help young people develop skills and self confidence. There are now many examples of where group work has successfully contributed to more young people friendly services.

Practice example – Department of Health – teenagers to work programme

- In the summers of 2000 and 2001 the Department of Health encouraged local authorities to employ looked after young people and care leavers to work for four weeks on projects to promote young people's participation. Many local authorities adopted the scheme to carry out a range of tasks including the production of leaving care guides, the development of web sites for looked after young people and to organise consultative events.

For it to be an effective method of involving young people certain conditions must be met:

- The group should have a specific focus, purpose or task. As such it is a means of promoting and achieving involvement not the involvement itself. Wherever possible the focus should be decided by young people. However, as a start has to be made somewhere, pragmatically some thinking must have happened in advance to attract young people to a project. If the outline task does not appeal to young people they will not join. There must be some possibility of young people designing the detail of the task and altering its parameters if necessary.
- If a group has the purpose of advising the department on a range of policy and practice issues the means by which this will contribute to overall policy development must be clear.
- Agreement should be reached about how the work of the group is communicated to other young people.
- Young people and adult supporters should agree the process for new young people to join the group.
- Young people should receive training on how to conduct groups and how to ensure that groups function effectively. Recognition or if possible some external accreditation should be available for this.
- There should be a budget for the group over which young people have some control.

- Young people should not be expected to service the group themselves. Arrangements for arranging meetings, finding venues, providing transport and refreshments, sending out minutes and other administrative tasks should be provided.
- Young people should have input into what happens to the group when its agreed lifespan is over or task completed.

Practice example – Leeds Children's Rights Service

- Leeds Children's Rights Service provided by Save the Children facilitated a shadow social services committee of young people. They were able to discuss issues on the social services committee agenda and choose the methods they would use to feed their views into the committee discussion. This was usually by meetings with the chair of the committee.

Research and surveys

Surveys and research of young people's views have become more popular as the expectations on local authorities to adopt a more responsive style of working and new funding has made the investment needed more affordable. They have disadvantages as instruments of involvement. Traditional academic style research and market research techniques are not empowering to young people. They become the recipients of, rather than, active participants in the process and research has in the past reflected adult preoccupations and concerns rather than young peoples. They also take time and require specialist skills if they are to have validity and credibility.

In recent years, however, new approaches and methodologies have sought to overcome the limitations of surveys and research as a means of empowering rather than disempowering young people. They place young people in the position of leading research rather than being exploited by it.

The methods allow young people to be able to make choices about the level of their involvement. Some choose to be researchers, others may want to contribute to the analysis or dissemination of findings, others are content to be interviewed or fill in questionnaires as their contribution.

Practice example – take care, take control

- Take Care, Take Control is a partnership between Lewisham SSD, The Children's Society and First Key. It receives funding from the local Health Action Zone. The first stage of the project was to recruit and train young people to research the health services and attitudes to health of looked after young people. The young people researchers defined the scope of the research, designed the questionnaire and carried out interviews with young people. They were then responsible for the analysis of the data collected and formulated the recommendations from the research. The second stage was to develop services that would meet some of the concerns and problems the research identified. The young people decided that the most effective way of achieving this was by the production of a health promotion video that would then be distributed to all looked after young people. A video production company was hired to help with this.

(Take Care, Take Control. First Key, Childrens Society and Lewisham SSD 2000)

Many local authorities have adopted or adapted the principles of user led research to collect information. Local circumstances, time or resources have dictated how far agencies have enabled the involvement of young people but successful projects follow a number of principles:

- Young people require training in how to research. This training should include research design, questionnaire design, interviewing skills and data analysis skills. It should also, include the possible issues of transference and projection which can both impact on the objectivity of the research and affect young people on a personal level.
- Young people should as far as is possible within the specification for the research define the research objectives. An example of the benefits of this was described earlier in the example of the research with disabled young people.

- Young people should be involved in the design of questionnaires and other media used to conduct the research.
- Young people should be involved in the collation and analysis of data. It may, however, not be efficient or useful for young people to be expected to carry out mechanical analysis of statistical information.
- Young people should be involved in the dissemination of the findings and recommendations.
- All young people who take part in the research, not just the interviewers, should receive preliminary findings and be given the opportunity to be involved in the analysis and formulation of recommendations.
- Research on its own will not improve the service young people receive. It should be followed by involvement in implementation and other initiatives arising out of the research. Follow up work on the outcomes of the research on services and young peoples satisfaction with the action which has been taken should be built in to the project.

Newsletters

Newsletters for care leavers and other groups of young people are becoming an increasingly popular means of both informing them about services and entitlements and young people communicating with each other. They are usually produced largely by young people with necessary adult support and assistance. They have the benefits of providing for different levels of involvement from editorship to casual reader and young people can use them to develop writing, IT and design skills.

Practice example – Lewisham Getting it Right

- Getting it Right is one of the longest established young peoples' newsletters. It is edited by a group of care leavers with the support of the Children's Society Rights and Participation Project. The design and layout is done on computers and professional software provided as part of a sponsorship arrangement with a magazine publishing company. As part of the deal young people are also provided with training in design and use of the technology. Much of the content is provided by other looked after young people and care leavers.

Newsletters are an effective communication tool but are limited on their own in their capacity to provoke change. They should be regarded as part of a wider strategy and a way of reporting on involvement and advertising other initiatives.

Anyone embarking on the production of a newsletter with young people should do so with their eyes open. It is a time consuming process in which young people will need a great deal of support. These days we all, young people included, expect production values and sophistication of design which may not be possible for the amateur to reproduce. Expecting young people to provide copy on time and of a quality they are happy with is not always realistic. Early results may not satisfy either adults or them. To develop the expertise and experience takes time that few can devote.

Perhaps more importantly a newsletter can quickly take over from all other activities, diverting valuable energy and resources which ought to be spent on carrying out other initiatives.

Conclusions

Involving young people is not a fad or a fashion. As we have seen it is a way of working, as much enmeshed in organisational culture and confidence as it is in policy. What we have described here are the outward manifestations of a listening, learning culture. As Omri's advice has shown, what young people want more than anything else are effective, caring, responsive services. They cannot have these unless a local authority is listening and seeking to empower the young people receiving the services. The conclusion, perhaps, if it can be summed up, is that involvement is neither a help or a hindrance – it is far more fundamental than that.

References

Department of Health. (2000) *Overview of Management Action Plans for 2000–2001*, DoH.

Croft, S. and Beresford, P. (1990) *From Paternalism to Participation: Involving People in Social Services*, London, Open Services Project and Joseph Rowntree Foundation.

UNICEF. *The Ladder of Participation*, UNICEF.

6. Advocacy for Young People and Redress When Things go Wrong

Nicola Wyld

Introduction

This chapter looks at the way in which care leavers can be empowered to achieve their human rights under the Children (Leaving Care) Act 2000. It starts off by looking briefly at the notion of empowerment and participation. It then looks at advocacy, why it is needed, its development and present government responses to its development. Finally it looks at ways in which young people can seek redress when things go wrong. This will primarily look at the Children Act (1989) complaints procedure but will also touch on legal action where this may be a more appropriate alternative.

Participation and Empowerment

The 2000 Act builds on the principles of the Children Act in giving prominence to the principle that young people should be fully involved in planning for their transition to independence and adulthood. It requires the local authority to consult with young people and take all reasonable steps to enable the child's participation in meetings, in carrying out the needs assessment, and the preparation and review of the young person's pathway plan. It also extends the Children Act consultation duty to relevant children.

These principles are also consistent with article 12 of the UN Convention on the Rights of the Child concerning the participation of children in decisions concerning their lives and article 8 of the European Convention on Human Rights which includes the notion of procedural fairness in the decision making process concerning private and family life.

A young person's right to participation in decisions about their lives is therefore firmly enshrined in law. It is also a key feature of the Government's Quality Protects Programme in which priority is given to:

... the participation of children, young people and their families in the planning and delivery of services and in decisions about their everyday lives. Particular attention should be given to the involvement of young people collectively and to enhancing their individual voices, for example through the development of individual advocacy services.

The Government's Objectives for Children's Social Services, Objective 8, 1998.

The question is how can this best be achieved. Lessons can be learnt from existing practice under the Children Act in relation to planning and reviews. Analysis of recent research studies (Department of Health, 2001) showed that:

- The Children Act has made a difference to the participation of children and young people in planning and decision making that affects their lives but that that practice remains variable.
- Review meetings should be only part of an ongoing programme of skilled direct work with children; many children and young people objected to having to talk in front of a room full of strangers.
- Children participate best in meetings when they are prepared, meetings are small and there is a structured child friendly agenda.
- Meetings should be used as vehicles for participatory decision-making and should focus on young people's wishes and feelings.

You don't really want to sit and talk to a whole room full of people about your problems, though, do you?

There's like people you don't know who are going 'How are you coping with your past experiences?'

Well, it's none of your business.

The more people, you get scared. You get shy and try not to make a mistake in what you are saying.

The Children Act Now:
Messages from Research, 2001.

In our experience many young people continue to feel that they are not properly listened to and that decisions are made about their lives by adults without reference to them.

> *The foster parents were lovely but social services wouldn't listen to me ... I've now been given a full apology by social services.*
> Shout to be Heard, 1998.

How then can participation be made real? Learning the lessons from research and improved training for social workers and other relevant professionals should help improve practice on the ground. Above all the provision of independent advocacy support for young people is essential to help empower young people themselves to express their views and so participate effectively in decision-making. The involvement of an advocate at early stage can often sort things out and avoid the need to embark on a formal complaint or indeed legal action. The acknowledgement of the legitimacy of advocacy support for young people should also contribute to the change in culture that is needed not only in making participation a real experience for young people on an individual level but also in developing policies which are sensitive to the perspective of children and young people.

> *Having an advocate helped me get things off my chest ... it felt like people started to listen.*
> *I'd been put in care to be protected from my dad and then I'd suffered worse.*
> *The advocate helped me ... if anything happened to you in care I'd say get out and get help.*
> Shout to be Heard, 1998.

Advocacy

The need for advocacy

Over the past decade there has been an awareness of the need to provide independent advocacy for looked after children so that this vulnerable group of children and young people have an effective voice in decisions affecting their lives especially in relation to statutory child care reviews and the complaints procedure. Increasingly, the provision of advocacy has also been seen as an essential safeguard in protecting from abuse those children who live

away from home in a number of different residential settings.

Young people themselves see access to independent confidential advocacy services as a key element in equating the imbalance between powerful adults and bureaucracies and potentially vulnerable and isolated young people (see *Shout to be Heard*, 1998).

The development of advocacy on the ground

During the course of the 1990s a wide range of advocacy services have been developed by the voluntary sector. These include:

- Local authority children's rights services. The majority of these are now managed by voluntary agencies and have proliferated as a result of funding from the Government under the Quality Protects Programme. They combine advocacy with more general children's rights and participation work and may contract out some advocacy referrals to the independent agencies.
- Specialist children's advocacy organisations. The two organisations in England are Voice for the Child in Care (VCC) and National Youth Advocacy Service (NYAS) and its predecessor Advisory and Representation Service (ASC). VCC provides direct advocacy and visiting advocacy to children's homes and many secure units. NYAS also provides direct advocacy and visiting advocacy and provides legal representation for children involved in legal proceedings concerning the breakdown of their parents' relationships.
- Local projects run by the large children's charities.

However, provision is patchy as a result of local authority attitudes towards advocacy for children and in relation to lack of funding. With no central government funding for these services provision has been largely dependent on the ability to contract with local authorities or to spot purchase in relation to individual cases.

In 1999, all the major children's advocacy providers formed the Children's Advocacy Consortium. The aim of the Consortium is that every local authority should have a children's rights and advice service as part of the Quality Protects Programme (see below) and that every child looked after should have a statutory right to an independent advocate. These services should be provided according to an agreed standard. The Consortium initially drafted national standards of good practice including key issues of independence and confidentiality which have been agreed by all its members.

The National Overview into the third year of the local authority Management Action Plans (MAPs) (DoH, 2001) states that many more local authorities have reported an increase in the availability of advocacy. It also shows that there has been an increased appointment of children's rights officers. That certainly mirrors our experience at VCC but the report does not reveal any quantitative data nor more details about how these services are operating. It does however highlight the 'most striking development is the insistence in many MAPs that participation and consultation should be real, and have a real impact on services and lives – no more "listening" and not hearing.'

Official recognition and government response

The development of advocacy on the ground has been mirrored by a plethora of official reports over the past two decades published following scandals of abuse in residential care. These all highlighted the need for advocacy.

- The Wagner Report *Residential Care: A Positive Choice*, proposed that children in all forms of residential care should have access to an independent advocate.
- The Scottish Review *Another Kind of Home*, recommended that children 'should be able to call on someone to act as their advocate'.
- The Warner Inquiry Report *Choosing with Care*, said that children in children's homes should 'have the support of their own advocates when pursuing serious complaints against staff'.

In 1997 Sir William Utting, the former SSI Chief Inspector in his report, *People Like Us* commended the role of children's rights services for all looked after children and recommended that children wishing to use the formal complaints procedure should be entitled to independent advocacy. The findings of this report which yet again condemned inadequate safeguards for children living away from home

no doubt contributed to the Government's decision to launch its Quality Protects initiative in September 1998. One of the six initial Government priority areas for securing funding in meeting Government social services objectives for improving outcomes for looked after children and children in need is listening to the views and wishes of children, young people and their families. In the second year of the Quality Protects programme this priority was extended to highlighting the involvement of young people and the development of children's rights services and independent advocacy (Stationery Office, 1998).

In its response to the Waterhouse Report on abuse in care and foster homes in North Wales (DoH, 2000) the Government has accepted the recommendation that children should have a statutory entitlement to independent advocacy when making a formal complaint under section 26 of the Children Act. This proposal has been included for consultation in its discussion document on the review of the complaints procedures under both the Children Act and the 1990 NHS and Community Care Act (see *Listening to People: A Consultation on Improving Social Services Complaints Procedures*, 2000, para 8.1–8.3).

Key features of advocacy

Three features particularly distinguish advocacy from other forms of personal social services, and these features are essential to an effective advocacy service:

The child's view

The Minister for Health, Lord Hunt, confirmed to Parliament during the passage of the Care Standards Bill that:

Advocacy is about effectively articulating the child's view, right or wrong. It is not about what the advocate thinks is best or in the child's welfare. Advocacy is grounded in Article 12 of the UN Convention on the Rights of the Child, which assures children capable of forming their own views the right to express those views freely in all matters affecting them.

The advocate's role includes informing and advising the child, but only where a child is incapable of expressing a view would advocates represent their own interpretation of the child's best interests.

Independence

The Quality Protects guidance emphasises the need for independent advocacy. Children are entitled to an advocacy service which can demonstrate from the outset that it is free of all pressures or conflicts of interest which could prevent the advocate from being single-mindedly on the child's side. This has clear implications for purchasers (both statutory and voluntary) in terms of the management and location of advocacy.

Confidentiality

Independent advocacy services offer a significantly higher threshold of confidentiality to children than social workers or others in social services. Like those working in the law, advocates will breach children's confidences only where circumstances are such that urgent action is needed to protect them or others from serious danger. They will not necessarily breach confidences by the child about significant harm or unlawful activity but will always work with the child or young person to make these disclosures themselves. In our experience the vast majority of young people want those in authority to take action for their protection but wish to retain control over the process; the circumstances in which confidentiality is breached are very rare. Indeed, by building up trust with children and young people by means of a confidential relationship, advocacy aids the protection of children. The Department of Health seems to recognise that independent advocacy services should be able to offer a higher level of confidentiality to children and young people than social workers under their statutory responsibilities but expects that they should be consistent with the Government's statutory guidance on child protection in 'Working Together'. This is a complex debate which, at the time of writing, has not yet been fully resolved.

My first thoughts about an advocate was that they were very similar to social workers ... Once I met her I relaxed straight away. She seemed to be really at ease with young

people ... My advocate explained her role and the issues she would be taking up for me. She was there for all my important meetings. When she saw that social services weren't looking after my needs, she made them TOTALLY aware of their faults. When it was announced to me that I would be moved, a week before Christmas, to a strange unit, it was my advocate who forced social services to stop the move.

Shout to be Heard, 1998.

Personal advisors and advocacy for care leavers

With the statutory requirement to appoint a personal advisor (PA) to all young people who qualify under the 2000 Act does there remain any need for care leavers to receive advocacy support? The Children (Leaving Care) (England) Regulations 2001 state that PAs must provide advice and support (Regulation 12(a)). These are key features of the advocacy task. The guidance to the Children (Leaving Care) Act 2000 states that one of the roles of the PA is to act as advocate for the young person when they need help in making a case both in formulating it and in presenting it (Ch 10, Para 7).

The answer to this question is yes but the circumstances will vary depending on the PA scheme in place, the date of appointment and the issues involved. Readers should refer to Chapter 21 for fuller details about the role of the PA but the following points are relevant to the relationship between PAs and independent advocacy support.

First, the boundaries of the PA role are unclear both in regulations and guidance. It is clear that they carry no budget holding responsibilities but they are appointed by the responsible authority and depending on the nature of their contractual relationship may not be perceived by young people as being independent. The advice and support that the PA can provide may therefore be limited so far as the young person is concerned.

Second, there is no requirement in the regulations about when the personal advisor is to be appointed. Regulation 13(b) refers to the participation of the PA in the needs assessment and preparation of the pathway plan 'where applicable'. It is possible therefore that there may be no PA at the time of the needs assessment and initial pathway planning process. This is the crucial time for the young person's full participation so that they can fully own their plan. There are also implications for financial support since it is only those matters identified in the pathway plan that the responsible authority is obliged to fund.

There is also an issue concerning the PA's role in the review of the pathway plan. It is suggested in guidance that they should chair the reviews of relevant children and former relevant children. In these circumstances there would be a conflict of role for them in also providing advocacy support to the young person. Again, where the young person is in dispute with the authority about any aspect of their plan, advocacy support may be necessary.

The guidance recognises that it would be inappropriate for the PA to advocate for a young person bringing a complaint against the local authority or indeed against their PA. This being the case, it is strongly arguable that independent advocacy should be available for any young person who requests it in the circumstances set out above.

Is there a statutory right to advocacy?

Despite intensive lobbying by the Children's Advocacy Consortium and the Action on AfterCare Consortium there is no right for children and young people to access independent advocacy in the 2000 Act, the Children (Leaving Care) (England) Regulations nor elsewhere. The Government took the view that it was not necessary to legislate as it was committed to the development of independent advocacy through its Quality Protects Programme. It was also concerned that there was inadequate service provision to meet the needs of all care leavers if enshrined in legislation. Furthermore, it did not want to pre-empt the outcome of the Department of Health consultation on the complaints procedure, '*Listening to People*'.

That consultation document states that:

The Government recognises how vital it is to listen to children and is committed to

encouraging the development and use of high quality advocacy services for those children who really need them.

Children and young people are particularly susceptible to pressure when they want to raise problems. Their interests may best be served by having a right to a champion, in the form of an advocate, who could help them in whatever way needed, including framing their complaints and pursuing them vigorously. It is arguable that access to advocacy would enable the procedure to operate more effectively than it does at present giving greater protection at an earlier stage for a child or young person wanting to air concerns.

Listening to People, DoH, 2000, p17.

It asked whether or not the right to advocacy should be introduced as a statutory feature of the Children Act complaints procedure.

The Children Leaving Care Act statutory guidance has, however, highlighted Government expectations that:

(When making a complaint) ... the responsible authority should make sure that young people have access to independent advocacy services to provide this help for them. Young people's wishes should be taken into account in choosing an advocate. The Quality Protects programme encourages the growth of high quality independent advocacy services.

The Government expects advocacy services to be available to all care leavers who request it. Services should be friendly, safe, welcoming and there should be clarity of role and purpose.

It is important to make sure that young people with communication impairments have full access to the complaints procedure.
Children (Leaving Care) Act 2000 Guidance and Regulations, Ch 10, Para 8–10.

While the statements in the guidance are to be welcomed it is the view of VCC and the Children's Advocacy Consortium that this is not enough. It has fallen short of ensuring a legal right to advocacy. This is significant because it is still open to local authorities to refuse children and young people the right to an advocate. It is our experience that local authorities may resist giving children support to access an advocate and sometimes they actively discourage it or even ask an advocate to withdraw after starting work with a child. This usually affects younger children but by no means exclusively and we find also that children and young people may be denied the opportunity to make a choice about the advocate or advocacy service they wish to approach. These difficulties may be compounded by the confusion in the role between PA and advocate.

Nonetheless the existing guidance is statutory which means that local authorities are expected to follow it unless there are exceptional circumstances locally which would justify its departure. Local authorities are not justified in refusing to provide advocacy because there are no local services with which they have contracted. Both VCC and NYAS offer a national service which between the two agencies can usually ensure the provision of an advocate on request. Even where there are local services, local authorities should be willing to listen carefully to the reasons why a young person would prefer an advocate from another agency.

Sarah's Story

Can you explain a little bit about what happened to you when you were leaving care?

I am just 21. I was in care from the age of five for most of my childhood. I was 16 when I first came to VCC. I had things I needed to sort out and needed help to do it.

I had been placed in a B and B having just come out of hospital and I did not feel safe there. I knew that I had to get out of there. I also wanted to get back to my original area (I had been living out of the borough for about six months). I wanted my advocate to get me away from this place but then I had to go back to the hospital and after that I went to a children's home. I think it was probably a combination of the two things which led to me being moved.

Then my advocate was trying to get me a social worker. The old social worker had closed my case without telling me and I was then referred to the Leaving Care Team. I didn't get a social worker for about nine months and I felt that they didn't know anything about me and

then were making decisions about what should happen to me.

They wanted me to move from my children's home to semi-independence. I felt that I was not ready to move on. The home felt that I needed more help with them too but social services wanted me to move. I felt that I had to take drastic action for them to listen to me and so I went into myself so I could stay at the children's home. I had recently come out of hospital for being assaulted and so there was a big court case coming up too. There were tons of meetings. My advocate and the home both managed to persuade social services that independent living was not the right thing for me at that moment.

I stayed for about six months in my children's home and then social services suggested supported lodgings. I didn't want to go but they said that my place was needed for younger children. I even met with the Director of Social Services. She went on about money being tight and the needs of younger children and this made me feel bad for wanting to stay.

I spent a year in supported lodgings. It was a nightmare. They had misled me about what the placement would be like and the conditions for me living there. I felt stuck. They never paid the money every week they had promised for my education at college. They said come and pick it up from them but I had no money to get to social services.

When I was 19 I got my own place. It was a hell hole. The house was falling apart even though they had sent round their assessor to say that it was alright. The toilet didn't work, there was no heating and the gas didn't work. There was no carpet either and my leaving care grant was not enough to cover this.

What has been your experience of advocacy?

I have had one main advocate who has helped me sort out a lot of things. And then there were visiting advocates at the two children's homes I was living in.

To begin with it was freaky to have an adult talking to you on your level. It is not something that I had experienced before because adults don't and social workers can't. Once I got used to this different way of approaching me I felt that my issues were being addressed. My advocate wrote letters to the local authority asking for things to change, set up meetings with social services and helped me make complaints. I have had to complain more than once. With the help of my advocate I have been able to sort things out in the end.

Do you think you could have managed to sort things out on your own?

I couldn't have sorted things out without the help of an advocate. I would have been nine feet under. I think that other care leavers have the same needs. One of the things that was really helpful was that my advocate was able to protect me from social services by helping me get things that I needed. Social services were not willing to provide a safe haven let alone a service for me. I needed to know that the things they were doing were not right and to stop them from doing it. My advocate was able to do this for me.

What sort of qualities do you think are important in an advocate?

I felt with my advocate that she was really there for me. I felt that I could bounce ideas off her and that she was listening to me. It is really important that an advocate does not give off an image of being judgmental about young people and their problems. I think that they also need to be quite balanced in understanding about how social services work. A sense of humour is really important too because things can just get too much at times.

It is very important that advocates are independent of social services so that you feel that they are doing things for you without worrying about what social services think.

My advocate told me about confidentiality and it is really important that you can trust your advocate and say things to her without thinking that she will tell social services. I also knew there were things I couldn't say in one of my children's homes because I thought that the visiting advocate would go to social services. Some of the young people in the home were having sex. This did not affect me personally but I was caught up in the culture of the home and I thought that if I said anything the visiting advocate would have seen it as a child protection issue.

Do you think that young people should have a legal right to an advocate?

Yes. I think that all young people should have a right to an advocate. Not everyone would use it. There needs to be a lot of publicity for young people to know about advocacy. Social services have only got in house help. I didn't know how to find out about advocacy. There was a leaflet at social services about NAYPIC (National Association of Young People in Care). I rang them up to talk to them but they had closed and left a message about VCC on their answer machine. So it was a fluke that I found out about VCC.

Did you know that you had the right to make a complaint?

No-one from social services told me about the complaints procedure or how it would work. My advocate explained this to me. I didn't know you could complain against social services. If I hadn't had an advocate I wouldn't have made a complaint and things would not have moved on for me.

How did you feel about making a complaint?

When the complaint was in process I figured out what the complaint would involve. I was very worried about the repercussions on me about what would be said. I was worried about rubbing people up the wrong way. But I didn't think about stopping the complaint because I am stubborn and I had the support of my advocate. For people who are not stubborn they definitely need support.

It is difficult making a complaint because you worry about what is going to happen afterwards. After making the first complaint I felt that the staff would treat me differently. They would know me. I felt awkward and worried that they would all hate my guts. I found that social services were also aggressive towards my advocate. The social workers took things as a personal attack.

How did you feel about the way in which your complaints were handled?

I don't think that the complaints procedure is young people friendly. When the complaints officer was trying to sort out things informally by having me and the social worker together she was very defensive and argumentative.

It was okay when I got to see the Independent Person. I think there is often a language barrier between social services and young people. The IP tried to explain things in a way that I could understand. My advocate has done this too. My social worker did not.

What do you think about the Government changes for children?

A lot has changed for the better over the past three or so years. I am very pleased about this but why has it taken so long? It is difficult for us ex-care leavers who have been through the old system. I am bitter and feel a kind of unbelief that so many mistakes were made continuously for young people in care. I feel that us ex-care leavers need recognition of what has happened to us under the care system as it was. They should give us an explanation about why things that are so obvious (like listening to children and letting us have advocates) were not done before. Or perhaps they should give us a nation-wide apology to say that they have messed up the lives of so many children.

Right of Redress When Things go Wrong

The primary source of redress is by making a statutory complaint under the Children Act. However, this may be premature or it may not be sufficient. With advocacy support, young people can negotiate with the local authority to reconsider their decision or there may be other sources of redress such as mediation. Advocates should also be alert to the necessity of taking legal action where for example a complaint cannot be heard in time to prevent the decision in question being implemented and there is no agreement by the local authority to 'freeze' the decision pending the outcome of the complaint. This most usually happens in relation to cases in which young people are being moved against their wishes.

The difficulties for young people in accessing and effectively using the complaints procedures are well documented and accepted by the Government (VCC, 1997; Aires and Kettle, 1998; Wallis and Frost, 1998; DoH, 2000).

Children Act complaints procedure

The existing Children Act complaints procedure has been extended to care leavers qualifying under the 2000 Act although not to eligible children presumably because they continue to be looked after children with access to the Children Act complaints procedure. It enables care leavers to make complaints about any actions the responsible authority has taken or not taken in relation to its new duties under the 2000 Act. There may be disputes about which local authority is responsible for the young person in an emergency. In those circumstances the young person should probably make a complaint to both authorities.

Local resolution

The Act amends the regulations as they apply to care leavers only by introducing a statutory 14-day local resolution stage prior to a formal complaint. This incorporates a recommendation made by the Government in its consultation document *Listening to People* by putting the informal stage of the complaints procedure on a statutory footing. Any person in the local authority who receives a complaint by a young person must put that complaint in writing and give a copy of the complaint to the designated complaints officer (DCO). If the complaint is not resolved to the complainant's satisfaction within 14 days the person looking at the complaint must notify the DCO who will then institute a formal complaint (regulation 13(3) of the Children (Leaving Care) (England) Regulations).

This new local resolution stage provides important safeguards to the existing way that informal complaints are handled. Not only is it often unclear whether an informal complaint has in fact been made but the process frequently takes a great deal of time before resolution. This is highly unsatisfactory and is particularly difficult for children and young people to deal with. The new statutory scheme ensures that the DCO is aware of the complaint and can then immediately institute a formal complaint. In 'Listening to People' it was recommended that children and young people should be able to have the support of an advocate at this stage.

It was originally intended that this procedure would not apply to complaints about financial arrangements but this has now been changed and it applies to all matters under the 2000 Act.

Proposals for further change to the Children Act complaints procedure

Issued in June 2000, the Government consultation document '*Listening to People*', on improving social services complaints procedures draws on issues identified in (Social Services Inspectorate) SSI national inspections carried out between 1993 and 1996 and heeds the difficulties for young people in using complaints procedures as highlighted in the Waterhouse Report. Its main remit is to achieve consistency as far as possible between the procedures under the 1989 Children Act and the 1990 NHS and Community Care Act. In addition to the points made concerning advocacy and the local resolution stage the following are the main points that emerge from the document. There is a clear recognition of the difficulty for children in making complaints and while acknowledging the need to make changes to a system that is not working properly this should not be done at the expense of children and young people:

- Complaints made by children and young people, or those who received services while a looked after child would be exempt from a new time limit of 12 months for adult complainants in which to submit a complaint.
- Complaints made directly by children or young people should continue to be concluded within the existing statutory 28-day period. In addressing the difficulties of getting complaints dealt with within this time scale it is suggested that complaints brought by adults under the Children Act should be completed within three months.
- There was some discussion about the future role of the independent person service. Present regulations ensure that the DCO must appoint an independent person to take part in the investigation of the complaint and that an independent person sits on any review panel. It is understood that this will remain as at present.

- Proposal for strengthening guidance requiring local authorities to 'freeze' decisions which have a significant impact on the life of the individual, pending the outcome of the complaint unless good reason can be shown otherwise. This is presently recommended by Government guidance but is frequently not done (The Right to Complain, (1991), Department of Health, Para 3.9–3.10). VCC has argued that the provision to freeze decisions should be contained in regulations. We have had to initiate judicial review proceedings in a number of cases where the DCO did not have the power to override the decision of the local authority to continue with its decision notwithstanding the submission of a formal complaint.
- Local authorities should identify who is responsible for taking action to implement panel recommendations.
- Complainants should be kept informed about implementation progress.
- Review panels should propose remedies they think appropriate.

Proposals made by the Waterhouse Report in relation to children's complaints

In addition to the recommendation that children and young people should have a statutory right to independent advocacy, the Waterhouse Report *Lost in Care*, 2000 recommended the appointment of Children's Complaints Officer (CCO) to make the complaints procedure more child friendly. The function of a CCO would be to act in the best interests of the child. They should be required to meet with all child complainants and all children who were the subject of an adult complaint. They should also notify and consult with appropriate managers about the further handling of the complaint including taking any necessary interim action in relation to the child, the complainant and the person who is subject of the complaint. They should also involve other procedures such as child protection or disciplinary procedures including any necessary involvement with the police or other agencies. The Government has not accepted these broader recommendations. However, from the most recent MAP report it would appear that some authorities have taken this idea on board.

Adoption and Children Bill 2001

There has as yet been no Government response to 'Listening to People'. However, by clause 111 of the Adoption and Children Bill the Government has created the statutory framework to draft new regulations concerning the introduction of a local resolution stage for all Children Act complaints. It has also introduced the time limit in making complaints although regrettably it appears that there is no exemption for children or complaints made about issues which arose during childhood. The regulations also include an extension to the complaints procedure whereby complaints about child protection procedures and court proceedings can be dealt with.

Again, there is no provision for a statutory right to advocacy. VCC has drafted amendments for this which will be tabled in conjunction with the Children's Advocacy Consortium.

Complaints under the Care Standards Act 2000

The Care Standards Act (2001) has introduced a new system of registration and inspection of children's homes and fostering and adoption agencies. This is to be carried out by a new government agency, the National Care Standards Commission (NCSC). The Act will come into effect in April 2002. New regulations have been drafted for children's homes and foster care which extend and strengthen the existing regulations. These regulations are accompanied by a set of national minimum standards. Decisions about registration by the NCSC will be made on the basis of compliance with both the regulations and the minimum standards while breach of regulations alone is an offence which ultimately gives rise to criminal prosecution.

Since some care leavers will continue to live with their foster carers or possibly in their children's homes it is important for them to be aware of these new changes.

The children homes regulations require the home to set up a complaints procedure. Independent fostering agencies are also required to set up a complaints procedure while children placed in local authority foster care can continue to use the Children Act complaints procedure. These new complaints procedures give an additional right to complain and do not exclude the use of the Children Act complaints procedure. However, the new procedure itself is less regulated and does not require the involvement of an independent person nor time limits for the hearing of the complaint. The relationship between the complaints procedure of the children's home or fostering agency, the Children Act complaints procedure and the monitoring function of the National Commission is highly complex. It will be very difficult for most people, particularly children and young people, to understand which procedure to use and we would certainly hope that guidance will be issued by the Department of Health and The National Commission.

VCC's model for an integrated complaints procedure
Local resolution

The representations procedure set out under the 2002 Children's Homes Regulations and the draft 2001 Fostering Services Regulations applies to all children irrespective of their legal status. This procedure should focus on local resolution. A time limit of 14 days should be inserted to comply with recommendations in the government consultation document on the Children Act complaints procedure 'Listening to People' and to regulation 13 of the Children (Leaving Care) (England) Regulations 2001.

Formal complaint

- Children should be able to take their complaint to the local authority and have the safeguards of the Children Act complaints procedure such as strict time limits, the involvement of an independent person, a response to each and every aspect of the complaint and access to a panel hearing. They should not have to utilise the children's home or fostering agency internal procedure before doing so.
- Information about the complaint should be passed by the placing authority to the National Commission so that it can exercise its monitoring function and consider matters

in relation to compliance or otherwise with the regulations and/or standards.
- If the parent places the child, the parent should approach the National Commission direct.

Advocacy

Independent advocacy of the child's choice should be available at every stage of the complaints procedure at the point of request (i.e. in the children's home or through the social worker or designated complaints officer in the local authority).

Children and young people need access to information about all this. VCC has proposed that children's homes managers should ensure that they have information about the complaints procedures of all the local authorities who place children in their care.

Legal Action

There are very limited circumstances in which young people can use the courts as a means of redress since the framework of the Children Act has generally excluded this being done apart from in specific circumstances.

Children Act applications

Young people under the age of 18 may use the courts if they wish to discharge their care order or apply for contact with members of their family or other people who are significant to them. There may also be circumstances in which they may wish to apply for a residence order to live with an adult who is not their parent. Matters concerning contact or residence are better dealt with through the courts since the court can impose its decision on the local authority in contrast to the complaints procedure where the recommendations of the investigation may not be acted on by the local authority.

Young people have a right to apply to discharge their care order. In some cases they also have a right to seek a contact order. In all other cases they will first need to ask the court's permission to make their application. This should be granted where the court considers that they have 'sufficient understanding' to make the application.

Legal advocacy

Where legal action is considered, legal advice should be sought on behalf of the young person from a lawyer on the Children Panel. They will be represented in court by a lawyer who should act on their instructions unless the lawyer thinks that the child is not 'Gillick competent' – that is, as a result of learning or communication difficulties, they are unable to understand the nature of the proceedings. Depending on the type of proceedings there may also be a children's guardian or Children and Family Court Advisory and Support Service (CAFCASS) officer to make recommendations to the court about the young person's best interests. Where the young person does not agree with this recommendation their lawyer should continue to act on their instructions.

Human Rights Act 1998

Care leavers may wish to make a complaint about their treatment in care which involve issues of abuse or other maltreatment. This is complex and advocates should be alert to the fact that there may be a claim under articles 3 and/or 8 of European Convention on Human Rights which has been incorporated into English law under the Human Rights Act. Again they should seek a lawyer to advise the young person.

Judicial review

This is a discretionary remedy brought against the local authority in the High Court when it can be shown that it has acted unreasonably in law. This means that it has taken into account things it should not have done or left out things it should have done or acted so 'unreasonably that no reasonable authority would have acted in that manner.' A great deal of thought needs to be given to whether this is a suitable approach and it is essential that legal advice is urgently found for the young person.

This remedy is most useful in an emergency when an injunction can be obtained to stop the local authority taking action such as moving a child or to require them to act, for example to provide accommodation to a child or young person who is homeless. The courts usually require a complaint to have been concluded before considering an application for judicial review but they would not expect this when an application for an injunction has been made. The local authority should always first be asked whether they are willing to 'freeze' the decision pending the outcome of the complaint.

Judicial review can also be used where the local authority has failed to follow the recommendations of the review panel without a justified reason. Sometimes this may be more appropriately dealt with by making an application to the local government ombudsman arguing maladministration on the part of the local authority which has resulted in injustice to the complainant.

We would anticipate that the use of judicial review will follow the pattern that has been developed in relation to issues in dispute under the Children Act. Much will depend on local authority policies in relation to implementation of the Leaving Care Act and whether they are being reasonably followed. There may also be issues in which the content of the pathway plan does not reasonably follow the outcome of the needs assessment. This issue has given rise to considerable interpretation and litigation in relation to the community care legislation.

Jack contacted VCC when he was shortly about to turn 16. He had run away from his family as a result of physical abuse. VCC submitted a complaint and asked that Jack should be accommodated pending the outcome. Jack was adamant that he would not go home. The local authority consistently refused to listen to our representations that they should accommodate Jack pending carrying out a full assessment of his needs. We considered that the local authority was behaving unreasonably in law sufficient to justify an application in judicial review. The advocate acted as Jack's litigation friend and filed a detailed statement setting out her understanding of his situation. The local authority was given notice of the intended application but gave no indication that they would attend. Having read the papers the judge not only gave permission for the application to go ahead but also made an order without the need for any court appearance.

Conclusion

There has been considerable Government activity over the past few years in trying to ensure that children are properly involved in decisions affecting their lives. As Sarah says in her story this has been for the better. However, there is still some way to go. Practice on the ground remains variable and we continue to hear young people tell us that their views have simply been dismissed without any recognition of their worth.

The provision of independent advocacy for all children and young people who want it can be one significant way of improving practice. Not only can young people be empowered to properly participate in decisions affecting them personally but this can also contribute to the necessary cultural change in social services departments and the development of sensitive policies affecting children and young people. In its Quality Protects Programme, the Government has prioritised the development of children's rights services and independent advocacy. However, while statutory guidance for care leavers reflects the expectation that young people should be able to access independent advocacy of their choice in order to make a complaint there is as yet still no legal entitlement to do so. While this may be most significant for younger children it will still have an impact on some young people particularly those who are isolated and with communication difficulties.

The proposed changes to the Children Act complaints procedures are on the whole to be welcomed as are the new requirements on children's homes and independent fostering agencies to introduce their own internal complaints procedures. However, the way in which these different procedures inter-relate is likely to be complex. Without clear information and support children and young people will continue to be disadvantaged. And making a complaint will no doubt continue to be a very stressful experience for them. Advocacy support is absolutely essential so that in Sarah's words they will not be 'nine feet under'.

References

Aires, A. with Kettle, J. (1998) *When things go Wrong: Young People's Experiences of Getting Access to the Complaints Procedure*, NISW.

Children (Leaving Care) Act. 2000 Guidance and Regulations, Ch 10, Para7.

Choosing with Care The Warner Inquiry Report.

Department of Health. (1991) *The Right to Complain*, London, Department of Health.

Department of Health. (2000) *Learning the Lessons*, London Department of Health et al.

Department of Health. (2000) *Listening to People: A Consultation on Improving Social Services Complaints Procedures*, Department of Health.

Department of Health. (2001) *The Children Act Now: Messages from Research*, Department of Health.

Department of Health. (2001) *Transforming Children's Services: An Evaluation of Local Responses to Quality Protects Programme Year 3*, Department of Health.

Residential Care: A Positive Choice, The Wagner Report.

Stationery Office. (1998) *The Government's Objectives for Children's Social Services*, Stationery Office.

Stationery Office. (1998) *The Government's Response to the Children's Safeguards Review*, Stationery Office.

Stationery Office. (2000) *Learning the Lessons: The Government's Response to Lost in Care*, Stationery Office.

Stationery Office. (2000) *'Lost in Care': Report of the Tribunal of Inquiry into the Abuse of Children in Care in the Former County Council Areas of Gwynedd and Clwyd Since 1974, Recommendations 1–7*.

Utting, Sir W. (1997) *People Like Us: The Report of the Review of Safeguards for Children Living Away from Home*, London, Stationery Office.

Voice for the Child in Care. (1998) *Shout to be Heard*, VCC.

Voice for the Child in Care. (1997) *How do Young People and Children Get Their Voices Heard?* VCC.

Wallis, L. and Frost, N. (1998) *Cause for Complaint: The Complaints Procedure for Young People in Care*, The Children's Society.

7. Foster Caring and Throughcare or Aftercare: A Personal and Professional View

Polnacha O'Mairthini

This chapter looks at my role as a foster carer and how my work developed when I became the manager of a leaving care project.

I chose to become a carer because of two boys I got to know very well at the time through my job as an assistant manager at an outdoor activity centre. I was working with all ages of children and young people on a daily basis, and felt I knew it all. How wrong I was.

I was the eldest of five children who were well fed and loved. Both my parents worked very hard to provide for us and instilled a strong work ethic in all five of us. We had the usual childhood arguments and fights and to top it all I was unbelievably wild. Or as my Mother would say, well I can't say it in print so use the imagination, but it was not very nice and at the time (12–16 years) I was not a very nice person. In fact I would go so far as to say that if I was my parents then I would have placed me in care, but they didn't. They stuck in there and my gratitude to them is unending. These early adolescent experiences allowed me to relate very well to young people who were experiencing what we call now 'challenging behaviour'.

I believed that my life and family experiences would benefit young people who may not have had the family life that I had growing up. I wanted to share my life with others for the benefit of others. Of course my family, and in particular my mother for a couple of years, thought I was mad, and kept hinting that if I were to get married it would be easier and then I would have children of my own to look after. But through it all, despite their misunderstanding of my motivation to care for other people's children, they supported me and to be a foster carer you need the support of your family.

I could talk for hours about my experiences and anecdotes of caring, the ups and downs, the frustrations and anger, the pain and happiness. Foster caring for me has been a continuous learning curve that is unending. Each day brings new challenges. I valued a day that I did not have to deal with new issues for the young persons I cared for. I recognised a few years ago that the difficulties the young people I was caring for presented far exceeded the knowledge I had at the time. Many times I felt out of my depth and frustrated that I was only able to contain the behaviours and emotions of young people. I was unable to assist them in moving forward in their lives. I was aware at the same time that I was doing something right, yet I did not have a hook to hang my practice on so I was unable to develop my fostering skills. I took the decision to return to college and find out more. I chose to do the Diploma in Social Work initially and the BA and currently the Masters. I met a teacher from the secondary school I attended recently who was confounded as to how I managed to achieve what I have. In the eighties at secondary school I was classed as 'not very bright' and more suited to practical applications.

When I started studying again in the nineties I was by this stage a carer of five years. I informed the young people I was caring for what I was doing at college, and one turned to me and said 'that's all I need, its bad enough having to see a social worker, never mind living with one'. That statement made me pause for thought. However, what I learned on my course gave me an insight into my work as a carer, theories became tools which reinforced my direct work. I was developing skills which gave me the opportunity to assess and plan my own caring, and the quality of care I could offer a young person.

I have always advocated that foster carers in today's society require preparation and training which allows the carer the opportunity to look at caring techniques and skills, away from the needs of a particular child. It needs to be proactive rather than reactive, which will enable carers to offer quality care to children and young people. The fostering service needs the recognition of being a service that is regulated yet not over-regulated, we never should forget that foster carers look after children in our own homes and this should not be removed by insensitive over-regulation.

Fostering services for the millennium will require a multi-disciplinary pool of staff and carers that reflects the diversity of needs and challenges that children and young people present. It is becoming increasingly difficult to recruit carers for all ranges of children and young people. The recruitment, assessment and approval process requires evidence-based methods of assessing the potential carer's skills, abilities and qualities for fostering. This process, from my own experiences, can be oppressive in its presentation and delivery, yet necessary to ensure it meets the needs of children. However, the delivery of the service needs to be as non-oppressive as possible.

Fostering is a key service for looked after children and young people. Yet in a recent report to the UK Health Select Committee (HMSO, 2000) on looked after children it points to the fact that foster care lacks recognition and attention on a national basis. It also highlights that there is an acute shortage of foster carers in many areas, demographic and social pressures are working against the recruitment and retention of foster carers, they receive no pension, training is patchy and support from statutory bodies is weak.

This is a pan-European difficulty and not just in the UK and Ireland. We hear the term multi-disciplinary practice bandied around, what is it? I like to think of it as a throughput of not only social work services supporting carers in their role with children and young people but also health, education and training and employment services. Any child or young person who has to be looked after in public care is through logical processes disadvantaged and requires a multitude of services to promote their welfare and needs.

We are in a period of recognition for the fostering services, however let us not forget that the only experts on foster care are the children and young people who are the receivers of the end service. Those who have been through the care system need to be involved in the process of deciding what is a good carer. Children and young people often have the ability of offering common sense and a reflective analysis of the carers that they are living, or have lived with. Let us be open to user involvement in the decision making process.

Following my qualification as a social worker I went to work for Fostering Networks (previously known as National Foster Care Association) in Scotland as Project Leader for the Stepping Out and Moving On Project for Scotland. This was my dream job, and as a foster carer I cared for mainly 13–18-year-olds with a specific remit of preparing them for adult living. Easy task it was not, and I discovered that all of the young people I cared for were desperate to escape the care system, similar to how I wanted to escape the school system at that age.

In Scotland, young people upon reaching 16 can request to be discharged from their care orders. It was common practice to let young people leave with little or no support offered. Some were lucky and received a setting up home grant, but my experiences of this were negative – just giving a sum of money to a young person was a recipe for disaster. However, I certainly had the belief that this was an exciting and new opportunity for foster carers, young people, birth families, local authorities and the voluntary sector to proactively work in partnership in the transition from childhood to adulthood.

In the criteria for the UK National Standards in Foster Care (NFCA, 1999) the standards acknowledge the role of foster carers in the preparation of young people for adult living. It states that foster carers should receive training, ongoing support and guidance to assist the young person preparing to leave foster care. This is a task that many foster carers at present undertake, on an informal basis, and in tandem with local authority social workers and independent living project workers.

The National Standards document recognises that foster carers can, and should, have a role in this important aspect of a young person's development. Research has shown that many young people who leave foster care struggle to live as independent adults. As often as not they have the necessary skills in place to deal with everyday problems and events such as food buying, cooking, paying bills, claiming benefits. Very practical but how do you prepare a young person for the emotional loneliness they may feel.

Think back, to the first time you had a place to call your own, the exhilaration, excitement and happiness of going it alone. Can you recall the first crisis you had to cope with, and who did you turn to for advice and help? Your parents perhaps, or a trusted family member or friend. Did you have someone to help you out when times were hard? Who do young people who leave care turn to when they have left the protective network of social services?

Young people I have worked with feel that every time they call to see their social worker that they are too busy to assist and their pride won't allow them to say that times are hard. They may not be able to rely on the support of birth family members. The advice line or drop in centre feels cold and alien and they don't have a relationship with the person to whom they are speaking.

Foster carers are in a unique position in that they usually have intimate knowledge of the personality, likes, dislikes, habits and attitudes of the young people they have cared for. In most instances the carer and the young person have had the opportunity to develop a good working relationship with each other. Continuing on this theme, it would seem the perfect scenario that a young person's foster carer could support the young person in the latter stages of development into adulthood.

The Stepping Out and Moving On Project aimed to reduce the instances of homelessness among young care leavers in Scotland through proactive involvement of young people and carers in determining the service the young person will require in adult living.

Young people who committed themselves to the project could expect to develop self-esteem and belief in themselves, to develop the ability to build and maintain satisfactory relationships with carers, support workers, birth families, landlords, neighbours and employers. Most importantly the young person can expect to

receive assistance in developing the skills and knowledge they will require for independent adulthood.

In Scotland a local authority has a duty to advise and befriend young people in care, and this provision extends to care leavers. It is covered under section 29 (1) (2) of the Children (Scotland) Act 1995 (HMSO, 1994). Of course the range of aftercare support is discretionary, however guidance suggests that it could include advice and information. If the young person is between 19 and 21 years of age, they will have to apply to the local authority, requesting that the local authority provide them with the same service. Unless, that is, the local authority are satisfied that the young person's welfare would suffer from such assistance. I have always failed to understand how a young person who is reaching out for help could be refused because it would be detrimental to their welfare.

Further guidance to the Children (Scotland) Act 1995 stipulates that a young person should be fully involved in discussions and plans for their future. The young person needs to have choices made available to them. This planning, I believe, does not start 12 or 6 weeks prior to the young person leaving looked after status. It can, and should, be ongoing in the development process. Are we really so eager to see the young care leaver in independent living at 16, 17 or even 18 and what is the hurry? The average age for a son or daughter leaving the parental home in Scotland is 24, so why are we trying to pack seven years development difference into a twelve-week preparation programme. Guidance on the Children (Scotland) Act 1995 also suggests that a leaving or continuing care plan should be formulated with direct input from the young person. This should specify the type of help the young person will be receiving and from whom. Parents and foster carers should also be involved in devising the leaving/continuing care plan.

The Stepping Out and Moving On project aimed to address these issues in the following way. It would provide the young person with an individual preparation package whilst they are in care, this will consist of an assessment of needs which the young person, birth family, foster family, local authority services and the young people's project will contribute to. The project would provide the young person with information and training materials as is necessary including the handbook '*Stepping Out*' (NFCA, 1998) which can include local information and a copy of the local authorities' written information to 'Looked After' leavers.

Basically we aimed to utilise the skills and the resources of the young person and their carers, to ensure that the young person is adequately prepared for adult living. We provided the young person with after care support from the project and their carer, which is flexible, clearly described in terms of availability and purpose and available up until the age of 21.

Through partnership with local housing departments, housing associations and voluntary housing consortiums to provide good standard, affordable accommodation that meets the young person's stated wishes so far as is practicable in terms of locality, size and proximity to family, friends, work and leisure networks.

Our care leavers are the providers of our millennium generation. I do not want to see them as the receivers of the millennium criminal justice, mental health or social work services. My ambition is to see our care leavers as the responsible, educated and stable adults of the new millennium.

A young person who I cared for, on his own insistence, was discharged from care shortly after his 16th birthday to live with extended family members. He received very little preparation for his discharge, in the main due to his failure to co-operate with through-care workers. After a couple of weeks he became homeless following difficulties with his family. He came back to our hometown and moved into a hostel for the homeless. Unfortunately he did not like the rules of the establishment and failed to make his contribution from his state benefits and ended up in debt to the hostel, which had to terminate his agreement. He then went from friend to friend, staying a couple of nights here and there, never being able to settle down for longer than a couple of weeks. The following year of his life mirrored the previous through long periods of homelessness and not knowing where he was going to stay the night.

He turned to alcohol and drugs to try and obliterate his pain and loneliness. The last time I saw him he wanted to stay, and I explained to him that I was unable to accommodate him but offered him advice on what he could do to help himself.

He decided that he would move to England to try life down there. That was four years ago. I do not know if he is happy or unhappy, dead or alive. I don't like not knowing but what can I do? I reported him missing, but on doing this I was informed that over 2000 young people in the UK go missing each year. Who has responsibility for this lost and lonely 20-year-old?

This young person is one of many who have lost their way in life through an eagerness to escape the 'in care' profile and stigma of a young person in care. I want him to be the last and we all need to work together to achieve this and if you're reading this I need your help to achieve this.

The project that I managed for Fostering Networks was hugely successful in meeting its aims and objectives. The basis for this I believe was the holistic approach we took by involving all stakeholders in the planning and implementation of a throughcare service and we embraced the philosophy of a caring society. I have outlined below the highlights of the project and what we achieved. None of this could have been achieved without the full participation and involvement of the young people who made it work. I only provided the engine but they provided the drive.

Since December 1998 the project has worked with 346 young people who are endeavouring to make the transition into adulthood. Each young person brings a fresh individual sense of purpose and destiny. They are coming to terms with the changes in their lives and trying to set solid foundations for successful adult living. We offer young people the opportunity to grow, the chance to take risks and be supported in doing this with the knowledge that they will gain valuable experience, understanding and responsibility.

Each area that we work in requires individual needs to be met, so that in some areas we act as a provider of training services to young people, their carers, social workers, housing officers and education staff on the needs of

Table 1.

Work Undertaken	Female	Male	Total
Direct Referral for assistance and advice	86	74	160
Attendance at workshops in local authority areas (8 LAs)	61	43	104
Development Forum (Training Participation)	15	11	26
Consultation of young people on throughcare and aftercare services	38	19	57
	200	147	347

young people preparing for adult living. In others we act as a consultant on the planning of young people's services particularly on throughcare and aftercare planning.

The table above identifies our main areas of work with young people since December 1998.

The project valued and upheld the belief that young people who have experienced the 'looked after' care system are the key to providing quality training and advice for foster carers, social workers, children's panel members (in Ireland the closest but inaccurate similarity would be Juvenile Courts), education and housing staff.

In most of the areas where we worked we built solid working relationships with young people who acted as co-facilitators for workshops and training events. This system of co-facilitating allows the participants the opportunity to view the looked after system through the eyes of a user and reinforces the value of young people in providing training and advice.

It is my belief that the project's greatest strength has been our ability to offer an open translucent service to all sections of the social services and housing communities in Scotland. We endeavoured not to predetermine what we can do for our clients and service users and instead aimed to provide through consultation a holistic service involving partner organisations, young people and carers.

In January 2001 16 young people from across Scotland took part in a training development weekend in Kilmarnock. This course focused for two days on the stress young people face while part of the care system. The preparation period was followed by a presentation to 50 foster carers and social

workers. For all those in attendance the presentation was graphic, factual and humorous and based on the experiences of the young people.

Young people are the only experts when it comes to providing information and advice on what it is like to be part of the care system. Audiences respond to their input and the honesty of their presentation is heart rendering yet endearing and allows the audience a fuller appreciation of the challenges young people face.

Key Development Areas

The Scottish Throughcare and Aftercare Forum

Since its inception the project has made links with other key childcare organisations in Scotland. The main focus of this work has been the Scottish Throughcare and Aftercare Forum, a voluntary organisation that has been founded to promote good practice in throughcare and aftercare in Scotland. Organisations involved include NCH Action for Children, Barnardos, Church of Scotland, Dean and Cauvin Trust, Glasgow Care Leavers Alliance, Residential Childcare Training Initiative and National Foster Care Association. In August 1999 the forum established a management committee, the project worker representing Foster Networks (previously NFCA) was duly elected as Secretariat for the Forum. This has resulted in Fostering Networks (NFCA) being recognised as a Key Development partner in Throughcare and Aftercare services in Scotland.

As a result a funding partnership of Fostering Networks, Church of Scotland, NCH Action for

Children and the Centre for Residential Childcare (now defunct) was formed with the aim of employing a development worker to further the work of the Forum and secure future funding.

Training for Young People as Trainers

Several groups of young people who have experienced being looked after and two who are birth family members of fostering families took part in a training course for trainers in Glasgow. The young people came from Moray, Aberdeenshire, Fife, Highland, Glasgow and North Lanarkshire.

All of them passed the course with flying colours and had an extremely stimulating and hard working weekend. All of the young people took part in two 45-minute presentations that they researched and formulated. Both presentations reflected the work of the project, the first being The Role of Sons and Daughters in Fostering Families and the second the Needs and Desires of Young People Leaving Care.

All of the young people have now been booked up to co-facilitate workshops, meetings and training in another key area of participation.

Conference Work

Bridging the Gap (Sons and Daughters and Looked After Young People)

This conference was held in Glasgow over two days in September 1999. The conference brought together 36 young people from the Republic of Ireland, Wales, England, Northern Ireland and Scotland who had been part of a fostering family. The conference explored the issues for the Sons and Daughters and those in placement with a family. The most striking thing that came from the conference was that it was very difficult to distinguish birth family members from those who had been in fostering placement.

The event was featured on Scottish Television, Evening Times and the Scotsman; Glasgow City Council kindly hosted a civic reception at the City Chambers.

As a result of the conference it was decided that joint events should take place biennially

with the venue changing to a different nation every two years. The Northern Ireland Foster Care Association will host the next conference in Spring 2002. The conference report also helped the project workers in compiling their report for the board on the participation of children and young people in the work of Fostering Networks.

As a result of this conference the group were invited to present at the International Foster Care Organisations European Conference in Cork, Ireland, during 2000. Four young people from each nation attended. Our Irish hosts kindly arranged a three day pre-conference planning and activity holiday in Skiberrean West Cork. The three days were organised by two foster carers, Marie Creggan and Jill Kennedy who attended the Glasgow conference with their families, and many thanks for their kindness and assistance.

Looked after children training conferences

The project and Karen McDiarmid (Y/P) took part in three one day conferences across the country that highlighted the use of Looked After Children's Materials. At each conference the project facilitated two workshops that looked at the role of fostering services in preparing young people for adult living. As a result of the work undertaken at these conferences the Scottish Executive requested the project develop an information guide for young people between 15-18 years on Action and Assessment Records. This was done with the help of young people in Orkney, Fife and Shetland and is now used by all 32 local authorities in Scotland.

Children's panel members training conferences

The project was commissioned by Aberdeen University (training co-ordinators for North of Scotland) to undertake a series of workshops and full day events for children's panel members on the needs of young people leaving the 'looked after' system. In total the project presented to over 300 members over a series of dates. Feedback from the University of Aberdeen has been very positive. The project worker and a young person facilitated each event.

Members of Children's Panel can be instrumental in ensuring that adult living preparation and appropriate supports are in place for the young person before they are discharged from orders thus meeting our aim of reducing the instances of homelessness among young care leavers.

I took a great personal pride in how young people I worked with promoted their needs. We gave them the opportunity to have a voice and they used it well. Many of the young people we trained in the early years of the project are now employed in the service area. Two are part of Scottish Parliamentary Committees and advise politicians and civil servants.

The crowning point of my involvement with young people and the project was the day we received the news that the project had been awarded The John Chant Award for Services to Young People by Community Care Magazine, a social work publication in the UK. To everyone the award and the £8000 prize reinforced that we were getting it right. At the award ceremony two young people collected the award and it was a proud moment for me, from being a foster carer who was unhappy about leaving care provision in Scotland to making a change and redressing the status quo albeit in a small way. The project, I feel, proved that although young people leaving care are needy and they will take risks that many judged to be inappropriate, we supported them through these risks just like a normal family household would do with their son or daughter. My own parents played a big part in this for me and never turned their back on me no matter how bad it got.

The model we developed for the project is a simple one and can be easily replicated in any country, local authority or voluntary organisation. We were fortunate in that we had a National Lottery Grant of £180,000 over three years to enable us to achieve our objectives. Recently the project was awarded a further £400,000 to progress the work over the next three years. This will allow for the employment of a young person who has left care to work with the project and gain skills they may have been otherwise denied.

I have now moved on to working in the Orkney Islands. However, I hope the project will continue in the future as long as it is needed. I also hope that others may learn from the work in order to help all those leaving care to succeed in their lives.

References

HMSO (2000) *Children and the Public Care System*, HMSO.

NFCA (1999) *UK National Standard in Foster Care*, NFCA.

NFCA (1998) *Stepping Out Guide for Care Leavers*, NFCA.

8. Leaving Care Support Groups

Carol Florris

When first asked to write this chapter my reaction was not to be too phased by the term 'leaving care support groups'. However, as I began to consider more about what I would actually write, I began to realise that the term was actually an evolving concept, which could mean a group with one of several structures and purposes. The uniform idea of the group being made up of care leavers is from current experience, also being adapted with several 'forums' being developed which have a membership of young people looked after as well as a membership of care leavers.

I concluded that the chapter would look at some of the main different models and purposes of the leaving care support groups, which currently exist or have recently existed in Wales. The chapter will examine some of the strengths and weaknesses of the various models, as well as outlining some of the challenges which are constantly present in working with young people, particularly with what can often be a diverse group of young people who may be undergoing the life changing experience of learning to live independently, but within that they may have very varied needs.

Voices from Care

Voices From Care is seen by many as a peer-led support group. In reality this is only one of the functions of the organisation. Currently the main provision of advice and support is located within the Advice and Support Service. In many ways this operates in a similar method to the Advocacy projects in existence in Wales at this time. The main differences are that the Voices From Care Service is delivered by Advice and Support Workers who have personally experienced the care system themselves as children or young people.

We also uniquely offer a policy of 100 per cent confidentiality, which is often viewed controversially by some people. Basically, in the instance of care leavers in danger, Voices From Care would work with the young person to deal with the danger at their own pace. Obviously, our aim would be immediate safety. However, Voices from Care believes that child protection procedures often do not offer this. In fact some independent living facilities can put young people at risk – supported housing facilities where there are no staff present during evenings and week-ends are often targeted by pimps and drug dealers; young people are left supporting each other around issues such as self-harm. These are some of the experiences of Voices From Care. With a lack of willingness to listen to young people and a shortage of accommodation options, Voices From Care does not feel confident that statutory child protection responses will protect young people. A 100 per cent confidentiality policy gives us time to empower young people to look at their own safety issues and to look realistically at their options for keeping safe.

However, Voices From Care strongly believes that if we do not offer this young people will not feel able to bring issues to us. We strive to deal with issues at a young person's pace and in an empowering context.

Voices From Care is open to all young people who are or have been looked after in Wales to become members of the organisation. Several of these also become volunteers for the organisation and currently the organisation has approximately twenty active volunteers. Peer support is an important part of volunteering for Voices From Care. The organisation views the idea of young people gaining support from each other as essential, as well as young people learning skills of empathy, understanding, listening and other support skills.

However, Voices From Care believes that peer support cannot exist in a vacuum. It has to have a purpose. Within Voices From Care, members and volunteers are involved in working and campaigning to achieve the aims set out in the organisation's Mission Statement:

to provide opportunities for young people, to improve the conditions for young people, to promote the voice of young people and to protect the interests of young people. Peer support is one of the vehicles which help achieve these aims, but it is also simultaneously one of the achievements of this Mission Statement.

The organisation has also set up for itself policies and procedures around peer support. Young people may have a shared vision for improving the looked after system, but are not always in agreement about how to bring about this change. Voices From Care is clear that young people need to engage in informed debate amongst themselves and to be supported to understand and reflect the range of experiences and views about the looked after system.

Young people in and leaving care are the foundation of Voices From Care. However, to keep that foundation strong requires a whole organisation of resources, skill and commitment. Leaving care support groups are in many ways working to achieve the same aims as Voices From Care, but within a much more minimal structure and time-frame, and perhaps in a way which is not so independent from the local authorities.

The questions facing Voices From Care reflect very much the experiences of the leaving care workers and leaving care support groups in Wales I spoke to for the purposes of writing this chapter – model of group, purpose, transport, funding and staffing etc? Whilst many of us have managed to grapple with these issues, or at least have learnt to accept that they are a recurring challenge of working in this field, there are still other issues for which we have yet to find an acceptable solution. The issues of how to empower/motivate young people in groups, how to achieve representation on *all* issues, how to avoid tokenism and exploitation? – these are issues which Voices From Care deals with daily. These are the challenges also currently facing local authorities in Wales.

Models

In seeking to explore the workings of leaving care support groups – I spoke to or visited several groups of young people, voluntary sector workers and local authority representatives. What I discovered was that there are in operation a number of models of the leaving care support groups. Some of these models included the actual meeting of a group, others involved a conscious decision not to be centred around a group and to locate support into community based services. The reasoning behind the various models is something I will discuss as well as outlining the models.

'The preparation group'

This is a time-limited group with the specific purpose of looking at the skills needed by young people to achieve successful independence e.g. budgeting, cooking and other household skills, bill paying, and health care. This type of set up also aims to inform young people of their rights and their responsibilities as independent young adults, and to distribute essential information such as where services are located (e.g. housing, health, benefits etc).

The reasoning behind this type of leaving care support group is that a certain level of preparation can be achieved for all young people coming up to the age of leaving care. Young people can be 'advised' of the benefits of attending. Difficulties that young people face in leaving care can be raised and talked through. Young people can meet others in the same situation.

The major anxiety about this type of leaving care support group is the question of can you teach someone (whether they have been in care or not) the skills for living successfully on their own in the time frame of what is essentially a course? What about the emotional skills needed? The diversity of young people who could potentially be attending this preparation group also needs to be addressed. The group would certainly be very diverse in terms of support needs, interests and learning abilities – presenting a challenge to the most qualified of educators.

Managers and practitioners faced with some of the appalling statistics of outcomes for care leavers have over the last ten years realised that preparation for independent living needs to take place over a number of years. Whilst several of the practical skills can be ticked off as learnt, the assessing of emotional skills is much more elusive. Voices From Care works daily with young people who are unable to put skills into practice when faced with the stress of debt, loneliness and general lack of support and direction. There is perhaps still a place for leaving care preparation groups, but these have to be very time limited, well constructed and viewed as only a stage in leaving care preparation.

'The working group'

This type of leaving care support group is the most modern model. Combining support with the current focus on service user consultation and participation, this is an active group and an asset to any local authority. This model is peer led, with young people taking a lead on organising the programme of work and activities, supported by staff from one of the large voluntary organisations who are contracted by the local authority to provide the leaving care team.

This model of group meets frequently – either weekly or every two weeks, has a steady membership (in the groups I spoke to this numbered from six to 12 young people) and has firm ground rules on involvement – decided by the young people. The groups I spoke to had a varied programme – one meeting may be taken up with a social issue, with a speaker being invited in. The idea of these meetings was generally to inform young people, generate discussion and to prevent the issue discussed from being a problem area for young people (addiction, housing, health related issues).

The following meeting may be set aside to concentrate on a work area, possibly negotiated with the local authority. In Swansea the 'Feedback' group have been involved in developing a 'What You Need To Know' pack for 11–16-year-olds and for carers, in improving leaflets on the complaints procedure and in looking into setting up a website for young people looked after and leaving care. At Network 2000 in Blaenau Gwent young people have met with Children's Commissioner for Wales, Peter Clarke, to raise the issues with him

that they feel he should be addressing. The group also met with the Director of Social Services in their local authority and with the Social Services Inspectorate. The Network 2000 group have also been involved in interviews for leaving care workers and a Project Manager. The focus of these activities for young people has been to help other young people looked after and leaving care by raising issues and improving services.

A rolling programme would designate the next meeting as being organised around a social activity – cinema, ten pin bowling. The activity would usually be decided and organised by the young people. As well as having a social element, such activities help to build skills of organisation and to build confidence. The groups I spoke to had strong ground rules, composed by the young people, that members needed to attend other meetings to be able to participate in the social activities.

The working group is arguably the most 'successful' of the leaving care support group models. It is an active group, at times high profile and certainly a grouping of which local authorities are proud. However, some may question the representative elements of such groups. Six to 12 young people in most local authorities is a small portion of the number of young people eligible to attend a leaving care support group. The fact that the group is small may also make it more difficult for other young people to join. A regular, consistent membership may mean that the group comes to be regarded as a closed group (even if this is not the case). Coupled with questions over representation may be concerns over tokenism. Pressure on local authorities to evidence service user participation and consultation can mean that it is an all too obvious choice to point to the leaving care support group. However, one could question whether such a small group constitutes what is expected of service user participation and consultation.

'Working groups' are on occasions asked by local authorities to consult with young people. Whilst this may be an innovative and laudable practice in some respects, it is valid to question the training given to young people to undertake this work. Are they informed enough to explain the looked after system/care issues to the young people they are consulting, are the members of the group able to put their own views aside enough to really record the points other young people are raising, particularly if the views expressed are not in agreement with their own? In Blaenau Gwent young people undertook a trainers course to help them develop the skills and methods needed in working with groups. This of course means that leaving care support groups need to have access to staff with these skills and access to appropriate resources.

The running of the 'working group' can be another area of concern. Most of the local authorities in Wales are rural with poor public transport systems. The groups in Blaenau Gwent and Caerphilly were certainly dependent on transport being provided by staff (or if sufficient funding is available, taxis). Staff felt that the survival of groups was dependent on proactive individual staff as well as key young people. However, in times of staff shortages the leaving care support group was one of the first areas of service to suffer, especially if the group was very dependent on staff for not only its running, but for its transport requirements as well.

The final point to make about what I have termed 'the working group' is that the support received by young people from such a group is potentially very different to that which the term 'Leaving Care Support Group' suggests. Attention to individual issues and support needs is not central to these groups, but is something which may happen if young people feel the subject is acceptable to the group or feel comfortable in the group. 'Working groups' can exist quite successfully although the young people may have severe problems, which would be worked through and seen as necessary to discuss in all traditional psychiatric based support groups. In a consultation/campaigning group problems may be acknowledged and either put aside or debated in pursuit of the cause. However, the degree of support received by young people around their individual issues and situations is varied in this kind of campaigning situation.

As I have stated the 'working groups' that exist in Wales are usually run by one of the large voluntary organisations -National Children's Homes, The Children's Society, Barnardos – as part of their contract with the local authorities. This may mean that there are issues here for young people around confidentiality. These voluntary organisations have child protection policies which offer a high degree of confidentiality but which still have to report to social services on situations of harm or likely harm. In Voices From Care's experience many of the issues young people would like to discuss in terms of support are those which involve risk to themselves or others – drugs, self-harm, sexual relationships (ranging from non-abusive to those that are on a high degree of abuse). Voices From Care's confidentiality policy allows young people the space to talk about these issues and their personal situation. Whilst other voluntary organisations may be very clear with young people about what their policies of confidentiality are, it may mean that the individual issues with which young people need support are not actually being fully addressed in the leaving care support groups.

Community-based leaving care support

Some local authorities in Wales have made a deliberate decision not to set up a leaving care support group. Managers in these areas believe that setting up a group falsely assumes that care leavers share a common identity and needs, when in fact their lives and issues may be very diverse. Such local authorities have worked to establish support mechanisms and networks within the community by working with drop-in facilities and groups set up for all young people and by targeting these services at where young people are – colleges, courts, police stations, health services such as GP surgeries, drug agencies, family planning. This type of community-based support can be more viable for small local authorities where the numbers of those leaving care are minimal. In larger local authorities such services would be essential, as well as perhaps having in existence one of the models of an actual leaving care support group.

The problem with community based leaving care support is one of communication. Often services set up for young people are on occasions not well informed or staff trained in issues for care leavers. The other danger is that young people leaving care can end up being passed around services as their needs may be complex and require a variety of input. However, there are some good quality one-stop drop-in facilities offering a variety of services like that operating in Rhyl in Denbighshire. If the communication of such projects with the leaving care team is regular and informative, the support needs of young people leaving care can be well met, assuming that young people are aware of the resource and able to get to it.

Of course some will argue that the empowerment aspect of the leaving care support group is missing from this community-based support. The assumption is that young people leaving care need to have a problem to make use of the service. This type of service may not facilitate much contact with other young people and often lacks the element of young people seeking to improve the care system and leaving care services.

Conclusions

Having looked at the various models for 'leaving care support groups' throughout Wales, their programmes and the problems they face, it is a difficult task to argue one against the other. It seems there may be a place for something which combines all the models. I would argue that to be truly effective and beneficial any model needs to look widely in terms of participation and consultation. The groups also need to have well-developed links with community resources and other forums and organisations for young people.

When young people are preparing to leave care it may be an opportune time to introduce young people to a group. Group work can serve an important role in preparing young people to live independently and in a group young people can have the chance to make links and friendships with those in similar positions. Attending a group from the supported base of residential care or foster care can assist young people in terms of transport, advice and someone with whom to talk issues through. Introducing young people to a group at this stage would be an essential opportunity to explain to them the new leaving care legislation

and what it will mean for them – personal advisors, pathway plans etc.

To acknowledge the limitations of 'the preparation group' in actually equipping young people to move into successful independence this group could become an on-going leaving care support group. The identity could then become more that of a working group–ensuring that young people have the continued opportunity of addressing social issues but also enjoy the empowerment and satisfaction of participation and consultation to influence the looked after system. Of course, it would need to be decided if local authorities have one larger leaving care support group incorporating the different preparation groups and ages or whether the groups carry on separately. This would have significant resource implications. Any group should be strongly linked to community based support projects for young people, so that they are aware of issues for care leavers who, for one reason or another, are no longer members of the leaving care support group. Such links would also perhaps assist in young people re-entering the group.

There should be well established policies and procedures for working with other forums and organisations for young people. This would give young people choice over where to get advice and support. For example through the leaving care support group a young person could learn of organisations offering confidential advice on contraception and family planning and could choose to turn to one of these. This would also be part of the encouragement of young people taking control in seeking advice and support for themselves. It would also mean that whilst the leaving care support group provided a more open forum for looking at issues, the overall aim was to ensure that particular difficult areas were sorted for the individual involved.

Any leaving care support group which is successful, should have inspired some of its members to want to continue being involved in work to influence the looked after system. Most leaving care support groups have an age limit. Links with other forums and organisations, such as Who Care's Trust, A National Voice and Voices From Care would give young people somewhere to go onto if they want to carry on campaigning. Links with educational establishments would also provide an additional outlet. Voices From Care regularly meets young people who hope to gain a social work qualification as a route to making a difference.

Investment

The leaving care support group I have outlined in my conclusions would require significant investment. Rather than being viewed as an aspect of the leaving care support service which can be cut in times of resource and staff shortages, or left to the goodwill of staff for its resource/time/transport requirements – this leaving care support group would need to be a foundation stone of the leaving care service. Its setting up could serve several of the functions of the new leaving care legislation. The group could become an important time and place for personal advisors to keep in touch with young people. Much of the work the leaving care service needs to do to improve outcomes for young people leaving care could be done via

the group. With proper and committed planning, resourcing and staffing the leaving care support group outlined could achieve real empowerment of young people and avoid being a tokenistic and exploitative exercise. By employing strategies and links which encourage the membership of as many young people as possible the group can ensure that it is fully representative. The potential of such a leaving care support group and the importance to young people leaving care is immense. Any local authority not making a proper investment, and continuing to treat its existence as something peripheral, is missing an essential opportunity to make a real difference to the lives and futures of young people leaving care.

Thanks to those spoken to:

Young people at Voices From Care, Feedback Group – Swansea, Network 2000 – Blaenau Gwent, Merthyr Local Authority, Vale of Glamorgan Local Authority, Denbighshire Local Authority and Caerphilly Local Authority.

9. Learning the Lessons from the Past – Leaving Care from 'Out of Area' Placements

Peter Sandiford and Cathy Glazier with Caroline, Mary, Trevor, James and Rachel
(James and Rachel are the names chosen by the young people concerned)

The children and young people who come to the Caldecott Foundation are amongst the most vulnerable in our society. They come from all parts of the United Kingdom having been placed by local authority social services, education or health departments. They are children and young people who have experienced extremes of hardship and suffering in their short lives – lives that have been literally devastated by physical, sexual or extreme emotional abuse and, much too frequently, all three. Deprived of the capacity to thrive in their own families, they are the children no one wants to know. They have often experienced many placement breakdowns and, far too often, many school rejections as well – coming to Caldecott often is their last chance before becoming one of the harrowing statistics relating to those in public care.

A placement at Caldecott is about providing a safe and consistent bedrock that will enable all the children and young people to work with staff, from a range of disciplines, towards achieving their true potential, both on leaving and in the years to follow. Everyone at Caldecott aims to ensure all those we look after live in settings which both recognise and respect their individuality, racial, cultural and religious identities.

The therapeutic approach that the Caldecott Foundation adopts is one that is constantly evolving and embracing new ideas. It is particularly based on psychodynamic theory with additional inputs from other therapeutic models including, but not exclusively, systemic and cognitive. That is to say that the adults employed in the task of caring for and educating our young people seek to understand behaviour rather than solely reacting to it. Understanding behaviour is essential if staff are to avoid re-enacting

previous patterns of the child's experience of adults, which, ultimately, will have been rejecting.

We endeavour to understand the root of children's and young people's troubles and help them, when they are ready, to better understand their past experiences and help them take control of their lives. The development of relationships to ease this transition is essential. An attachment theory model is employed to provide the child or young person with a secure base from which they may take risks in remembering, forgetting and re-living past traumas and happy times. Children and young people, through their relationships with staff have an opportunity to internalise these experiences and develop a more contained emotional inner world, which can sustain them through further traumas, disappointments and successes.

We seek to provide a facilitating physical environment, which ensures the physical safety, stimulation and nurturing of the child/young person. We provide a quality environment with pleasing colours, soft furnishings, good quality furniture, personalised individual space, good quality home made food, soft lighting and open fires. The physical environment is an extension of the relationships with adults, and is central to our therapeutic approach.

For many, before referral to the Caldecott, education has been a poor experience often ending with permanent exclusion. The Caldecott school provides the opportunity for children and young people to renew their confidence and self-respect through achieving, both academically and vocationally, their full potential.

We recognise that leaving is a difficult transition for all in public care. In order to finish the work we have begun, a Family Placement service and a Throughcare service have been established.

Leaving care is often seen as relating to young people leaving public care at, or above, the age of 16, to live in some form of independence. However, the vast majority of care leavers are much younger and leave to move on to other care settings or indeed, back to their own family. This is particularly true of 'out of area' placements which provide a specific intervention that is increasingly time governed with a focus on the child or young person returning to their locality once 'the work' is completed. In this chapter we will look at how the use of 'out of area' placements has developed over recent years and some of the issues relating to how children and young people might be prepared for the transition back to their own community and, or a new family. The chapter has been written by Cathy, the manager of the Caldecott Foundation Throughcare service and includes comments made by a range of people who are living or have lived at the Caldecott. I have had the relatively simple task of writing an introduction and conclusion.

Children and young people in public care are increasingly being recognised as one of the most vulnerable groups in society. In the public eye this is largely due to the high profile abuse cases detailing their experiences whilst being looked after by the 'corporate parent'. This seems to be a weekly occurrence in our local and national press. Undoubtedly it is this public face that has led to Government interest resulting in the setting up of task forces and the resulting Quality Protects initiative. Since these were created, many working in the field have wondered what the final result will be in terms of legislation and guidance.

As a result, on the statute books are the Care Standards Act 2000 and the Children (Leaving Care) Act 2001. In order to support these there are new public bodies, the National Care Standards Commission and the General Social Care Council. It is these bodies that have the authority to ensure services provided to this most vulnerable group are of a high standard. About time you may say! You would definitely say this if you were a care leaver in the 1980s and 1990s, particularly if you had been living out of your home area.

As a residential social worker since the early 1970s I have frequently been amazed at how little thought and expenditure (both financial and energy) was put into helping young people leave a placement that had been extremely expensive and in which they had resided for many years. Whilst a range of interventions had been made to help them through their childhood, the transition into adult life was not recognised as important. The statistics of education failure of those in public care bear this out and when related to statistics about rough sleepers, the prison population and mental health we are left with a desolate picture. I have wondered whether we would have even more running away from care if children and young people knew how their chances of a positive move into adult life would be disrupted if they became the corporate son or daughter.

For 'out of area' placements the picture has not been too much different to all others. We know that outcomes have been similar to those from 'in area' placements. However, this should perhaps be seen as an achievement as those referred are frequently the ones social workers have given up on and need to find a 'bed' where they believe they will be safe. A purchasing manager from one social services department has said to me that it was not a major consideration what an 'out of area' provision charged, what mattered was that they would maintain the placement through difficult times and that 'they' would be safe. I have wondered whether the 'they' referred to the worker or the child!

If it was the case that finding a 'bed' and making the child 'safe' led to a consistency of placement that could well be in the child's best interest, during the latter years of the 1990s, however, we have seen placements shorten and children and young people being brought back into their local authority provision. Whilst this is going on there have been targets to be met regarding lowering numbers of 'out of area' placement and also reviews looking at where the authorities' money is best spent in receiving quality services. Hence many local authorities' children and young people have had their placement disrupted well before the work with them has been completed – another placement move with the resulting disruption.

As a result, the population of many 'out of area' placements has changed. Gone is the time when a child would be referred between five and ten years of age and remain there until adulthood. The length of placement is frequently down to less than two years with three years often being a maximum, which means that children and young people are not leaving to adulthood and independence but to go to a family or an 'in area' placement. A leaving care service meeting the needs of an 18-year-old moving into adulthood is very different to one helping a child at 10 move to an alternative family, or a 12-year-old move into a local authority children's home!

It is within this context that the Caldecott Foundation, like many other residential establishments, has struggled with the issue of how best to prepare and support its leavers. Services provided have included a semi independence project, organised individual and group work programmes, and an outreach service for leavers until their mid 20s and in some instances, beyond. However, in recent years, the shortcomings of what essentially has been a somewhat piecemeal provision, together with the importance of addressing the need for continuity during a young person's transition through residential placement and preparation for adulthood, have increasingly been recognised. This in turn has led to a new model of working gradually being developed in the Caldecott Foundation.

Influential in the development of the new model for practice has been not only our own experience and understanding of the particular needs of our leavers, but also the views of leavers which were canvassed to help guide the services we offer. Most striking in their responses were the comments about loneliness, the absence of stable support, and how unprepared they were for independence following the secure and protective world found at the Caldecott.

Caroline

Caroline is 30. She came to the Foundation at the age of 5 and left at 17. She remained in the local area after leaving and now lives in a local authority flat:

I left the Foundation when I was 17. I didn't really think about leaving beforehand. I was doing a YTS scheme and I moved from the Foundation to a halfway house in the town. I didn't have an outreach worker before I left but a worker got involved when I left. There was a drop-in centre outreach ran in the town and I used to go to this. About six months after I left I was introduced to a new worker and this worker started visiting me at home.

Before I left the Foundation I didn't really do any preparation for leaving. Me and another girl used to do the washing and drying-up and we went into town on the bus but when we went to the dentist we went as a group and we never went to the doctors surgery because the doctor came to the house. Nobody ever really talked to you about what it was like to leave. I felt discouraged from going to College because they didn't think I would manage. I was quite scared about moving. It was scary but exciting at the same time.

Moving to the halfway house was a bad mistake, I got blamed for damage that other residents did and was told I had to pay for it. I left there after about a year.

When I left the Foundation I found it really hard to manage the money I had. All I had to live on was the dole cheque and there was all the hassle with filling out forms, again and again. When I got a job it was still really hard, I once got caught without a TV licence, that was another scary thing.

The worst time was when my electric was cut-off. I spent several nights in the dark. It was horrible, I felt totally alone. In the end I made a reverse charges call to my outreach worker. He came and phoned the electricity company and got a key meter fixed. He also took me out shopping to get me some food and helped me clean up the flat. He helped me with lots of things. I knew I could call him whenever I needed him but sometimes my pride stopped me.

I didn't really have any close friends after leaving the Foundation. I remember once when there was a fire in the block of flats I was living in, all the other people had people who invited them back to their place with them, or stayed with them. I was the only person who went back on my own.

Throughcare finally stopped visiting me about three years ago but I've kept in contact and I still go to their leavers' Christmas meal. I know they prepare people for leaving now and I think they should carry on doing this. They should also get people who have left care to talk to those who are leaving.

Another factor that has been influential in our thinking is changes in the profile of children at the Caldecott, which is consistent with the national picture of children and young people in public care. Up until around the mid 1990s it was common for children and young people, who were resident at the Caldecott to have lived with us for a large proportion of their childhood and adolescence. It was also the case that many of the young people did not leave until 16 plus and a considerable number moved out of the Caldecott and settled in or round the locality or London area. This is no longer the case for the majority of children who come to the Caldecott. Increasingly, local authorities are placing children in the Foundation for much more limited periods than they used to. In addition, they also often leave earlier and do not remain in and around the locality, but return to their local authorities, which are often many miles away, or even across national boundaries. These changes have made us look again at the leaving process for children and the kind of aftercare service that a residential resource such as ours, servicing young people from widely disparate geographical areas, can realistically provide.

In addition, to these changes in the profile of young people the Foundation provides a service for, it has also clearly been necessary for us to take into account new policy initiatives that have taken place relating to leaving care, including Quality Protects and the Children (Leaving Care) Act. In particular, the increased obligation on local authorities to provide a 16 plus service has supported a move towards us having more of an advocacy role than being providers of aftercare support services ourselves.

At the centre of the model of practice we have developed, is the recognition that the work with the children at Caldecott is part of a continuum of care, and that the history, present and future should dovetail together when forming plans. We have adopted the notion of

'Throughcare' as a way of underpinning the process of preparing children and young people for adulthood and supporting them through the process of a residential placement and beyond.

Mary

Mary is 20 years old and left Caldecott 3 years ago to live independently, locally. She was at Caldecott for 9 years.

Throughcare first became involved when I was 16. I was helped with budgeting, shopping and leisure activities, we spent time talking, we talked about anything.

Throughcare helped me with finding a flat and then helped me budget my leaving care money to furnish it. They helped me fill out application forms for jobs, get on the housing register, fill out benefit forms and stuff. I also got help when I was upset. They kept on even when I gave them a hard time!

I still see Throughcare about every three weeks but I can get in touch whenever I need to, if I've got a problem.

If Throughcare had been involved earlier I would like to have done more cooking. Caldecott cook for you too much and you don't learn.

When I left Caldecott I found paying bills hard, cooking and being on my own. It took ages to get used to not having people around all the time. I think I did a pretty good job of looking after myself though. Social services were also really supportive, because I left when I was 17, they helped me with paying my bills and rent but it was hard when they stopped.

If money was no object I would want cooking lessons.

The early development of the Throughcare service took place in 1997–98. It was supported by substantial funds from a charitable trust which enabled the recruitment of three social workers and a team manager. Initially it was decided that workers would commence working with young people in the Foundation from the age of 14. This involved the provision of individual and group work programmes in partnership with school and residential staff. It also embraced participation in all reviews and professionals meetings which related to preparation and planning in regard to the young person's future. Other elements of the work included building links with the wider Foundation, which provided greater opportunities for young people at the Foundation to experience wider value systems through leisure, social and work experience programmes, and training programmes for our residential and education staff, to enhance social and practical skills training within the children' home and school.

Trevor

Trevor is 18. He came to the Caldecott at the age of eight and left at 16 to return to live with his parents in a neighbouring county.

I started thinking about leaving the Caldecott when I was about 14. It was decided I would be going home to my parents rather than to foster parents and I was really pleased. I wouldn't have wanted to go anywhere else.

The first major step was going to mainstream school, that was before Throughcare were involved. Group staff helped me with that, Throughcare became involved when I was about 14½. They and the group staff did lots of things with me, like helping me learn to get the train home, budgeting, cooking, talking about jobs and what you wanted to do when you left school, sex education and talking to people. Oh yes, and I started doing my own washing and ironing and had more freedom around bedtimes and going out.

Throughcare and group staff also helped social services get my mum and dad a bigger house from the local authority so I had my own room when I stayed with them and took me to careers and for interviews at the college where my mum and dad live. They also used to have meetings with me, my mum and dad and social worker to talk about how everything was going.

When it came near to leaving I knew I'd miss it at the Caldecott but I knew it was time to leave. I would spend most of my time out with my school friends as all those in the group were younger and I used to wait for them to go to bed and then I could talk with staff and have a laugh.

When I left I had mixed feelings. I was sad and happy. I had to do a lot of work on my own. It's the biggest thing I've had to do in my life. I never used to have any confidence but I can do anything now.

It took a while to get used to the different rules at home. The hardest thing was finding mates. I was on my own. Then I made a couple of friends at football and college. My first big step at home was getting a part-time job when I was at college.

I went through a down phase about making friends. I was given support but it was suggested I tried going to youth clubs and I didn't think I would make any friends that way.

When I first left Caldecott my Throughcare worker used to visit about once every three weeks and I felt I could phone the group any time. Social services also helped financially. Now I'm visited about four times a year. I could contact Throughcare if I had a crisis or problem but now I feel I can cope with most things myself or with the help of my parents or friends.

If money was no object then I think Throughcare should get a place in Ashford where 15 and 16 year olds could go and practise living by themselves. They could be given money and learn to budget and pay bills. Staff would visit but wouldn't live there.

Following on from the service provided for young people within the Caldecott, continued support was offered to young people who left the Caldecott from the age of 16 plus to maintain a link right through to independence and up to the age of 25 or so, if necessary. The support offered included emotional, practical and, on occasions, financial, and was provided in conjunction with local authority and other voluntary and statutory services.

The benefits of the new Throughcare Service soon became apparent and a more cohesive and co-ordinated approach to the preparation and planning for young people for leaving the Foundation and for adulthood began to emerge. In addition, awareness around the importance of taking risks and preparing young people for living in the wider community was increased amongst the residential staff.

Alongside this, the ongoing relationship with leavers meant more opportunities for preventative work with leavers rather than young people sinking into crisis, before being ready to accept our help. Another valuable aspect of the service that has become increasingly evident as time has progressed has been that of advocacy, which Throughcare workers were able to take on both for young people within the Foundation and leavers. Our position in not having either statutory responsibility, nor day-to-day involvement in the primary care of children, combined with knowledge of other agencies, meant we were often well placed to perform this role.

Although clearly a considerable advance on previous provision, it began to become increasingly evident by the end of 1999 that Throughcare's remit was not wide enough and that if consistency and continuity were to be achieved in both preparation and planning for leaving and adulthood, the Throughcare involvement should begin from the point of admission. The changing profile of young people at the Caldecott reinforced this. Currently, this means being involved at a child's admission conference and being available on a consultative basis to groups until the child reaches the age of 12, when they will be allocated a Throughcare worker. However, we are gradually working towards a far greater involvement in working and planning around younger children. This will involve a wide diversity of work including individual and group work with children, work with natural and substitute families and advocacy.

In regard to provision for those who have left the Caldecott, the model of practice has to be flexible due to the widely varying needs and circumstances of those who leave the Foundation. For a few 16 plus young people who remain relatively local we continue to provide a service which offers ongoing support with day-to-day practical, emotional and financial issues. We may also in the future in some instances be able, if so requested by a young person/local authority, to fulfil the role of personal advisor. However, for the majority of young people who return to their local authorities some distance away, the role of the service we offer is much more one in which the

worker can offer some informal support and act as a back-up or safety net within this role, can help young people advocate for services they are entitled to and, on occasion when there are difficulties between them and agencies who have a more formal involvement, act as mediators. Frequency and type of contact vary according to need and distance but can be ongoing until the age of 25. The possible provision of some financial assistance is also an aspect of the service. A fund is available to which leavers may apply for financial assistance in the form of a grant or loan. Items for which help is given are wide ranging and includes deposits on flats, educational fees/materials, unexpected repair bills on essential household items, clothes for interviews, etc. in fact, all the kind of help with items young people often look for from their parents.

James

James is 12 and has lived in the Foundation for 3 years. A foster placement is currently being sought for him.

I first started seeing my Throughcare worker about three months ago. We've started by getting to know each other and we've been out on some trips together. We've talked about learning social skills and I would like to do some baking. I don't want to go to a Throughcare group yet.

I think Throughcare got involved at the right time, although maybe they could have got involved a little earlier. I think Throughcare could help with school work. They could run a homework club so they could help with writing and reading.

The service for those below the age of 16 is still in the throes of being developed but we have begun to offer, when appropriate, a service to help bridge children and young people into their next placement. This can involve us in continuing to visit a young person who has moved into their new placement to help them through the transition and settle into the placement such as in the case of a child moving into a local substitute family or back to their birth family. It also could involve us being commissioned by the young person's local authority to do a particular piece of work with the young person. Clearly this kind of input does have cost implications and in these cases some financial agreement with the local authority has to be reached.

Rachel

Rachel is 13 and has lived in the Foundation for 2 ¼ years. It is planned she will move on to a foster placement and mainstream school next year.

I first got involved with Throughcare a few months ago when I started going to a group they run. It was about learning skills for when you are older, like skills with money and about learning how to co-operate and get on with each other. We did lots of things like going out to places, cooking together and a video evening.

I started seeing my Throughcare worker by myself a few weeks ago. So far we've done phone practice and talking about friendship and getting on with others. I'm doing another Throughcare group now and after that finishes I will be doing some cooking skills with my Throughcare worker and work on getting ready for mainstream school. I think it would be better if Throughcare got involved a bit earlier, maybe about 11. If they waited until I was 14 I would be going. I would like Throughcare to run an activity or sports club.

I don't know what kind of support I would like from Throughcare when I've left, it depends on what problems I've got.

Some common themes of the experiences young people and ex-residents talk about are:

- How preparation for leaving starts 'too late'.
- How scary it is.
- How lonely it is.
- How difficult it is to make friends.
- How to get a job.
- How to manage the day-to-day difficulties of living on your own!

By developing a leaving care service that becomes involved at the beginning of a care placement it is possible to plan from the earliest point how the leaving process will be managed. Whilst it is clearly the responsibility of referring authorities to provide a leaving care service to young people and for ensuring that those leaving a placement to move onto another placement it is, at the very least, good practice for any specialist 'out of area' placement to work at ensuring as smooth a transition as possible and to advocate on behalf of the young person when required.

In conclusion, I return to a point made early in this chapter, how can a referring authority jeopardise the impact of a placement by not providing a good ending – but on the other hand how can an independent sector placement ethically justify failing to champion the needs of a young person they have worked with and been financially rewarded for so doing? For all young people in public care, leaving a placement is a major life cycle event, for those living away from their home area this is even more acutely the case. A 'throughcare' type service can positively intervene in order to ensure as smooth a transition as is possible.

References

Hardwick, A. and Woodhead, J. (1999) *Loving, Hating and Survival*, Hampshire, Ashgate.

Little, M. with Kelly, S. (1995) *A life without problems?* London, Arena.

10. Becoming a Parent: Good Practice in Prevention Strategies and Support Services for Looked After Young People and Care Leavers

Kathy McAuley

Introduction and Context

Much has been written over the past few years regarding 'teenage pregnancy'– why it happens and what can we do about it? The Social Exclusion Unit summarised this body of knowledge, experience, good practice, research and statistics in their June 1999 report Teenage Pregnancy. For the most part it presented a fairly bleak picture. In England there are 90,000 conceptions a year to teenagers; around 7,700 to girls under 16 and 2,200 to girls aged 14 or under. In the UK teenage birth rates are twice as high as in Germany, three times as high as in France and six times as high as in the Netherlands. Such teenage birth rates are far higher in the poorest areas and amongst the most vulnerable people, including those in care and those who have been excluded from school. Teenage parents are subsequently more likely than their peers to live in poverty and unemployment and be trapped in it through lack of education, childcare and encouragement.

The Social Exclusion Unit rightly attributes these high rates in the UK to the low expectations of young people who have been disadvantaged in childhood and have poor prospects in terms of education or the job market and to the ignorance of young people regarding accurate knowledge about contraception, sexually transmitted infections, what to expect in relationships and what it means to be a parent. The highest risk factors to becoming a teenaged parent are poverty and being a child in care – a quarter of care leavers had a child by the age of 16 and nearly half were mothers within 18 to 24 months after leaving care (Biehal et al., 1995). Other risk factors include being the child of a teenage mother, having educational problems/low achievement, being unemployed; earlier and more intense exposure to high risk behaviour e.g. experimentation with alcohol, drugs, smoking, sex and violence; having previous experience of sexual abuse; experience of mental health problems and involvement in crime. The link between disadvantage and early parenthood also impacts disproportionately on ethnic minority groups. 41% of African Caribbean, 82% of Pakistani and 84% of Bangladeshi people have incomes less than half the national average (Health Education Authority, Analysis of Health Education and Lifestyle survey, 1994). People from some ethnic minority groups (particularly African Caribbean) are also disproportionately likely to be in the high risk groups, i.e. in the care system or excluded from school.

For those of us working in the 'In and Leaving Care' Sector, such statistics are not a surprise. Looked after children and care leavers are over represented in all the risk factors identified above – initially due to the reasons why they came into care and then, to our eternal discredit, often compounded by the system that is supposed to be caring for them. Whilst this chapter will be discussing good practice in relation to support for looked after young people/care leavers who become parents, it is crucial that we first look at some preventative strategies that need to be delivered within the system itself in order to ensure that looked after young people/care leavers have other positive alternatives to early parenthood.

The remainder of this chapter looks at the role of fostering services for young parents; preventative strategies as well as pregnancy and parenthood. Appendix A is a document on teenage mothers and fostering produced in consultation with Fostering Networks.

Preventative Strategies

Development of resilience

Some interesting research on the development of resilience in children and young people in need by Gilligan (2000) is of particular value when applied to increasing the motivation and choices of looked after children/young people. According to Gilligan:

> A resilient child is 'one who bounces back having endured adversity, who continues to function reasonably well despite continued exposure to risk.
>
> Children and Society, 14: p37–47.

Although the qualities of the child/young person are important in understanding resilience, so also are the experiences that the child/young person encounters and how they process those experiences.

Development of positive relationships with adults

In Gilligan's view a small change or favourable experience in a child or young person's life may be a turning point in their development. This would seem to have a particular resonance for those of us working with young people in or leaving care. For a young person in or leaving care, a network of social support based on work, social, educational, recreational and professional helping relationships, is essential to their overall personal development. Even one positive relationship or experience in childhood or adulthood may do much to counter the harm of negative relationships or experiences. As carers we know this is true – for example an ex-Coram young person said 'When I left here, I remembered the things you told me and what you did for me and its helped me learn what I have to do. I thought you were just hassling me but you weren't – thanks'.

Involvement in activities

Similarly, success in an activity that the young person values, may do much to overcome a sense of failure in other areas of their life. According to Gilligan it is in 'the everyday and ordinary that may be found many such supports and opportunities. The naturally occurring opportunities in daily living may ultimately prove more therapeutic than ones which are specially contrived or engineered'. Consequently, a caregiver's commitment and perseverance can help young people to develop one crucial and positive thread in their lives that can have an enormous impact on their self-image and behaviour.

At Coram we had a young man 'C', who though small and slightly built, had the capacity to destroy everything around him when he had taken alcoholic drink. After much persuasion we managed to involve him in our *Get a Life* sports and leisure programme and he suddenly discovered that he had a natural ability for badminton and could play better than the tutor. The turn around in his behaviour was extraordinary – his self-esteem rapidly increased, his drinking decreased along with the violent outbursts and he began to find a sense of purpose in his life. Activities such as dance, singing, involvement with animals, sport, helping and volunteering and part-time work are all areas that as carers we need to support and encourage looked after young people and care leavers to become involved in. Attention to the detail in the present makes the prospects for the future more promising and more attainable for looked after children and young people. They need an investment of interest and concern by adults personally committed to them, so that they can develop the personal resources to make more informed and positive choices in their lives.

Support for educational achievement

As indicated earlier, the research shows that childhood disadvantage, experience of the care system and low educational prospects and achievements are all-powerful factors associated with teenage parenthood. Clearly education is the key to improving the prospects of looked after young people and care leavers and to increasing their options beyond that of early parenthood. The Government's Quality Protects programme (November 1998) put education at the top of the agenda for looked after young people/care leavers. For the first time as Corporate Parents we were all exhorted to 'be ambitious for them'. The appalling educational outcomes for looked after children and care leavers are all too familiar to those of us working in the sector, as detailed elsewhere in this book.

Developments such as designated teachers for looked after children in every school, tighter deadlines for identifying school places when a child or young person is taken into care, greater emphasis on keeping children/young people in their existing schools and reduction of placement moves will all contribute to the improvement of the above outcomes. As carers we have to actively encourage and support looked after children, young people and care leavers with their education. We need to constantly ask ourselves the question 'would this be good enough for my child?' We should help with, and check on, homework, liaise with the schools, attend open evenings, check on test results, familiarise ourselves with course content requirements and help with accessing information, identify extra support where needed, facilitate involvement in extra-curricular activities and show a genuine interest in their achievements and goals.

Given the lack of positive educational experiences of looked after children and care leavers there is much work to be done to enable those whom the system has already let down, to catch up and compete equally with their peers. At Coram we identified that many of our service users were experiencing serious difficulties in accessing and sustaining education, training or employment, because they lacked the necessary level of literacy and numeracy skills. Such difficulties were primarily due to their experiences of a disrupted and inadequate education, caused by multiple placement moves. They then left school without adequate basic skills or qualifications. In addition we had noticed an increase in the number of young women in this disaffected group who became pregnant at an early age. We now run a specialist one-to-one and group teaching service for care leavers (single, pregnant and parents), that will assess and meet their needs and offer a safe, supportive and private environment where they can begin to tackle their basic skills needs, without losing face in front of their peers. We also run a range of accredited courses, education, training and

employment advice/information and homework support and ESOL (English Speakers of Other Languages). The service aims to raise their basic skills, enable them to gain qualifications and then progress onto further education courses, training schemes and employment opportunities.

One young woman who had not attended school for two years and had disrupted every foster and education placement found for her, attended our education service regularly and achieved her first qualifications. The predicted outcome for her, by her previous carers and to a certain extent herself, had been early parenthood. She has now gone on into further education and is receiving homework support. Our experience shows that it is not too late for young people who have already been through the system. With the right kind of teaching, guidance and support they can still find the motivation to succeed and achieve their full potential, instead of taking the route to early parenthood.

Good sex education

Another of the Government's Quality Protects objectives was 'to ensure the number of pregnancies to girls in public care under 16 is the same as the rest of the population'. The Children Act 1989 highlighted the importance of sex education for looked after young people and this expectation was further emphasised and extended by the Children Leaving Care Act 2000. Most of the research points to the effectiveness of sex and relationships education in delaying sexual activity and promoting safe sex (World Health Organisation). For the most part this is generally consistently and effectively delivered in schools (particularly where linked with local sexual health agencies) albeit in uneven quantity and quality. However, as mentioned earlier, as many looked after young people significantly miss out on school due to multiple placement moves, they are most likely to miss out on what sex education is available. The challenge for carers therefore is to ensure that such information is made available to them in the most appropriate and accessible ways. Carers must be informed themselves; be flexible; admit when they do not know; have a 'let's find out approach'; be non-judgemental; be un-patronising; know their own limitations and boundaries; be prepared; be able to listen; make the young people feel safe and challenge prejudice in a non-confrontational manner. However, this will not happen if carers are not given appropriate and on-going training in sex education and how to deliver it to young people.

Kanwal and Lenderyou's publication *Let's Talk About Sex and Relationships*, identifies the core elements of good sex education for looked after young people as:

- **Attitudes**: we need to enable young people to identify what they believe in and why, and to learn to respect the beliefs of others.
- **Skills**: we need to teach young people communication and personal skills, to enable them to develop successful relationships and to make informed choices about sexual health and emotional well being.
- **Knowledge**: we need to provide easy to understand, age appropriate information on how bodies develop and work; sexuality; the Law; sexual reproduction; sexual behaviour; sexual health; emotions and relationships.

It is important as carers that we understand the varying needs of young people in or out of care. Such young people often become sexually active as a way of seeking physical affection and affirmation of themselves as desirable and attractive individuals. They may also have a distorted view of sex and personal relationships due to their experiences of neglect, abuse etc. by parents and carers. They therefore often lack the necessary skills, self-esteem and confidence to negotiate and sustain positive personal relationships.

The key, therefore, is the development of social skills. Looked after young people and care leavers often find it difficult to ask for help, access services, ask questions or to talk about feelings and relationships. They need sensitive, confident carers, other professionals and mentors to develop these skills. At Coram we use a multi-disciplinary team of social workers, teachers, youth workers, aftercare workers, group workers and adult and peer mentors, to develop a range of age-appropriate methods

and resources, including one-to-one teaching, group work sessions, residential sessions, leaflets, books, videos, computers, media, games, art, theatre, drama, poetry, storytelling, role-play, music and singing etc. to engage and sustain the interest of young people. We run both single sex and mixed groups and give equal emphasis to the importance of sex and relationship education for young men as well as young women.

In our experience very little will change if young men are not enabled to take responsibility for their sexual behaviour and make informed sexual choices. In order to achieve this young men need positive male role models using non-stereotyped resources who can give positive feedback and inspiration. A focus on personal development as well as sex education is needed for young men and young women, in order to increase their self-esteem and confidence and to teach them how to communicate about sexual and emotional matters within personal relationships.

An example of some focussed work with young men is the Coram Boys2MEN (B2Men) group-work programme that was developed two years ago with the aim of tackling the issues associated with the social exclusion of young men in the care system, particularly black young men, by preparing them for fatherhood, relationships, career and social development. Devised as a 'rites of passage' outlining the development stages from boyhood to manhood, the B2MEN programme has used a wide range of psychological theories, as well as music, video, computers, the expressive arts and experiential and motivational techniques. Young men have been encouraged to reflect on their experiences of their own fathers, what they wanted and received from them and what sort of a father they would like to be. Through this process they have developed more positive attitudes, raised their self-esteem, had their personal and social values challenged, built up their resilience and set goals for future life commitments. Fifty per cent of the group have now moved on into education and employment. Group members have also contributed to a planned publication detailing the stories, memories and recollections of what life was like growing up without a father.

The issues of identity, knowing where they are coming from and where they are going to, a key focus of all of our group-work programmes and a fundamental issue for looked after young people and care leavers, is closely related to feelings of self-worth, values and young people's ability to commit and maintain responsible relationships. In the words of a Boys2MEN group member:

> If I didn't come to the boys2MEN project I don't think I would have gone to see my father. Before I would just ignore him and pretend he did not exist, but coming to the project, because it was there all the time, I could not avoid it and realised it was something that I had to do.

If we can provide these kind of programmes for looked after young men/care leavers at an earlier age, then they will have a better chance of competing on a level playing field and maximising their potential in the future, all of which can contribute to the possibility of a decrease in early, unplanned parenthood.

Pregnancy and Parenthood

The reality of teenage pregnancy is that even when young people have been provided with the necessary knowledge and information on sex education, they do not always put this into practice. Consequently the phrase 'it just happened' often accompanies the revelation of an unplanned pregnancy. It is hard for most young people, but particularly looked after girls and young women, to match the idealised images of romantic love, with the realities of sex and relationships. This is confirmed by Corlyon and McGuire's (1999) research *Pregnancy and Parenthood: The Views and Experiences of Young People in Public Care*, where most of the young people interviewed were inclined to think that teenagers became pregnant not because they did not know how to use or where to obtain contraception, but because they were careless and considered themselves invincible.

It is crucial that as carers we respond sensitively to a looked after young person or care leaver's disclosure of their pregnancy. Whilst most early pregnancies are in fact unplanned, it is important that we do not make this assumption. We need to be caring and

supportive and to encourage the young person to talk about their feelings rather than rushing in with information and advice on what the options are. The young person is likely to feel shocked, fearful, anxious and distressed and initially wants non-judgemental reassurance. Most of the looked after young people in Corlyon and McGuire's research, (and this is confirmed by our own extensive experience of working with pregnant young women and young mothers), did not receive objective information about their options or counselling to help them make their decision. Instead they experienced a judgemental response and considerable pressure to have an abortion, which is rarely the option taken by looked after young people and care leavers, because they perceive it as similar to the rejection they themselves experienced from their own parents. In addition, looked after young people and care leavers are not accustomed to making long-term decisions and therefore going through with the pregnancy is usually the easiest choice in the short term. Our experience also shows that even when a looked after young woman has made a considered choice to have an abortion, she can sometimes be subjected to such moral judgement from her peers, that she blames others for her decision and subsequently becomes pregnant again very quickly in order to absolve herself. As with any parent receiving news of their teenaged daughter or son's potential parenthood, carers have to deal appropriately with their own feelings of disappointment and failure, as well as how to convey their concern for the young person and their future. Ultimately, we have to support the decision they make and then ensure that we provide them with the support, care, guidance and information that they need, to ensure a healthy and informed pregnancy.

Corlyon and McGuire's research, and our own experience of working with young mothers, shows that pregnant young women generally and looked after young women and care leavers in particular, rarely access antenatal or parent-craft classes at their local hospitals or health centres. The very nature of adolescence means that most young pregnant women will feel ill at ease with their bodies and embarrassed at the changes taking place. They often cannot talk to anyone about what is happening to them, or their fears and fantasies about giving birth. They rarely feel able to turn to their parents, carers or non-pregnant peer group for help, and consequently many resort to a denial of what is happening, often due to a lack of knowledge and understanding about their bodies and the belief 'it could never happen to me'.

According to the Social Exclusion Report on Teenage Pregnancy, as a group, pregnant teenagers tend not to have well managed pregnancies. They go to their doctors much later in pregnancy and consequently miss out on important early health measures, and during pregnancy they are the most likely age group to smoke. For many young pregnant women, any kind of conventional ante-natal planning is very difficult, as they face huge problems of family conflict, probably change of care or fostering arrangements, relationship stress or breakdown, and problems with education, housing and money. One alternative to conventional ante-natal care for such hard to reach pregnant teenagers, is the development of specific support groups for pregnant young women and young mothers. Whilst such groups are labour intensive, time consuming and require the provision of transport to get the young women to and from the groups, they have proven to be a life-line to those young women (mainly care leavers) who do not use other services, The young women attending the young mothers groups run by Coram over a 15 year period, recorded on video their very negative experiences of pregnancy, ante-natal care and childbirth. They rejected the institutionalised and professional atmosphere of hospitals and clinics, feeling that they were disapproved of and treated like naughty children. Consequently they tended not to use these services effectively and therefore experienced pregnancy and birth as a time of ignorance, anxiety, fear and helplessness.

Coram subsequently ran community based Pregnant Young Women's groups for 10 years, as part of a much needed network of accessible support services for vulnerable and looked after young women/care leavers. The focus of these groups was on encouraging a positive self-image in the young women, valuing what they felt and what they wanted in their lives, as well as providing much needed information on pregnancy, childbirth and on-going parenthood. These groups were run in informal settings, by staff using an accessible youth work approach. The young women felt confident and relaxed to share their anxieties and hopes without fear of ridicule or misunderstanding. They enjoyed being with other pregnant young women and gained a sense of status at belonging to a group where they received special attention. As with Corlyon and MaGuire's research, the looked after young women/care leavers using these groups, had family experiences that were often characterised by violence and arguments, virtually no teaching about family life, poor parental role models, inappropriate expectations of them by their own parents, virtually no contact with their fathers and frequent rejection and neglect by mothers. They therefore had few positive family experiences or support to draw upon and consequently felt ill prepared for what they were taking on.

The groups also covered issues about relationships with boyfriends/the father of their baby, their families, how to deal with the medical profession, racism within the hospital system, how they would cope physically and emotionally with a baby and what support networks they had and would need in the future. The role of the baby's father was a sensitive issue within the groups. During their pregnancy most of the young women wanted the baby's father involved, but many experienced considerable difficulty in sustaining his interest. The young women felt insecure and fearful that they would be abandoned – a familiar experience that many had gone through with their own families. Where possible the group workers encouraged the fathers to attend some of the groups' mixed sessions and where this was successful, some of these young men supported their 'babymother' during her labour. Unfortunately they were very much in the minority and most of the young fathers were absent during the pregnancy and subsequently not welcomed by the young mothers, once the baby had been born.

An additional learning tool for the pregnant young women was to invite new mothers back to the group, to give an account of their labour and birth. The other group members then had the chance to ask very specific questions and to gain reassurance from the new mother on how she had coped with her labour. They also had an opportunity to handle a new-born baby and to talk about what it was like feeding and caring for them. The bonus for the new mothers was being transformed into 'experts', which gave them a confidence boost and much needed affirmation that they could manage and were not alone. The principles and content of such community based pregnant young women's groups can be effectively applied to individual support sessions and small groups within residential settings, using the support of external specialist agencies, as needed.

Once pregnant teenagers become young mothers, they often have difficulty in getting the right balance between needing and resisting help. They want to feel cared for, and to have someone to take an interest in them and their child, but they can also be defensive and view such help as interference. They have to prove themselves and show they know it all because they are terrified of being viewed as inadequate parents and of having their child taken away from them. Many care leavers are encouraged to spend some time in a mother and baby unit, before moving with their baby into their own flat in the community. However, this type of resource is often disliked by the young parents themselves, because they feel they are treated like children. It is difficult for such projects to get the right balance of accommodation that allows self-reliance, as well as providing useful parenting information and advice, together with support and company if needed. The Social Exclusion Unit's report on teenage pregnancy highlighted the need for supervised semi-independent housing with support, for under 18 lone parents, many of whom would be care leavers. It is planned that the Department for the Environment, Transport, Local Regions (DETLR), Department for Work and Pensions (DWP) and Department of Health (DoH) will work together to identify necessary revenue funding for such projects through the Supporting People programme, which officially commences in April 2003. The challenge is for experienced care leaver organisations, in consultation with their users, to produce creative and flexible project proposals that will appropriately meet the needs of young parents.

As mentioned earlier, care leavers who are parents are often fearful of social services involvement. This was borne out by young women attending our Young Mother's groups:

Just because we are very young mothers they expect us to batter our kids: I wouldn't tell them anything.

Such young mothers need to be supported to make more effective use of statutory and other mainstream agencies, (e.g. Sure Start and Home Start) whilst maintaining control over their own lives. Young Mother's groups have proven to be especially effective for looked after young women and care leavers who, as mentioned earlier, lack a network of family and peer support. Such groups can give these young women a source of friendship, support and tolerance, where they can share issues of childcare and relationships and help each other look for solutions. Where crèche services are provided, the young women have the added opportunity of participating in structured, personal development, group-work programmes with their peers, without the responsibility of childcare. The role of the crèche workers is very important in providing the children with stimulating play experiences, as well as giving the young women positive feedback and advice on the development of their children. Home visiting the young mothers and picking them up and dropping them home, are also important components that help the young mothers remain in contact with the group workers, even if they could not always attend the group.

The Coram group-workers made concerted efforts to involve the young fathers in the project, where appropriate and desired by the young mothers. We were most successful in achieving this when organising family day-trips for the groups, where the fathers were explicitly invited and some did in fact attend, but mainly those who were still involved with the mother of their child. As with Corlyon and McGuire's findings, most of the young women were dismissive of their baby's father and saw them as a liability, immature and:

... like having another baby in the house.

The need to find ways of engaging young fathers is borne out by the experience of the Coram Boys2MEN project which demonstrates how the 'absent father syndrome' denies children, particularly male children, the role model of a good father, thus influencing how they themselves approach parenthood in their own adult lives. It is known that a poor parental attachment in childhood, especially amongst males, makes it harder for them to cope with the responsibilities of parenting and to attach to their own children.

Coram's experience with Young Mothers groups dispels the myth that most very young women become pregnant to gain housing, that they are automatically bad parents because they are young, or that they are happy to remain at home on benefits, rather than undertake training or education. On the contrary, many of the young women tried very hard to 'do their best by their children', which included ensuring they were well stimulated and talked to, and had time with their peers. The looked after young women and care leavers in particular, often wanted to 'improve' themselves through education, training or employment, in order to provide their children with a better childhood than their own. Ann Phoenix's study *Young Mother's* (1991) showed that a negative focus on mothers under 20 is common because little attention is paid to the circumstances in which most of them live. Consequently any problems they experience are attributed to age rather than to the structural factors, such as their employment histories, housing conditions and income levels. Most of the young women in Phoenix's study (which included care leavers from Coram's groups) were fairing well despite high rates of poverty. Good outcomes were mainly linked to the degree of social support that the young women received and their ability to access good childcare, education, training and employment opportunities.

More recent research by Dawson (1997) and Coleman and Dennison (1998) also questioned the assumption that adolescent parenthood is inherently negative. They too highlighted that the main factors influencing positive outcomes for the young women who became pregnant at an early age, were limited economic and educational opportunities. One of the key

factors according to Pugh, De'Ath and Smith, (1994) is also how the experience of pregnancy and parenthood is managed and an available network of family, friends and professionals.

Currently a number of Early Excellence Centres are piloting DfEE funded Teenage Parents projects, with the aim of establishing whether 'an increase in the education participation, completion and achievement for teenage parents', can be achieved through the provision of paid childcare. As one of the pilot projects, the Coram Parents Centre (in conjunction with Coram Leaving Care Services) is providing a package of high quality, appropriate childcare, education assessments, advice and teaching provision, transport and parenting support, for the young people involved in the project. The outcomes so far indicate that the issues surrounding whether young mothers return to education, following the birth of their babies, is much more complex than just the provision of paid childcare. The barriers to education for teenage parents also include:

- The young parent's prior history of missing out on or disaffection with school (i.e. care leavers), or offending.
- Refugee or asylum seeker status.
- Limited English, or low basic skills.
- Preoccupation with housing problems and the effects of poverty.
- Poor health associated with inadequate housing and health care.
- Breakdown of family relationships or partner relationships.
- Low self-esteem and high levels of anxiety and insecurity.
- Limited ability, because of present immaturity, to plan for the future.

Nevertheless, the provision of paid childcare has been of immediate benefit to some young parents who already had appropriate 16 plus qualifications and the necessary skills to be accepted onto such courses. However, due to some of the barriers listed above, most of the young parents need a more gradual return to education and consequently access services at the Coram Parents Centre (e.g. I.T. course and other classes, crèche and drop-in) as a precursor to moving on to a college course at a later stage. Other participants who missed out on education prior to becoming pregnant (e.g. looked after young people or care leavers) need to increase their skills levels before being ready to access mainstream courses. Consequently they attend the centre for basic skills or English Speakers of Other Languages (ESOL) classes, whilst some are being given regular one-to-one tuition in their hostel accommodation or at the Parent's Centre.

Both the earlier Coram Leaving Care Services Young Mother's groups and the current Teenage Parents Project have found that most of the young parents want to spend quality time with their babies and do not immediately want to leave them with carers, so that they can return to, or catch up on, education. However, improving their education remains part of their overall plan. In addition, 16–17-year-old young parents are able to take part in Education Maintenance Allowance Pilots (where available and eligible), and these pilots are looking at how to meet the particular needs of teenage parents.

Very few of the care leavers using the Teenage Parents project have taken up the explicit parenting training on offer at the Coram Parents Centre. They, more than the other young parents, have strong fears about being labelled bad parents if they show any sign of what they perceive as weaknesses. However, they have gained many important skills from their interactions with Centre staff, especially in the crèche and drop-in. Their preference was for informal parenting support, which they had more control over. Given the social isolation resulting from institutionalised care, and lack of family or extended family support, it is very important that we introduce care leavers who are young parents to the range of parent/child services in their local area and to support and encourage them to make use of these services.

Corlyon and MaGuire found from their 1999 study that some of the care leavers with babies received support from ex-foster carers, staff from residential homes and semi-independence units, as well as aftercare workers. The aftercare workers were often the only continuing support for young mothers living in the community and they provided a source of support, friendship and reassurance. In addition, the informal parenting support provided by aftercare workers was found to be more acceptable to care leavers than support from social workers. Social workers were not available enough and also represented a conflict of interests between the needs of the young mother and those of her child. An aftercare worker was viewed as being able to support and advocate for the mother, particularly if there were child protection concerns being addressed by the social worker. However, aftercare worker input is often mainly available when the young parent's baby is very young. Such support tends to decrease as the child or young parent both get older, as the aftercare worker's limited time is then devoted to the new care leavers moving into the community.

Whilst most aftercare workers continue to provide some ad-hoc contact, this is rarely sufficient to meet the needs of a young parent, as their child moves from the more manageable baby stage to that of the more active toddler. The support of a specially trained mentor can be particularly beneficial to such young parents, both in terms of receiving informal parenting support, but also that such support is provided by an adult who has been through similar experiences themselves and understands what the young parent is going through. Currently, most mentoring projects for care leavers focus on improving the educational prospects and social inclusion of the mentees they are supporting. Consequently, whilst most mentors are not selected or trained to provide parenting support, many tend to do so in order to support the mentee where they can. Our experience has shown that it is very difficult for mentors without a parenting mentor brief and/or training, to properly meet the needs of the young parent and their child. However, the mentors do try to increase the confidence and skills of the young parent in more indirect ways e.g. helping to improve the basic skills of a young parent, so that she could then read to her children. Additionally, it is of considerable value to young parents to receive support from members of their local community, who can then introduce them to a range of services and experiences, which they might not have accessed by themselves. Work is currently being undertaken to develop specialist parenting mentor services for care leavers who are parents, as a much-needed adjunct to aftercare services.

Conclusion

At the beginning of this chapter, I quoted the statistics from the Social Exclusion Unit's report on Teenage Pregnancy, which presented a 'bleak' picture on the high numbers of teenage pregnancies in the UK and the high proportion of looked after children or care leavers in these figures. In order to develop appropriate responses and services to looked after children and care leavers, who might, or do, become young parents, we need to move away from a 'knee jerk', negative reaction to teenage sexuality and young parenthood. As indicated earlier, young people will experiment sexually and in the case of looked after children this tends to happen earlier than their peers in the community. We therefore need to be pro-active in putting in place preventative strategies that offer genuine opportunities to looked after children/care leavers to develop positive and consistent relationships with adults; access a range of stimulating and nurturing activities and receive support, encouragement and high expectations for the maximisation of their potential and their educational achievements.

As professionals working with looked after children or care leavers, we must always have in our minds the question '*would this be good enough for my child?*' If the answer is '*no*' then we must take positive action to redress the situation. We need to use this question as a tool to improve our practice and services. We must respond appropriately and sensitively to a young person's disclosure of teenage pregnancy and ensure that accessible information is provided, pulling in a range of acceptable supports and services of the types mentioned in this chapter. We must be positive about their future options, help them achieve their goals of 'doing it better' than their own parents. We must ensure that they have a goal in terms of education and if we can't provide the support they need then we must find services and people that can. It is not the end of a young person's life if they become a parent at a young age. As parents we would ensure we

supported our child through this stage in their lives – as corporate parents we must do the same for looked after children and care leavers.

Appendix A – Becoming a Parent and Fostering

Fostering Networks (previously NFCA) also work in this area. They have produced information on the subject and part of this is reproduced below:

Why foster care?

P and P have been foster carers for over 25 years but now they focus mainly on mother and baby placements. This came about accidentally when the girlfriend of a young man they were fostering became pregnant. Sadly she had had limited mothering experience herself so was unprepared to become a mum. P and P converted a downstairs room into a bedsit for the young couple, P acted as birth partner and was on hand to offer guidance and support in the early days following Jamie's birth. Within six months the family were ready confidently to move on. Ten years on they are still in close touch and although the relationship didn't last, Jamie has been continuously well cared for by his young mum.

Since then many young women have been part of the 'family' – mainly they come from dysfunctional families and/or a care background. Whatever the reasons they need support and guidance at a critical stage in their young lives. What are their needs, what problems do they face?

Immediately:

- Support and guidance in preparing for parenthood at a time when many are still developing their own maturity.
- Dealing with changing relationship with their partner or having to accept that they will be coping alone.
- Dealing with family conflict- intergenerational conflicts that are heightened by pregnancy and may lead to rejection by own parents.
- Unresolved feelings around past abuse and childhood trauma.

Longer term:

- Coping with the daily demands of a baby or toddler.

- Managing on welfare benefits.
- Difficulties in accessing educational and employment opportunities.
- Lack of adequate move on options with limited or no support.
- Fear of failing so their own child comes into public care.

What does a foster home offer?

- *It's flexible*: foster homes, like young people, are different so it becomes possible to offer a resource which:
- *Can provide individual care* – not all young people want to be together with others or some need special individual care package.
- *Scope for matching* to meet cultural, religious and racial needs.
- *Scope for working* with young fathers, making them welcome as part of the 'family' whether joining in at mealtimes, caring for the baby or babysitting. Boundaries are needed but these can be set to meet individual circumstances.
- *It's based on experience*: from evidence provided by local authorities usually, carers offering this resource already have fostering experience – with that comes many skills that are highly useful.
- *It's local*: carers often do not move around – they can provide continuity of a young person's social, family and other networks which will be important when the mother and her baby move on.
- *It enables* carers to support the young mum in establishing relevant health and other networks and resources.
- *It provides some element of normality*: that is important both during pregnancy and in preparation for the future.
- *Care and support* given takes place within a family environment.
- *Placing in a two parent family* enables both mother and baby to have experience of a male role model around everyday, often something which has been or will be missing from their lives.
- *Carers provide a valuable role model* for the boyfriends or fathers – 'his interaction with the babies is lovely and it is not resented' so he both acts as a role model as well as being willing to talk to the young parents.

- *Providing normality* helps to reduce the stigma attached both to being a young parent and being in care.
- *It's preventative*: being flexible, being local and providing some normality which allows for better assessments, and the establishment of supportive local networks and ongoing support.

What works well?

- Foster carer support groups should meet regularly, co led by the family placement team and be well attended.
- Importance should be placed on shared support as well as benefiting from outside specialist speakers.
- Realistic planning: detailed planning meetings and agreements avoid confusion by setting realistic tasks and responsibilities and off set some potential problems e.g. the foster carer is a glorified baby sitter.
- Outcomes: overall these have been good with young women moving into their own accommodation and being able to care for their child. In some instances it has been possible to use a fostering placement to reunite a mother and her child.
- Carer's ability to work well with grandparents – pregnancy and birth often bring to the forefront unresolved conflicts that can impact on the developing relationship between the young woman and her own child. It can also highlight gaps in the mothering she has received and needs at this critical and vulnerable time in her life.

What are the difficulties?

Managing risk: there is sometimes tension between the district staff and fostering staff and carers around managing the risk. This may result in reluctance on the part of social work staff to end a risky placement and maybe instigate care proceedings. Foster carers get frustrated when their concerns are not acted on.

In many authorities more work is needed around the after care support provided formally by foster carers, the role and relationship with the leaving care team and accessing suitable accommodation for a young parent who is also a care leaver.

Working in a transracial context – many of the young parents are white and are or were having a relationship with a black young man. This often leads to problems around identity e.g. denial that the baby is black and what that means, problems of violence and allegations of racism against the foster carer. These have implications for training, contact arrangements in placement planning and support and guidance to carers.

What do local authorities need to provide?

Policy and practice guidelines covering:

- Financial arrangements for mother and baby placement including source of funding for equipment.
- Roles and responsibilities of foster carer, social worker and young parent.
- Complaints and representation procedures.
- Leaving care policy and guidance which outlines the corporate response to meeting the particular needs of those leaving public care who are either pregnant or already young parents.

Placement agreements: setting out the boundaries of the placement so that everyone is clear about their roles and responsibilities. Scope for misunderstandings and conflicts are reduced and inappropriately dependent relationships are not formed.

Written agreements should cover factors such as:

- The carer's roles and responsibilities.
- The social worker's roles and responsibilities.
- The mother's roles and responsibilities.
- Babysitting arrangements if any.
- Day care arrangements to facilitate young mother attending work or education.
- Family contact.
- Any specific arrangements in relation to contact with the baby's father.
- Financial arrangements.
- Equipment arrangements.
- Review date.

Support: both in policies and guidelines and individual placement agreements. It is essential that carers are informed of the support available e.g. respite, out of hours, groups for carers and young parents.

Training: general and specific to this type of fostering with emphasis on child development , assessment, recording and child protection.

Finance: these placements require a high level of skill on the part of carers and the risks can be high so carers must be well rewarded. Young people in care under 18 cannot claim benefits. Although the baby is not usually accommodated on most schemes the carer should receive the full allowance for the baby.

Monitoring: effective monitoring systems are essential at national and local level.

What everyone wants to achieve with, and for, young women in public care is that they make informed choices about when and why they are starting a family. Also, if they become pregnant that skilled support is available to assist them in pregnancy and early motherhood in theirs, and their child's, best long term interests.

Many of our placements are regarded as inappropriate for residential assessment as the young people need to learn parenting but also to be parented.

local authority representative.

References

Biehal, N. et al. (1995) *Moving on*, NCB.

Botting, B., Rosato, M. and Wood, R. (1998) Teenage Mothers and the Health of their Children, *Population Trends*, 93, Autumn.

Coleman, J. and Dennison, C. (1998) Teenage Parenthood, *Children and Society* **12**: 4, 306–14.

Corlyon, J. and McGuire, C. (1999) *Pregnancy and Parenthood: The Views and Experiences of Young People in Public Care*, National Children's Bureau.

Dawson, N. (1997) The Provision of Education and Opportunities for Future Employment for Pregnant Schoolgirls and Schoolgirl Mothers in the UK, *Children and Society* **11**: 252–63.

Department of Health. (1998) *Quality Protects Programme*, Department of Health.

Gilligan, R. (2000) Adversity, Resilience and Young People: The Protective Value of Positive School and Spare Time Experiences, *Children and Society* **14**: p37–47.

Health Education Authority. (1994) *Health Education and Lifestyle Survey*, Health Education Authority.

Kanwal, H. P. and Lenderyou, G. F. (1998) *Let's Talk About Sex and Relationships*, Sex Education Forum, National Children's Bureau.

Phoenix, A. (1991) *Young Mothers*, Cambridge, Polity Press.

Pugh, G., De'Ath, E. and Smith, C. (1994) *Confident Parents, Confident Children*, National Children's Bureau.

Social Exclusion Unit. (1999) *Teenage Pregnancy*, Social Exclusion Unit.

Werner, E. and Smith, R. (1992) *Overcoming the Odds: High Risk Children from Birth to Adulthood*, Ithaca, Cornell University.

11. Accommodation Issues Arising from the Children (Leaving Care) Act 2000

Keir Parsons with Bob Broad and Ena Fry

Background

Care leavers are over-represented in every aspect of social exclusion.

Young people leaving the care of local authorities are failed by the systems that are supposed to care for them and encourage them to fulfil their potential. The figures in relation to mental health difficulties, teenage pregnancy, homelessness, unemployment, substance misuse and time spent in custody, show a disproportionate number of care leavers amongst their number.

Research shows, time and time again (for example, amongst many, Biehal et al., 1995) that young people leaving care have a:

- Poor or difficult background before coming into care.
- Limited support at time of entry to care.
- Mixed time in care.
- Poor support and preparation for leaving care.

Many of these in-care problems and difficulties are simply compounded by the lottery of under-funded services provided by local authorities. Around 50 per cent of young people are unemployed after leaving care. It is known that every placement move is likely to lead to approximately six months loss of educational attainment. The effectiveness of supported lodgings depends in part on what has gone before. Clearly there needs to be more focus on the preventative use of friends and relatives and improving the quality of the care experience before reaching the preparation for adult life stage. Let us now look at accommodation issues.

Biehal et al.'s study (1992:43) found that young people leaving care experienced 'accommodation problems, including temporary accommodation, drift and homelessness.' There is also evidence (for example, see CHAR, 1995) that young black people continue to be over represented in the homelessness figures as a result of racism (CHAR is now the National Homeless Alliance). Additionally, and according to evidence submitted to the 1996 Inquiry into Preventing Youth Homelessness, two thirds of young people leaving care experienced homelessness (CHAR, 1996:56). The three main reasons given in that inquiry were; the (young) age at which most care leavers make the transition to independence, their disadvantaged position relative to other young people, and the lack of adequate support and preparation that they receive (CHAR,1996:56). In a general sense these findings, though alarming, are not new. One earlier survey (Broad for the After Care Consortium, 1993) pointed to the wide range of accommodation in which young people leaving care lived.

Many other studies have reported on both the unsatisfactory situation in general regarding the availability of housing, and inadequate housing finances for young people (see Darke, et al., 1994; Kirk, 1996), and in particular for young people leaving care (see Stein and Carey, 1986; Young Homelessness Group, 1991; McCluskey, 1994; Biehal et al., 1995).

The government response to this appalling situation was the consultation paper *Me, Survive Out There* which informed the process resulting in the new legislation, The Children (Leaving Care) Act 2000. This legislation, which amends the Children Act 1989 and increases local authority responsibilities toward care leavers, is long overdue but very welcome.

It is vital that local authorities are held to account in how they respond to the challenges this legislation creates for them.

One of the principal aims of the new legislation is to ensure young people remain looked after by the local authority until they are adequately prepared and ready to live in independent accommodation. The general trend of discharging young people from care soon after their sixteenth birthday needs to be addressed immediately:

> *Since 1993 there has been a small drop in the numbers of young people leaving care – from 8,900 to 8,400 – but whereas the proportion of young people leaving care on their eighteenth birthday has fallen, from 48% to 41%, the proportion leaving aged 16 has increased from 33% to 40%.*
>
> Wade and Stein, 2000.

Main Issues

Before the Children (Leaving Care) Act there was a financial incentive for local authorities to discharge young people from the care system once they reached 16 years of age. By removing young people from the benefits system and placing an absolute responsibility for the maintenance and accommodation costs of 16 and 17-year-old care leavers with the local authority, the financial incentive to discharge early should be removed.

> *For relevant children the 2000 Act requires the responsible local authority to support them, by providing them with, or, maintaining them in, suitable accommodation – unless they are satisfied that their welfare does not require it, (Section 23B(8)(b)); and former relevant children where the local authority is required to assist them to the extent that their welfare requires it (Section 23C (4)).*
>
> DoH, 2001, Ch 7.6.

Under the old benefits system there was confusion as to what financial support young people were entitled to. Now, the continuing financial responsibility towards care leavers until they are 18 years of age, irrespective of whether they remain in the LAC (looked after children) system, should reduce the confusion. The duty on local authorities to develop and publicise their transparent financial criteria will further assist in clarifying in which circumstances care leavers are entitled to financial support, as detailed later in this book.

> *It is important that young people are clear about the funding duties owed to them by their responsible authority, and about what the authority would normally expect to provide funds for.*
>
> DoH, 2001, Ch 9.5.

Although the duty to provide accommodation and maintenance costs is primarily towards 16 and 17-year-olds, the guidance specifically mentions circumstances in which this duty should be extended to young people aged 19 and over.

> *Former relevant children in further education may not have access to any other help – Income Support and Housing Benefit are not available for those aged 19 and over in full time Further Education – and in such circumstances the responsible authority would need to provide them with maintenance and accommodation.*
>
> DoH, 2001, Ch 8.22.

Practice within LAC systems will need to change if local authorities are to operate within the spirit of the new Act:

- It will require a fundamental change in the attitudes of local authorities towards the 16 and 17-year-old young people they accommodate.
- It will also require a cultural shift from senior managers through to social workers, residential workers and foster carers.

Only this will bring an end to the custom and practice adopted by many local authorities whereby care leavers are *encouraged* to move out of children's homes and foster placements once they become 16 years of age.

Historically the pressure on resources and placements has meant that many local authorities have devised leaving care plans for young people that were based on resources, rather than the needs of the young people. The new legislation clearly states that a comprehensive assessment of *need* must be carried out for each young person and sets out a timescale for this to occur within. It is crucial that this assessment is done by trained staff using the appropriate framework and tools.

The *Framework for the Assessment of Children in Need and their Families* covers the same developmental areas as the *Looked After*

Children materials and will be invaluable in assisting Young Persons' advisors to carry out the comprehensive assessment. The development of an *Integrated Children System* that assesses young people across the same areas and effectively combines the previous materials should aid in a smoother assessment and planning process as young people move into independence.

Accommodation Issues in Relation to Assessment

There is a new duty to carry out a needs assessment within 3 months of a young person becoming eligible or relevant. This assessment must look at the issues in relation to accommodation. The guidance clearly states that:

> *Young people living in and leaving care are a diverse group whose needs will vary according to their care experience, ethnicity, gender, sexuality, contact with their families, degree of preparedness for leaving and any disability they may have. It follows that their accommodation needs will be equally diverse.*
>
> DoH, 2001, Ch 5.2.

Consideration should be given to all of the following when establishing what the accommodation needs of a young person are:

- pre-care experience
- care experience
- family contact
- ethnicity
- gender
- sexuality
- disability
- how well prepared

The guidance makes it clear the assessment should identify the particular help required by the young person for them to live independently or in semi-supported accommodation.

> *The needs assessment will have identified what specific assistance a young person will need in relation to accommodation and what types of accommodation are suitable to meet a young persons needs.*
>
> DoH, 2001.

Many authorities are already struggling to provide appropriate placements for young people. The looked after children population has increased significantly since the mid 1990s with the non-surprising result that the pressure on placements has continued to grow. Unless local authorities take action now to develop accommodation options the new legislation will compound these difficulties.

Recruiting and retaining foster carers continues to be a national problem. (DoH 2000 Ch11.13). This shortage of family placements can create a tension within social services departments. It puts pressure on the childcare professionals to *free up* foster placements for younger children in the LAC system, rather than pursuing best practice in relation to meeting the needs of care leavers.

When it comes to education and health, it is well documented that, when young people are looked after, in 'out of area' placements, they do not always succeed as well as their peers accommodated 'within *local* provision'. The Quality Protects initiative on Placement Choice for looked after young people should begin to address these difficulties and facilitate the development of local provision where there is a shortage.

It is essential that local authorities act in a corporate manner when discharging their responsibilities to provide support and accommodation to care leavers. Social services departments – working in isolation – cannot hope to meet the accommodation needs of such a diverse group as care leavers. Only by working in partnership with the housing authority, housing associations and voluntary organisations can this range of accommodation be developed.

Links between the Guidance and housing departments

In relation to the all-important links between the social services department and the housing department, and supported lodgings, the Guidance (Department of Health, 2001, Section Three – The Role of the Housing Department, paragraph 23, page 25) refers to the Homeless Bill. It states (the obvious) (page 26):

Whilst the primary responsibility for securing accommodation for young homeless people rests with the local housing authority, it is essential that a corporate and multi-agency approach is adopted by the local authority to care leavers. Local authorities should develop a strategy in partnership with housing providers to provide a range of accommodation to meet the assessed needs of relevant children and other care leavers. The housing needs of care leavers should be addressed before they leave care and arrangements made for joint assessment between social services and housing authorities, as part of the multi-agency assessment on which an individual after-care plan or pathway plan should be based.

The Children Act 1989 Guidance
(Role of the Housing Department)

Under the guidance and amendments to the 1996 Housing Act, (under which care leavers are specifically named as a priority group) other changes about supported lodgings are likely to have an impact on young people leaving care. Housing providers have often expressed concern about re-housing care leavers whose vulnerability and lack of preparation make poor tenants, in some instances ending up losing their tenancies. Supported lodgings offers opportunities to young people to develop the life skills and confidence needed to assume and maintain their responsibilities as tenants.

Successful implementation of both these pieces of legislation will contribute to local authorities meeting their Quality Protects and Best Value targets and to meeting the government's objectives as set out in their social exclusion objectives and programmes. For the first time there is a climate of opportunity when the government is prepared to both listen and act.

Accommodation in pathway planning

There is strong evidence that a number of issues identified in the Children Act guidance in relation to planning accommodation for care leavers can significantly increase positive outcomes for this group (Hutson, 1995; 1997):

Councils will need to bear in mind the range of needs they may need to meet when they consider how they are going to meet their duty to provide accommodation for eligible and relevant young people. The development of accommodation resources will require formal agreements with statutory and voluntary housing providers to plan services, ensure access to a range of tenancies and partnerships or joint ventures to establish a range of accommodation options. Councils should take steps to make sure that young people have the best chance to succeed in their accommodation. They should:

- *Avoid moving young people who are settled unless it is unavoidable or offers clear advantages.*
- *Assess young people and prepare them for any move.*
- *Where practicable, offer a choice in the type and location of accommodation.*
- *Set up a package of support to go with the accommodation.*
- *Have a clear financial plan for the accommodation.*
- *Have a contingency plan in case the proposed accommodation breaks down.*
- *Ensure that the accommodation meets any needs relating to physical and/or sensory impairment and/or learning difficulty.*

DoH, 2001, Ch 5.27–28.

When the Children Act 1989 was implemented in the early 1990s, many childcare professionals thought it would provide a major breakthrough in the support available to care leavers and vulnerable young people assessed as in need. Unfortunately the use of these powers has been virtually non-existent. The new guidance accompanying the Children (Leaving Care) Act reminds local authorities of powers that they possess.

Local authorities should also note they have powers under section 20(5) to provide accommodation for young people aged 16–20 in their area if this is necessary to safeguard or promote their welfare. The provision of accommodation under section 20 may be a desirable course of action if it is not possible to provide suitable accommodation in any other way for a young person who has left care. There is, of course, a duty to provide accommodation if a child is in need and section 20(3) applies, and to provide accommodation for relevant children under section 23B(8)(b).

DoH, 2001, Ch 3. 27.

It would be interesting to know just how many local authorities have used their powers under section 20(5) since the implementation of the Children Act 1989.

Accommodation for young people leaving care includes:

- **Local authority and housing association tenancies**. These are provided, more often, according to the questionnaire data, in urban unified local authorities, than in county areas.
- **Supported lodgings**: see next chapter.
- **Voluntary sector schemes** which provide accommodation and support to young people leaving care and homeless young people – this is provided by Housing Associations working with voluntary organisations (such as Barnados or NCH-Action for Children). The type of accommodation can include floating support, or self-contained bedsits, or shared houses.
- **Private accommodation** in the form of bed and breakfast accommodation, for emergencies, or in other circumstances, private hostels are options, although because of the varying quality it is potentially dangerous – the term is not used lightly – if used unchecked and unmonitored.
- **Where young people can safely return to family or relatives** – they may be provided with emotional support and contact networks even if accommodation cannot be provided.
- **Extended stays in foster or residential placements**, if it was appropriate and if sufficient finances are provided, can provide additional stability and deliberately delay the often premature 'preparation for independence' phase which 'kicks in' at 16 years of age in many cases (see Biehal et al., 1992).
- **It makes sense for there to be contingent emergency housing strategy in place and accommodation available** and direct access to hostels and bed and breakfast facilities of some sort, and though not always appropriate they will be required from time to time.

- **Foyer accommodation** and training and employment can be used by young people leaving care as well as other young people seeking stability.

Regulation 11(2) defines what is meant by the term suitable accommodation and specifies areas that must be considered by the local authority. For accommodation to be suitable it must be accommodation that:

(a) So far as reasonably practicable is suitable for the child in light of his identified needs, including his health needs.
(b) In respect of which the responsible authority has satisfied itself as to the character and suitability of the landlord or other provider.
(c) In respect of which the responsible authority has so far as reasonably practicable taken into account the child's wishes and feelings as to his educational, training or employment needs.

DoH, 2001, Ch 7.11.

In the event of crisis and placement breakdown authorities will need to access emergency accommodation. Local authorities will need systems in place to ensure that appropriate character checks and references are obtained as soon as potential accommodation is identified. These checks will need to be swift and thorough so that potential accommodation is not lost through avoidable delay but is rigorous enough to safeguard vulnerable young people. Some authorities have established a register of accommodation providers, usually bed and breakfast providers who will also provide different tiers of support to young people if this is required. The guidance states that:

Bed and breakfast accommodation would not be regarded as suitable although very occasionally its use may be justified as a short-term emergency measure.

As well as reminding authorities of powers they possess, the new guidance also points out the new duties placed upon them. The duty to provide holiday accommodation to all care leavers that carry on into higher education will give care leavers greater confidence to continue in the education system, especially if they are required to move away to attend university or college.

> *The 2000 Act also requires a local authority to ensure that any local authority care leaver in full-time further or higher education has suitable accommodation if they need it during a vacation. The authority may discharge this responsibility either by providing the young person with accommodation or by paying them enough to secure suitable accommodation (Section 24B(5)).*
>
> DoH, 2001, Ch 7.7.

The guidance specifies further that this requirement is for every vacation not only the long summer vacation. It also states how much time local authorities have in which to identify an appropriate package of support.

> *These provisions apply to every vacation and are intended to ensure that the young person is not homeless during this time. An assessment of whether there is likely to be a need for this assistance should be undertaken when the young person is making a decision about which course to pursue and when the pathway plan is being reviewed to establish an appropriate level of student support.*
>
> DoH, 2001, Ch 7.18.

The majority of care leavers that go on to higher education come from stable foster placements. Many carers continue to offer emotional and practical support to former foster children when they move on into higher education. Some authorities have acknowledged these examples of good practice that were previously taking place in an isolated and unsupported way by the local authority. When individual foster carers continue to show this commitment to young people the local authority should:

- Recompense them and make allowances available to further encourage this practice.
- Develop procedures that allow for continuing support from carers if this is identified and agreed as appropriate.

A number of authorities have approached these challenges in an imaginative way that maximises the resources available to those delivering the leaving care service. The North West After Care Forum has facilitated the sharing of practice initiatives in a number of areas. The issue of accommodation provision and the chronic lack of supported accommodation options for care leavers nationally, has meant the inappropriate placement of many young people. For the individual young person the result of this has been the loss of their accommodation and in many cases a spiralling into the homelessness culture.

Chaotic young people

Most, if not all, authorities have a small but significant number of extremely chaotic young people who rapidly exhaust the limited accommodation options available to them. Anecdotal evidence from across the North-West suggests this particular group of young people who are least able to manage their own tenancy are perversely the ones most likely to obtain a tenancy.

Once they have been expelled from supported accommodation projects it is often the only option left open. Workers have little option but to re-house these young people, knowing well that in the majority of cases it will breakdown in months, if not weeks, due to rent arrears, or anti-social behaviour. Invariably the young person moves on, quitting the property in an unplanned way, losing furniture and possessions and having run up a huge debt in rent arrears, which will preclude them from obtaining a tenancy in the future. Even when young people give the specified notice they often struggle to store furniture and belongings and so lose the purchases made from any leaving care grant they may have obtained.

Accommodation Panels

Attempts have been made to tackle this problem in a number of ways. Stockport 16 plus Service has developed an Accommodation Providers Panel that brings together the main social housing providers (social services, housing dept., housing associations etc.). A multi-agency assessment form is completed on the individual requesting emergency accommodation. This assessment document informs the panel and they discuss which accommodation they consider is appropriate to meet the needs as presented to the panel. The panel are also aware which projects have vacancies and waiting lists, so are well placed to match the need to available resource in the short term, while looking at the longer term plans and aspirations of the young person.

Manchester Leaving Care Service are particularly concerned about the numbers of 16 and 17-year-old care leavers requesting their own independent accommodation. The vast majority of these young people have completely unrealistic expectations of what independent living would entail.

Evidence collected from the *Exit Interviews* (which are now offered to all those young people leaving the service) showed overwhelmingly that the young people who had requested their own accommodation at 16 and 17 regretted their decision.

They looked back at the difficulties they experienced (and in some cases continued to experience) because of leaving care early, and many wanted the opportunity to explain to current care leavers about the reality of independent living, perhaps via peer mentoring schemes. Anecdotal evidence from across the North West supports the Manchester findings that the majority of 16 and 17-year-olds who move into their own tenancies fail to maintain them without adequate support. Unfortunately this does not deter those looked after young people who are determined they want their own tenancy.

Manchester Leaving Care Service and the housing department aim to discourage young people aged 16 and 17 from leaving care and moving into their own tenancies. They aim to create an environment where the general expectations of both young people and the workers involved with them, is that no young person under the age of 18 is given their own tenancy. This will require a cultural shift away from the expectation of leaving care and moving directly into their own tenancy without any consideration of their preparedness for this level of independence. Only in exceptional circumstances would a tenancy be given to a 16-year-old and any 17-year-old would have to show an accommodation panel that they were capable of managing their own tenancy and understood the responsibilities involved.

Manchester Leaving Care Service is currently developing a programme aimed at better preparing young people for living independently. They hope this programme will award certificates of merit for successfully completing a range of modules. They hope to tie this in with the accommodation panel by making completion of the programme a condition of being allowed before the panel (Lever, 2000).

Oldham's after care service were concerned about the numbers of vulnerable young people with borderline learning difficulties. These young people did not meet the high threshold to access support from adult services but were still considered as too vulnerable to live independently in their own tenancies without support.

Oldham social services are developing a project in partnership with a voluntary organisation (KeyRing), which aims to place these young people into a supportive network of tenancies. The network uses ordinary social housing with each individual having their own flat. These networks consist of up to ten flats with one central flat identified for a 'community living worker'

The 'community living worker' carries out a range of functions with and on behalf of the network. They provide practical help and offer advice and guidance to the tenants occupying the other nine flats in the network. The worker seeks to build on the strengths of individuals within the network. The worker also has the task of building links between the network and the local community to ensure that tenants are utilising community facilities and resources. Partnerships with community groups and other agencies, allow tenants to receive appropriate services as and when needed. The structured support that KeyRing offers to tenants has helped make this model particularly successful at establishing and maintaining vulnerable people in the community in a cost effective manner (Simons, 1998).

Transitional Housing Benefit and Supporting People

The recent changes to the housing benefit system resulting in the splitting of monies into bricks and mortar costs and support costs means that forward thinking authorities are identifying gaps in provision and developing new supported accommodation options. When Supporting People takes over from Transitional Housing Benefit in 2003 the support element of any charges will be met from this pot of money. In the interim period Transitional Housing Benefit will cover these costs if the people concerned meet the identified criteria.

All *Relevant* care leavers under the Children (Leaving Care) Act are removed from entitlement to both the basic rent and the support charges from transitional Housing Benefit. However, *Formerly relevant* care leavers under the Children (Leaving Care) Act and young people only qualifying for services under section 24 are permitted to have their support costs met through transitional housing benefit where they are living in *social sector accommodation*. This will include where the landlord is a:

- housing authority
- non-metropolitan county council
- registered social landlord
- registered charity or voluntary organisation including non-registered housing associations

Payment of support charges must be a condition of the tenancy otherwise they cannot be met by Housing Benefit.

Where a young person lives in *private rented* accommodation they will only qualify for help with the support charge element of their rent if they have a community care assessment. If they are under 18 and are therefore unable to obtain a community care assessment the children's services department will need to make a decision about whether they will pay the support element of any charges.

In Stockport collaboration between social services and the housing department has resulted in the development of a post for a worker to offer floating support to a discrete selection of tenancies. This worker will offer support to vulnerable young people who otherwise would be unable to live in their own tenancies in the community. Although the bid was a joint venture, the direct line management of the post is undertaken via social services and the manager of the 16 plus team that operates

in Stockport. This floating support would only be available to those categories of young people specified in the previous paragraphs, but if we consider that the intention of the Children (Leaving Care) Act is to ensure most young people remain looked after (eligible) until they are 18 this development offers potential support to a large group of young people who will require a move into semi-independence after this.

In Oldham the imaginative collaboration between the social services department and a housing association has led to the development of *Independence Units* which offer supported accommodation and opportunities for young people to develop the skills necessary for them to live independently. Access to 24 hour staff support also enables vulnerable young people to move into short-term tenancies with the confidence that advice and assistance is available to them outside of office hours.

Conclusion

Securing appropriate affordable accommodation, with support offered, is absolutely vital for young people when they leave care, if they are to make the transition to a more independent life. To some the term 'appropriate' means a long term or permanent tenancy with either a housing association or local authority. For others it could mean more temporary accommodation, such as supported lodgings where a young person will normally live with a family and receive support from the landlord/lady and a social worker or project worker. There are many further accommodation alternatives available, some of which are desirable and some of which are not appropriate in terms of the rent or setting.

The issue of young people leaving care is not about bricks and mortar alone.

It is about the timing of the move, the suitability and maturity of the young person wishing to live independently, and the support available.

References

Broad, B. (1998) *Young People Leaving Care: Life After the Children Act 1989*, London, Jessica Kingsley.

Department of Health. (2000) *When Leaving Home is Also Leaving Care: An Inspection of Services for Young People Leaving Care*, Department of Health.

Hutson, S. (1995) *Care Leavers and Young Homeless People in Wales: The Exchange of Good Practice*. Swansea, University of Wales.

Hutson, S. (1997) *Supported Housing: The Experience of Young People*. Barkingside, Barnardo's.

Jones, G. (1987) Leaving the Parental Home. An Analysis of Early Housing Careers, *Journal of Social Policy* **16**: 49–74.

Lever, T. (2000) *Accommodation Proposals Paper*, Manchester Leaving Care Service.

Simons, K. (1998) *Living Support Networks*, Joseph Rowntree Foundation.

Wade and Stein (2000) *Helping Care Leavers: Problems and Strategic Approaches*, Department of Health.

For further references, see the end of the following chapter.

12. Sustaining Supported Lodgings: A Golden Opportunity for Growth

Bob Broad and Ena Fry

Introduction

This chapter will examine the factors that make for successful 'supported lodgings' schemes; what policy and practice questions need to be addressed; and how 'supported lodgings' fits in with fostering and leaving care accommodation strategies.

The chapter is arranged as follows:

- A working definition of supported lodgings.
- The benefits of supported lodgings.
- The factors that make for successful supported lodgings.
- Why does supported lodgings work?
- What research evidence there is about the use of supported lodgings.
- How the Children (Leaving Care) Act 2000 guidance supports supported lodgings.
- Legislative guidance, practice, and monitoring issues concerned with supported lodgings for young people leaving care.
- Relevant social care and housing legislation and guidance, but only in so far as it applies to supported lodgings, i.e. not to all housing issues for care leavers.
- How 'supported lodgings' fits in with fostering, and leaving care accommodation strategies.
- Developing best practice.

In addressing these questions we draw on the limited research available as well as the invaluable experience of those agencies nationwide that have already developed schemes. In particular we use data from two consortiums, covering the London and North West local authorities, that have established their own forum to share and promote good practice.

What are supported lodgings?

'Supported lodgings' schemes offer temporary lodgings with live-in support.

The term 'supported' or 'supervised' lodgings indicates that young people so placed require greater community supervision or support than the norm – e.g. because of their involvement in the youth justice system. Although schemes have evolved in different ways to meet local needs there are some distinctive features which make them different from other kinds of provision:

Each is made up of a network of local people who offer a room in their home with varying levels of support to vulnerable and or homeless people.

NWSLF, 1993.

The expansion of supported or supervised lodgings as an option for young people leaving care or homeless has brought many benefits. Its flexibility means that it can be of benefit to young people who are already reasonably self-sufficient through to those who require more intensive support. It can be a viable community based option for that small group of young people who find any group living situation untenable, needing to be left alone until they are ready to accept the guidance and support offered – a viable risk taking option with appropriate support.

The benefits of 'supported lodgings'

Supported lodgings is a transitional resource which offers young people:

- A period of *stability* in which to take advantage of educational and training opportunities so increasing their life chances and opportunities.
- *Consistent adult support* in varying degrees, which can change over time within the placement e.g. hands off approach at the beginning but at exam time or if ill, more dependence on the provider. Alternatively some require intensive support at the

beginning reducing as they develop confidence and skills.

- *Modelling* – learning how different households or providers work and how they deal with mistakes.
- *An opportunity to test and develop* the day-to-day skills needed to survive in the world.
- *A resource that requires negotiation* on both sides in itself a necessary skill to surviving in adult life.
- *Variety* – carers come in many shapes and sizes as do young people – backgrounds can match.
- *Normality* – local resource which allows for anonymity – reduces stigma of being labelled as mad or bad which is so often the layperson's understanding of being in care.
- *Continuity* (in some cases) – Conversion from fostering to supported lodgings allows for continuity of existing foster care arrangements. Many young people consulted as part of developing the National Standards for Foster Care (NFCA, 1998–9) stated their concern at age not needs-led policies which meant that they couldn't remain in foster care post 18 or until they were ready to move on. New ring fenced monies and a duty to assist until 21 makes this option of conversion more widely available. The implications of this are discussed later in this chapter.

These advantages fit well with achieving the Quality Protects and leaving care objectives but to be effective they cannot remain in isolation from other leaving care resources. However they are managed, whether they stand alone, are part of fostering or leaving care teams or are provided by a voluntary agency, this provision is part of the corporate planning that all local authorities must develop in order to be a 'good parent'. That raises several issues about what makes for successful supported lodgings.

Supported Lodgings: The Research Evidence

The Children Act 1989 created opportunities for 16 and 17-year-old homeless young people to access accommodation, support, advice, information and financial assistance from local authorities. However, the discretionary nature of the legislation and accompanying guidance led to widely varying interpretation by local authorities. Many set up their own supported lodgings schemes whilst others did so in partnership with voluntary organisations. For others it was never even an option. This ad hoc approach has led to 'supported lodgings' often being seen and treated as the Cinderella service compared to fostering. Partly this is due to it being seen as a cheaper option often favoured by young people and highly appropriate to their needs at a transitional stage in their lives – as opposed to a quality option.

In the 1994 After-Care Consortium survey (Broad, 1994) we see that of the young people leaving care whose accommodation situation was known 25% (n = 987) were in 'supported lodgings.' This was followed by local authority tenancy (20%) and 'shared transitory housing' (19%).

A larger independent leaving care survey (Broad, 1998) conducted four years later found an ever widening range of accommodation types for young people leaving care. That study showed that of the sample described (n = 2096):

- Local authority tenancies accounted for 23% of accommodation.
- Shared/transitional housing for 15%.
- Housing association tenancy 14%.
- Supported lodgings accounting for just 10%.

The same percentage (10%) of young people living in supported lodgings schemes was found in another survey (London Region Supported Lodgings Network, 2001).

These three surveys suggest that the actual use of supported lodgings has slightly declined since the Children Act 1989 was introduced. The reasons for the decline in the use of supported lodgings are not clear but agencies may need to review their financial payments to carers, use exit interviews to determine the reasons for the loss of carers and whether housing options have increased. Also the effect of changes at local level brought in by the 1996 Housing Act is important.

This is not the same as saying that 'supported lodgings' is not needed. According to Vernon (2000) one of the major gaps in services for young people leaving care (there were five gaps identified) was 'supported lodgings.' Vernon commented that whilst many London local authorities stated they were planning to develop such schemes, 'very few were actually currently operating such a scheme' (Vernon, 2000, p69). Vernon also identified a key issue about the recruitment and approval of those offering supported lodgings. In the conclusion to this most comprehensive audit of leaving care services in London the author commented (as Broad had done in the 1994 Consortium survey report, p13–4) that the audit had raised a number of issues which extended beyond the domain of individual departments and authorities, and require the attention of central government and these included:

> *The actual or potential loophole with respect to the arrangement for the approval and vetting of staff, from departments other than SSD, who are working directly with young people in supported accommodation situations.*
>
> Vernon, 2000, p126.

Vernon pointed to the Care Standards Bill regarding standards and inspection, a point to which we will return later.

Factors that Make for Successful Supported Lodgings

The ingredients of a successful scheme, according to Hutson (1995) are:

- Clarity about purpose and target groups.
- Staff time and expertise to manage the resource.
- A thorough approval system.
- Ongoing training and support for providers.
- Clear funding arrangements.
- Planning move on accommodation.
- Reviewing and monitoring outcomes.

Finally in this evidence section it is worth summarising what the London 'supported lodgings' network respondents to a questionnaire stated:
Why do supported lodgings work?

- It is seen as an integral part of the preparation work being done with young people.
- Offers emergency placements.

- Offers specialist placements.
- Support for young person in placement – low placement breakdown.
- Support and supervision for carers – high carer retention.
- Provides 'out of hours' support.

When we looked at what the London and South East supported lodgings network questionnaire respondents said about 'what works least well?' the answers were about two things. One was 'finance' – issues around housing benefit, personal income tax, and insurance. The other was 'move-on accommodation'- getting social services and housing to implement plans and undertake their responsibilities.

The 'headline' findings from that survey were:

- Supported lodgings is a valued option for young people leaving care which needs proper funding.
- An average of 10% of young people leaving care use supported lodgings.
- Quality Protects funding provides added value and generally made a real difference.
- Feeding back young people's views to policy makers and practitioners is still not regularly taking place.

Legislative Guidance, Practice, and Monitoring Issues Concerned with Supported Lodgings for Young People Leaving Care

The introduction of new leaving care legislation and related government initiatives including Quality Protects, Connexions and Supporting People offers an opportunity to review the concept of supported lodgings. We can consider its strengths and weaknesses and think how it can become an integral and valued part of every local authority's leaving care resource.

Thus research and practice strongly suggests that Quality Protects has provided a welcome but limited and short-term opportunity to put in place a framework for developing supported lodgings. The funding issues, for both supporting the young person and the provider, are complex, (e.g. housing benefit entitlements) and remain largely unresolved. In relation to The Housing Act 1996 young people leaving care are identified and post 18s qualify for transitional housing benefit under the Transitional Housing Benefit Scheme (THBS). It is our view that a support element should be reflected in the Housing Benefit system and Supporting People legislation guidance. In law there is limited direct reference to this provision – yet it is used widely both for young people in care and others not in care.

How the Children (Leaving Care) Act 2000 Guidance Supports Supported Lodgings

According to that Act (Section 23.2.a of the Children Act 1989) a looked after child can be placed with family, relatives or another person. Also the fostering regulations apply in that a looked after child may also be placed in accommodation that seems appropriate to the local authority (Section 23.2.f). In both situations there is a requirement to safeguard and promote the welfare of the young person, and 'safeguarding the welfare' implies some check or assessment. Let us now come onto the Children (Leaving Care) Act 2000.

Care leavers are seen as entitled to accommodation which safeguards their welfare. General accommodation issues are contained within the new Children (Leaving Care) Act 2000 legislation and guidance. Implemented from October 2001 it seeks to strengthen the Children Act 1989 and links with a number of wider government objectives including:

- Reducing the number of placement moves within the care system.
- Increasing placement choice.
- Avoiding early discharge from care.
- Improving outcomes for care leavers.

This legislation provides a context for, but not a blue print or resources for, delivering supported lodgings in that it:

- Requires that care leavers be in suitable accommodation.
- Sets a requirement for every young person to have:
  – an assessment
  – continued contact
  – a pathway plan
  – a personal advisor

However, it is not prescriptive about how supported lodgings is defined or assessed, and it does not state how it will be managed.

The Children (Leaving Care) Act 2000 guidance looks to the voluntary sector to be contracted in, or, become a partner with, local authority social services departments to provide various forms of accommodation such as 'sheltered' and 'half way housing', refuges for young people at risk, 'supported lodgings' and 'continued foster care' (Department of Health, 2001: Chapter Three, The role of voluntary organisations. Paragraph 11 page 23). Indeed as possible evidence of the role (and anticipated growing role) of the voluntary sector the Merseyside Accommodation Project (MAP), – a part of the charity Local Solutions (2001) is reported, in June 2001, (Liverpool Echo, 2001) in the following terms:

When the Children (Leaving Care) Act 2000 comes into force in October, our role will increase. We have 100 householders across Merseyside looking after 130 young people. They can stay for as long as they like but the average is a couple of months ... between 30% and 40% of the young people are reconciled with their families while they are in MAP households.

All referrals to MAP are described as having to come 'through social services' departments but it is reported that only about 25% of young people in the MAP scheme are care leavers. This points to a diversity of need, provision, referrals, and, possibly, regulatory needs, and points to the range of links between social services departments and the voluntary sector needed to establish supported lodgings.

Foster Care and Supported Lodgings

The practice of supported or supervised lodgings can be informed by the experiences of specialist teenage fostering. However the growth may not be entirely the result of recognition of good practice. We fear that its popularity has grown because it is seen as a cheap option. However, recent developments in supported lodgings have seen its increased professionalism and improving quality and standards.

There is evidence that there is still confusion about the relationship between supported/supervised lodgings and fostering, and a reluctance to openly address the issue. To date, this is a particular concern for the placing of 16 and 17-year-olds where a supported or supervised lodgings is mistakenly seen as a way of avoiding the Children Act regulations and costs governing foster placements. However, the provision of supported lodgings indicates that a young person has been assessed by a local authority as being 'in need' and comes within the terms of the Children Act 1989:

Whether or not the local authority has parental responsibility under a care order it adopts, in effect part of the role of the parent of the young person it is looking after.

Department of Health, 1991, Children Act 1989, Guidance, Vol 3.9.4.

and

Where children are to be placed in lodgings to enable them to enter work or further education the person or persons who own or manage or are otherwise responsible for the lodgings should be checked out. The premises should be visited, the landlord or landlady interviewed and a written report prepared.

Department of Health, 1991, Children Act 1989, Guidance, Vol 4.1.34.

We hope that the Children (Leaving Care) Act 2000 legislation with its ring fenced monies for 16 and 17-year-olds will redress this matter as well as establishing supported lodgings as part of the accommodation strategy.

Another major implication of the new legislation is that it should for the first time ensure all local authorities address the relationship between foster care and leaving care. No longer can the current ad hoc approach be maintained. Research findings (Collis, 1999; Fry, 1992), highlight that many foster families continue to provide a range of support to young people they have cared for, often out of their own pockets and not formally recognised or assisted by their fostering agency. However, there have been examples of good practice in which authorities have financed packages of support post 18 usually in relation to young people in higher education. Usually these are one-off packages. Now written into leaving care policies and guidance there will need to be clear statements about:

- The roles and responsibilities of foster carers in preparing young people for adult life.
- Training, support and information all foster carers will be given.
- Options open to young people and their carers.

Standard 12 UK National Standards for Foster Care Preparation for adult life (NFCA, 1999) states:

... each young person in foster care is helped to develop the skills, competence and knowledge necessary for adult living: she or he receives appropriate support and guidance for as long as necessary after being in foster care.

This standard reflects the principles underlying the new leaving care legislation and will inform the planned inspection of all fostering agencies under the Care Standards Act 2000 to be implemented in April 2002. So this means:

- Agencies addressing the current gulf that exist between fostering and leaving care services teams.
- Recognising that preparing for adult life starts from the point any child or young person joins the foster family.
- Recognising this work is an integral part of preparing and training foster carers.
- Operating an effective, 'child-led' service where disruption and early discharge is kept to a minimum, conversion of a fostering placement to supported lodgings must be considered as a serious or main option.

The implications for policy and practice can no longer be avoided or dealt with piecemeal. These include some of the following hidden fears and myths.

Fears and myths about supported lodgings and foster care

Preparation of carers is as important as preparation of young people. It shouldn't be the sword of Damocles waiting to descend on the foster carer. The supervising worker in supervision sessions should be addressing the leaving care policies and how they will impact on the carer. That includes the carer's fears, based in many instances on bitter experience that age means the end of a placement. Improvements in assessments should allow for negotiation and arrangements about transition that are needs led not resource led. The reality is that fostering is not the same as parenting with scope to put off indefinitely a point at which the young person leaves but being a 'good corporate parent' means negotiation and flexibility and treating foster carers as professional colleagues whose opinions and experiences are valued and respected. Otherwise experienced carers are not retained. A leaving care policy needs to clearly state the ways in which carer's interests in providing after care will be met and not as the following statement suggests:

We need the bed for a younger child or young person.

social worker.

Carers are professional colleagues not employees – failure to adopt a sensitive and responsive approach to carers who express an interest in supporting a young person can lead eventually to the loss of experienced carers. Part of a job well done is being able to see it completed. Fostering Network's Young Peoples Project has had frequent contact from carers who are suddenly informed that fostering payments will cease and the young person will, often at 16, be expected to move into more independent accommodation. The new leaving care legislation should prevent such unacceptable practices, facilitating more negotiated, better assessment and planning. Supporting carers to provide an after care service means they get the satisfaction of a job well done and it doesn't have to block a bed:

It is not helpful to train together foster carers and supported lodgings providers.

Clear policies and guidance on respective roles and responsibilities and expectations combined with improved assessment means each can respect and value each other and share and learn from each other. Experience in some agencies has shown it may be uncomfortable to begin with but the long term benefits far outweigh the initial difficulties.

Practice Suggestions

- Use carers annual review to ensure they are well informed and prepared about their tasks and responsibilities.
- Experienced carers have to retire at some point but maybe they too can do some transitional work as supported lodgings providers.
- With well settled young people maybe there is someone in the foster carer's wider family or network who could offer supported lodgings – well planned, this is a beneficial step onwards for everyone.
- Through joint training and meetings agency staff would learn of the many community based resources and networks that carers and providers are aware of and use – some of which may be new and valuable ones for other care leavers.

Conversion provides stability and prevents young people moving on before they feel ready to do so. The extensive consultation with young people undertaken when the *National Standards for Foster Care* were drafted highlighted this as a major source of concern to them (Robinson, First Key, 1998). Another key finding from this research was the importance of young people's own families.

Supported lodgings are time limited and not so time consuming in some instances as fostering, so exploring the young person's network or family could identify potential supported lodgings providers.

Developing best practice

Supported or supervised lodgings must not be seen as a second class, second tier service but as a valuable option in its own right. Getting that message across in policy and practice is essential at this critical stage in any care leaver's life. There are no short cuts. Young people using supported or supervised lodgings often have had a ragbag of previous life experiences, some very damaging. Each has different needs but the common need of all adapting to life outside care is to have a stable base from which they can confidently make the transition to coping in the adult world.

However unobtrusive the role of the supported lodgings provider is, comfort, care and skilled guidance must be available as and when the young person requires it. That means supported lodgings providers must be *well prepared, well supported and recompensed*. It is essential both for young people and providers that adequate opportunities for training are given.

Recruitment

Anecdotally, word of mouth remains the best way of recruiting new providers. So an effective service that supports and values providers will ensure retention and will encourage existing providers to recruit new providers. Other successful options include regular items or adverts in the local press, libraries, medical centres, shopping and leisure centres – even as in one authority – local hairdressers. The London Borough of Redbridge, for example, offers information evenings every six weeks together with the fostering team which has had beneficial results.

Assessing carers

A competency based approach to assessment and reviewing of providers is well suited to 'supported lodgings' with defined tasks and responsibilities that fit well within the competency framework. The following are some of the key competencies that are relevant to supported lodgings.

Caring for young people

Carers need to have the ability to:

- Provide a good standard of care, promoting their emotional, physical and sexual development as well as their health and educational achievements.
- Work positively with the young person's family and others who are important to the young person.
- Set appropriate boundaries.
- Listen and communicate with the young person appropriate to their age and understanding.
- Help the young person manage their *finances*.
- Help the young person achieve positive outcomes.

Providing a safe and caring environment

Carers need to have the ability to:

- Ensure young people are cared for in a home where they are safe from harm or abuse.
- Help young people keep themselves safe from harm or abuse.

Working as part of a team

Carers need to have the ability to:

- Work with other professionals and contribute to the authority's planning for the young person.
- Keep information confidential and safe.
- Communicate effectively.
- Promote equality, diversity and the rights of individuals and groups within society.

Personal development

Carers need to have the ability to:

- Use resources within the community as well as have people who can provide support.
- Relate how personal experiences can affect the provider's family.
- Learn from experience, past mistakes and improve skills and knowledge base.
- Work under pressure and periods of stress whilst maintaining effective relationships.

Using this model as the basis for the assessment report also provides a good foundation for the supervisory sessions to be undertaken regularly with the provider. It allows for identification of appropriate training, information and assists in matching a provider to a young person. Using this approach means regular meetings with the provider are purposeful, clear, supportive and help to develop a working relationship where the supervising worker can offer effective support and the provider feels able to ask for this whenever there is a need.

Written supported lodgings agreements

Who are they for?

- Local authority and the provider.
- Provider and the young person.
- Service agreement (if partnership with voluntary organisation).
- With housing department to secure permanent housing options.

Agreements are needed and work because they:

- Provide safeguards.
- Can be referred back to.
- Provide accountability (personal and organisational).
- Learning process for the future for young people (negotiating skills).
- Set boundaries.
- Set targets and goals.
- Describe roles and responsibilities.
- Provide a safe framework for talking about difficult issues.
- Can be matched against competencies.

Young person's agreement can become or complement their pathway plan.

What should an agreement cover?

- Household 'basics' including rules about keys, times, washing arrangements.
- Who supports who and how.
- Young person's goals and responsibilities.
- Financial arrangements.
- Insurance arrangements.
- Emergency support.
- Relationships to leaving care and other specialist resources.
- Moving on arrangements.
- Review dates.

Key Questions when Planning or Reviewing a Supported Lodgings Scheme

- Supported lodgings – the best or cheapest option?
- How can supported lodgings be funded to be a sustainable option?
- What will happen after Quality Protects?
- What extra support is needed for young people with a disability and what are the training and support issues for the provider?
- Why is practice monitoring of supported lodgings outcomes not happening and being used to inform and improve services?

Some considerations

- Services should protect and promote the welfare of the young person.
- Care leavers are vulnerable – and there is an argument that the most difficult to place are amongst the most vulnerable.

- We must have mechanisms to check and assess that a placement can safeguard the young person.

Outstanding questions

It is the case that some local authorities in London, and elsewhere, are using short-term Department of Health Quality Protects funding to try to develop supported lodgings for young people leaving care. Others are trying to introduce supported lodgings without specific funding. In relation to the former it is significant to note that whilst it is 'a good thing' that staffing, training, travel and administration costs are being covered using Quality Protects monies, payments to providers and 'top-up payments' are not covered by the way these Quality Protects based supported lodgings budgets are set up by local authorities. This raises the questions 'why not?', 'how can supported lodgings be funded to be a sustainable option?' and 'what are the accommodation options for disabled care leavers?'

Conclusion

We want supported lodgings to be chosen as 'the best option for the young person' (as agreed for example within a pathway plan) and not the 'cheapest option for the local authority' and offered in default. Supported lodgings are one of many important accommodation options for young people leaving care. So far as we are aware, views about supported lodgings from young people leaving care have not been systematically recorded and published, (unlike other housing options). However, there is a presumption that supported lodgings is a valued option. It is good news that some local authorities have developed supported lodgings schemes. Yet there remain substantial gaps in service provision. It is long overdue for central government to introduce policies, a funding framework for sustained development, and guidance about supported lodgings. Basic practice issues about checking, vetting, supporting and paying providers still remain a matter for local authorities to address or ignore. Also issues about the monitoring and inspection of supported lodgings are of considerable importance so that vulnerable young people are as safe as possible.

It would be a matter of considerable regret, if despite the repeated messages about the need for better safety checks for young people in supported lodgings, that either nothing is done, or that the system of inspection within the Care Standards Act 2000 is insufficient to this task. We must ensure that young people living in supported lodgings receive full support in order to be safe, and to continue to survive 'out there.'

References

Biehal, N. Clayden, J. Stein, M. and Wade, J. (1992) *Prepared for Living? A Survey of Young People Leaving the Care of Three Local Authorities*, London, NCB.

Biehal, N. Clayden, J. Stein, M. and Wade, J. (1995) *Moving on*, London, HMSO.

Broad, B. (1994) *Leaving Care in the 1990s*, A National Survey conducted for the After Care Consortium, Kent, RPS/Rainer.

Broad, B. (1998) *Young People Leaving Care: Life After the Children Act 1989*, London, Jessica Kingsley.

Button, E. (1993) *Supported Lodgings: A Guide to Good Practice*, Centrepoint/North West Supported Lodgings Forum.

CHAR. (1995) *Planning for Action: the Children Act 1989 and Young Homeless People: A Black Perspective*, London, CHAR.

CHAR (1996) *Inquiry into Preventing Youth Homelessness*, London, CHAR.

Collis, A. (1999) Unpublished survey of foster carers and the after care support they provide, North Wales, Fostering Network (formerly NFCA).

Darke, J., Conway, J., Holman, C. and Buckley, K. (1994) *Homes for our Children*, London, National Housing Forum.

Department of Health. (1991) *Children Act 1989, Guidance Notes*, FoH. 3:9.4.

Department of Health. (2001a) *Children (Leaving Care) Act 2000 Regulations and Guidance*, London, Department of Health.

Department of Health. (2001b) *Children Looked After by Local Authorities Year Ending 31 March 2000*, London, Department of Health.

Fry, E. (1992) *After Care. Making the Most of Foster Care*, London, National Foster Care Association.

Hutson, S. (1994) *Supported Lodgings: An Accommodation Resource for Young People: Points of Good Practice*, S & Mid Wales.

Hutson, S. (1995) *Care Leavers and Young Homeless People in Wales: The Exchange of Good Practice*, Wales, Swansea University.

Kirk, N. (1996) *Opportunity, Choice and Housing Benefit: A System in Conflict*, a briefing paper, London, CHAR.

Liverpool Echo (2001) The MAP that Put me Back on Track, *Liverpool Echo*, 5 Jun.

London and South East Supported Lodgings (2001) *Supported Lodgings Workshop Report*, London, LSESL Network.

McCluskey, J. (1994) *Acting in Isolation*, London, CHAR.

NFCA. (1999) *National Standards for Foster Care*, London, NFCA.

Robinson, S. (1998) *Consultation with Young People re National Standards for Foster Care*, First Key for NFCA.

Stein, M. and Carey, K. (1986) *Leaving Care*, Oxford, Basil Blackwell.

Vernon, J. (2000) *Audit and Assessment of Leaving Care Services in London*, London, National Children's Bureau.

Young Homelessness Group (1991) *Carefree and Homeless*, London, YHG.

13. Volunteer Mentoring For Care Leavers

James Cathcart

Introduction

Since 1998 over 50 new mentoring projects for care leavers have been set up in the UK. These use a mentoring model promoted and developed by The Prince's Trust's Leaving Care Initiative. By March 2002 over 1300 young people, leaving or who have left care, had chosen to have the support of a volunteer mentor in addition to statutory support.

This chapter will chart the development of this mentoring for care leavers model. It will describe what is involved, set out the steps that are necessary to set up a mentoring scheme and summarise the national minimum standards that are used to underpin its quality assurance.

Finally it will draw on the experience and evaluation of some of the mentoring projects to signpost key issues for the future. A source of further information is the York University report into the mentoring initiative (in publication 2002).

What is Mentoring?

The word mentor was used by Homer in his poem 'The Illiad' which described the adventures of the Greek hero Odysseus. 'Mentor' was the name of the character he entrusted to be the guardian and tutor to his son.

Today there is no universally accepted definition of mentoring although a dictionary will talk about a mentor as a 'wise and trusted advisor'. The UK Mentoring Strategy Unit, the Active Community Unit, and the National Mentoring Network share the definition that:

Mentoring is a one-to-one, non-judgemental relationship in which an individual mentor voluntarily gives time to support and encourage another. This relationship is typically developed at a time of transition in the mentee's life, and lasts for a significant and sustained period.

Mentoring relationships in general can be both informal and formal.

We can perhaps all identify the informal mentoring processes that have shaped our own development or career. These occur when another person says or does something that subsequently influences our lives for the better. We choose, often unwittingly, to take their advice, or follow their example, because they have an experience or expertise that we value and respect. We sometimes store the knowledge for future reference and it is often only with hindsight that we realise how significant their influence was.

The development of formal mentoring schemes derives in part from an appreciation of the influence of informal mentoring. The role and the skills required will be pre-determined rather than left to chance. Success will be measured against a specific set of aims and objectives within a given context.

Such mentoring schemes are popular in the fields of business, education, training, employment, unemployment, management, religion, and other socio-cultural groups. Each will have associated expectations, limitations, conventions and rules relevant to their community.

A more recent phenomenon is the growth in popularity of community-based or 'social care' mentoring schemes. These set out to influence or support specific groups such as young offenders and care leavers. A variation on the theme is the growth of peer mentoring support.

The growth of community and educational based mentoring schemes has been further stimulated by public policy initiatives and targeted funding.

Why Mentoring for Care Leavers?

There is no reason why a young person should not continue to derive support from a mentor or other significant person whilst also having a personal advisor, provided the roles are clear and agreed with all involved, including the young person, as part of the pathway plan.

Children (Leaving Care) Act 2000:
Guidance and Regulations

Care leavers are a disadvantaged group, both in terms of inequality of opportunity and negative outcomes. Whatever the causes, one of the consequences of an unsettled childhood is that those who leave care are less likely to have the naturally occurring support networks of family, friends and significant others. This is compounded by the fact that they leave care so young (between 16 and 18) compared to their peers leaving home (age 22). This is perhaps when they would most need to have access to a natural source of mentors from within their family and local community.

Although care leavers have role models in popular culture there are few who are identified as having had a care background to which they can relate or aspire to imitate. Although care leavers will identify key people in their care career whose advice was influential these people are often transient or tied to the care system which care leavers, by definition, will leave behind. This deficit has been acknowledged by practitioners, policy makers and researchers, and of course expressed by the young people themselves.

It is plain from what young people say themselves that what they most lack is someone trustworthy and resourceful that they can turn to after they leave care.

(Utting, 1998)

The final report of the three year partnership between the National Children's Bureau and Kent and East Sussex councils, which consulted practitioners, carers and young people, recommended the development and piloting of a volunteer mentoring model (1996).

The Prince's Trust opted to support the development of a mentoring model with the National Children's Bureau. The Trust was already familiar with the successful use of mentoring to set up small businesses. The aim is to help young people, who would not otherwise have the opportunity to succeed, not just to survive. Mentoring explicitly aims to make a difference through setting goals that

allow a young person to grow in self-esteem, experience achievement and celebrate success. The Trust commissioned pilots that developed a model that responded to the particular circumstances and wishes of care leavers.

This occurred at a time when some practitioners were looking to be more ambitious for care leavers rather than focus solely on the goals of survival which were beginning to be addressed by Quality Protects and the draft Leaving Care Act.

What is the Mentoring Model?

The process of establishing a definition of mentoring for care leavers was looked at in two workshops in 1998 – The *Partnership for Care Leavers Think Tank,* February 1998 and at the Action on Aftercare Consortium workshop – *An Introduction to Mentoring for Care Leavers* in May 1998. The Think Tank workshop produced a report containing a definition:

A mentor for a young person leaving care is a committed supporter, a private helper, who will look on the positive side of the young person's agenda and will move at the young person's pace.

Four pilot schemes were set up by The National Children's Bureau in partnership with Bristol, Lambeth, Brighton and Hampshire where the model was refined and its core principles established. Subsequently a set of Guidance and Standards were developed and a mentor training course accredited to the Open College Network. (Alexander 2000). The model was also influenced by number of existing befriending/mentoring schemes in Sheffield, Foyle and Hackney.

In the consultation phase, care leavers told us that they wanted a scheme that gave them:

1. An element of choice – an advisor who was clearly theirs and not shared.
2. Someone who did not know their complete care history or have low expectations of them.
3. Someone who was a committed supporter and who cared for reasons other than statutory obligation or remuneration.

4. Someone who was recruited from a broader community rather than the traditional circles of social work.

These views of care leavers influenced the ongoing development and definition of the mentoring model. The Prince's Trust Leaving Care Initiative subsequently supported the rolling out of this model, working in partnership with voluntary and statutory organisations. It also commissioned York University to evaluate the initiative and their report is due to be disseminated in 2002.

> *Mentoring for care leavers is the offer and availability of one to-one advice and encouragement at a time of transition and opportunity which focuses on the positive and future aspirations of the individual care leaver. Mentoring seeks to realise and fulfil potential, develop skills and promote new opportunities.*
>
> (Prince's Trust – Standards and Guidance Toolkit)

This model assumes that the encouragement, attention and advice of a trained volunteer mentor can best provide a unique form of support to young people leaving care – which is distinctive and complementary to statutory services.

Its main characteristics are:

1. It is delivered by local organisations who have a partnership agreement with the Prince's Trust.
2. The mentors are volunteers.
3. It does not duplicate other provision.
4. Young people are encouraged to get involved in its development.
5. There is a clear set of minimum standards underpinning its delivery.

Benefits to care leavers

- advice and encouragement
- opportunities to learn new skills
- sign-posting to other sources of support
- increased self-esteem and self-confidence
- reduced isolation
- help to access prince's trust grants and programmes
- individual time and attention

> *It's nice that you know they're not there for the money – they're there cos they want to help you.*
>
> care leaver

Benefits to mentors

- minimum 24 hours of training in mentoring skills
- accreditation opportunities
- experience in voluntary work with young people
- improved job and career prospects
- personal development
- the satisfaction of making a difference

> *I think my mentee is amazing. I've got a lot of respect for her and how she's running her life and surviving and having a go.*
>
> care leaver

What's Involved?

Mentoring projects are operated by an equal number of social services leaving care teams and voluntary organisations. They typically have a full-time co-ordinator but there are examples of part-time co-ordinators who are members of a team.

A project is set up following a 16 step process which crucially starts with an assessment of the need for the scheme in the light of other service provision. It is important that the concept of volunteer mentoring is both understood, welcome and will complement, not compete with, other existing options. Once in post a project co-ordinator, who will be skilled in managing volunteers, will recruit three stakeholder groups: the volunteers, the referrers and the care leavers.

1. **The Volunteers** who will be recruited, vetted and interviewed to a volunteer specification, will be asked to make a commitment to attend training and ongoing supervision. They should offer contact and support to a care leaver for a period of between six months and a year. In practice contact can be for a few weeks to over two years and volunteers may subsequently have several consecutive mentees.

   The average age of a volunteer is 32, the age range is 18 (peer mentoring) to 66 (retired), mainly female (78%). Two thirds are employed full or part-time and 16% from a Black, Asian or mixed origin. (Evaluation Report)

2. **Referrers,** which can include self-referral, will understand the role of the mentor, where they fit into the range of support, and understand that they are not a social worker, personal advisor, foster or residential carer, parent, family, counsellor. They are volunteers and offer only complementary support to which the young person is essentially sign-posted by the referrer. It is the young person who will then decide if they want to apply. Most referrals come from social services departments. On average it will take six weeks for a match.

3. **Care leavers** should understand the role of the mentor and be guided though the options within mentoring. They can request a mentor for general support; someone to talk to other than social services; to combat the loneliness and isolation of independence. They can also define in advance, or develop, a specific personal goal. This can range from learning a skill or hobby, acquiring relevant information, to accessing opportunities for work, training or further education.

   Similar proportions of young men and women use mentoring; the average age is seventeen, and up to a fifth are black, Asian or mixed origin. 89% of a sample of 39 care leavers said that their mentor had helped them and 82% recommended mentoring to other care leavers. Some of these relationships are still ongoing. (Evaluation Report)

Once the volunteers are trained and provided with sufficient information the matching process begins. Matching is a combination of paper profiling of both parties, group contact, and personal interview. The aim is to match what the volunteer has to offer with what the young person is seeking to get out of mentoring. One-to-one mentoring can only commence after vetting procedures are complete. From then on the participants set the pace of meetings and agree what they do. Contact is generally a few hours a fortnight for a minimum of six months. Activities will depend on goals if these have been set at the start, but all relationships will go through three phases:

1. Getting to know each other and establishing trust.
2. Mentoring contact and activity.
3. Endings and moving on.

Mentors will receive ongoing group support, supervision and training. The relationship will be reviewed regularly and a decision made about a formal ending. However some pairs remain in contact beyond this as friendships develop. However young people retain their social workers, personal advisors or other supporters. Pairs meet to talk, eat, do activities, learn skills, socialise and keep in touch by telephone, text message, email, postcards and letters.

   Mentors can be practical with their advice, or generally supportive by just 'being there' as a reference point and signpost at a time of transition. They can either help to equip and empower young people to overcome problems or they can offer emotional support to those who are unclear about what direction they want to take. Mentors can also signpost care leavers to other opportunities, and when appropriate refer a young person back to other leaving care services. Mentors have helped young people with education, occupation, accommodation, budgeting, communication skills, decision-making, self confidence and goal-setting. Skills have also developed in the use of leisure time such as starting a hobby or sport.

   Care leavers who lack the social and practical skills to cope with independent living can draw upon the experience of their mentor and those who are lonely, confused or struggling with challenges of adult life know that their mentor will offer a listening and sympathetic ear. The young people tell us they value the voluntary status of the mentor, their commitment and the fact that they do not have 'power' to make decisions about them.

The Sixteen Steps to Setting Up a Mentoring Project

Preparation and planning

1. Decide the level of need and consult.
   - How many eligible care leavers are there in the catchment area, both leaving care

this year, and in previous years but still age under 21. This is the target market. A rule of thumb is to divide the target group by the factor of four – this is the number, based on research who may be interested in mentoring.

- The actual number will also depend on other available provision – How are they currently supported? Do they already have a mentoring scheme, personal advisors, other leaving care projects, aftercare support? Although young people value volunteers, not all will need or want it, though this can change depending on what else is happening for that care leaver.
- Consult with young people and other agencies to ensure there is enough support for a scheme, that it would not duplicate others, and that it adds to the range of support and choice.

2. Set clear aims and objectives.

- What difference will it make to young people?
- What is the aim of the project and what objectives will it need to achieve that aim. Success will be measured against reaching both the process and outcome objectives.

3. Identify resources.

- Experience and expertise in the field of leaving care.
- Experience and expertise in volunteer management.
- A credible mentoring model.
- Finance for staff, capital and running costs that will cover all the stages required, including evaluation.

4. Establish an action plan, targets, timetable and budget.
5. Set up an advisory or reference group.
6. Recruit a skilled co-ordinator.
7. Establish the policy and procedures manual, and training programme, and get it checked for compliance to both legal and good practice standards.
8. Design and develop information resources for potential care leavers, referrers and volunteers

Recruitment and training

9. Recruit volunteers through local advertising, hold an information session, circulate a pack, interview volunteers and commence vetting procedures.
10. Recruit prospective young people, both direct and through referrers.
11. Deliver training to minimum standards and review suitability of participants at the end.

Matching and mentoring activity

12. Matching – over several months, using a mixture of complementary techniques including group events, personal interviews and paper profiles.
13. Agree initial goals for relationships – which may include getting to know each other with a view to establishing a goal.
14. Provide ongoing training, group and individual supervision opportunities.

Evaluation

15. Keep records and monitor turnover and outcomes.
16. Evaluate and review.

Minimum General Standards

The following minimum standards are recommended to ensure that mentoring is delivered to a consistent level of quality that values the volunteers and the young people:

Needed

1. A project based on consultation and identified evidence of need.

Focused

2. Have a statement of aims and objectives.
3. Have clear objectives for the mentoring relationships, including a personal goal identified by the young person.

Participatory

4. Voluntary to mentors and young people.

Complementary

5. Complementary to statutory duties of local authorities and boards.

Partnership

6. Working in partnership with other agencies and The Prince's Trust.

Integrated

7. Part of a range of leaving care support and not duplicating other individual support

Networked

8. Projects are members of a broader support network, in contact with other mentoring projects, and to The Prince's Trust.

Involving young people

9. Involving young people in its development.

Accessible

10. Accessible to those care leavers most in need – regardless of disadvantage, race, colour, religion, nationality, ethnicity, gender, marital status, sexuality or disability.
11. Ensuring care leavers can self-refer, as well as be referred, to the scheme (age range 16–21 only).
12. Have policies, procedures and staff for its operation in a safe and effective manner.
13. Have a clear criteria for the recruitment, selection, screening and ongoing support of volunteers.

Prepared

14. Ensuring volunteers are trained to the Leaving Care Initiative's specification and syllabus, and for a minimum of 24 hours, and care leavers are prepared about what to expect.

Confidential

15. To ensure that personal information is not shared beyond a designated boundary of the mentoring relationship.

Monitored

16. Recording of activity, and profiles of mentors and care leavers, their goals, contact, review and endings.

Evaluated

17. Recording, reporting and assessment of outcomes for both volunteers and young people.

Checked

18. Quality assurance through a range of systems to confirm 1–16 are in place.

Two of the general standards on training and monitoring are detailed at length in the polices and procedures supplied to each participating project partner. Quality assurance tools are also used to review whether projects are complying with the standards and whether the standards themselves are up to date.

What are the Themes and Opportunities of Mentoring?

Mentoring benefits care leavers, volunteers and service providers. It is a vehicle that offers new opportunities for innovation and must stay relevant to appeal to the care leavers who choose to use it.

Mentoring can reach some of the most disadvantaged of care leavers and help them to achieve their goals. It is a positive agenda that complements and goes beyond the goal of survival. It has brought benefits to the volunteers who participate and stirred the interest of social services departments who are not only able to now access a fresh option for continuing support, but are also experiencing a fresh input of volunteers from a range of new and diverse backgrounds. Their skills, training and voluntary experience puts mentors in a good position to successfully apply for posts in leaving care services.

In 2001 mentoring has been used to pilot the use of volunteers to enhance basic skills (literacy and numeracy) support and a Basic Skills Mentor training pack was developed in response to a study that indicated that over 70 per cent of care leavers were at level one. Recent proposals have indicated specialist innovations in the development of mentoring such as parenting skills and peer mentoring. We have observed that young people who have been 'mentee' are now asking to become 'mentors'. A significant number of adult mentors are also from a care background. All are in positions to influence the future direction of mentoring.

The influence and self-confidence of care leavers will result in a greater number willing to talk about their success if they are given the opportunity. More public information about successful role models will influence and change the stereotype public perceptions of care leavers and reverse some of the negative expectations.

The leaving care field is changing as the impact of new legislation is felt. The role of the volunteer mentor must be distinctive to the role of the personal advisor and the young person must be allowed to retain a choice of support.

In this changing environment it is important to stay fresh and relevant and to listen to care leavers.

One thing that mentoring has shown is that care leavers respond to encouragement. In this they are no different from their peers. As we stay in touch with care leavers for longer we will discover other unacknowledged needs of those in their twenties and beyond which will set new challenges.

However, as confidence grows, the care leavers themselves will increasingly play an active part in providing the solutions to the challenges they face. This will not only help the individuals but contribute to a climate where care leavers will ultimately feel more welcome in society.

References

Alexander, A. (2000) *Mentoring Schemes for Young People*. Pavilion.

Biehal, N., Clayden, J., Stein, M. and Wade, J. (1995). *Moving On*. London, HMSO.

Benioff, S. (1998). *A Second Chance*. London, Commission for Racial Equality and Crime Concern.

Broad, B. (1998). *Young People Leaving Care: Life after the Children Act 1989*. London, Jessica Kingsley.

Burke, T. and Loewenstein, P. (1998). Me and My Shadow. *Young People Now*. March.

Cathcart, J. (2002). *Mentoring for Careleavers Toolkit: Guidance and Standards*. Prince's Trust.

Cathcart, J. (1996). *Preparation for Adulthood: Standards in Residential Care*. NCB Final Report (unpublished).

Clayden, J. and Stein, M. (due 2002). *Mentoring for Careleavers: Evaluation Report*. Prince's Trust.

Department of Health (2001a). *Children (Leaving Care) Act 2000 Regulations and Guidance*. London, Department of Health.

National Mentoring Network (1999) *A Quality Framework: Ten Steps to Setting up a Mentoring Scheme*. National Mentoring Network.

The Prince's Trust (2002). *The Way it is: Young People on Race, School Exclusion and Leaving Care*. The Prince's Trust.

Social Services Inspectorate (1997) *Inspection Report Standards in Leaving Care*. HMSO.

Stein, M. (1997). *What Works in Leaving Care?* Barnardo's.

Stein, M. (1999). *Leaving Care Factsheet*. The Prince's Trust.

Utting, Sir W. (1997). *People Like Us*. HMSO.

14. Asylum Seeking and Refugee Children in the UK

Selam Kidane

At any one time there may be up to 100,000 separated children in Western Europe alone. As many as 20,000 separated children lodge asylum applications every year in Europe, North America and Oceania. The term separated children is used to define:

> Children under the age of 18 who are outside their country of origin and separated from both parents or their legal or customary primary care giver ...
>
> Statement of Good Practice: Separated Children in Europe, Para 2.1.

The term Unaccompanied Asylum Seeking or Refugee Children (UASC) is more commonly used in the UK to refer to children who flee and seek asylum alone. There are approximately 6,000 unaccompanied asylum-seeking and refugee children currently in the UK. Most of them are either looked after or supported by local authorities. The majority are in England – in London and the Southeast. (BAAF/Refugee Council, 2001).

A refugee is someone who leaves or remains outside their own country of origin 'owing to a well-founded fear of persecution for reasons of race, religion, nationality or membership of a particular social group or political opinion' (United Nations, 1951). In the UK an asylum-seeker is recognised and granted refugee status and usually given indefinite leave to remain under the 1951 United Nations (UN) Convention on Refugees (United Nations, 1951) upon demonstrating eligibility. A person who may be found not to meet the criteria of the 1951 UN Convention, but for whom removal from the UK is deemed to be unreasonable or impracticable, may be granted exceptional leave to remain for a specified period of time to be reviewed upon expiry. An unaccompanied child is a person who is under the legal age of majority and is not accompanied by a parent, guardian, or other adult who, by law or custom, is responsible for them (Department of Health Social Services Inspectorate, 1995).

Article 20 of the UN Convention on the Rights of the Child states that 'A child temporarily or permanently deprived of his or her family environment ... shall be entitled to special protection and assistance provided by the state' (United Nations, 1989).

A child who is seeking refugee status must receive appropriate protection and humanitarian assistance in the enjoyment of the applicable rights set forth in the UN Convention on the Rights of the Child. It is important to bear in mind, when reading about young refugees' experiences in care in the UK, that those rights entitles **an asylum-seeking child to the same level of protection as any other child deprived of their family**.

UK Immigration Legislation

Immigration legislation has seen various changes over the past decade resulting in the confusion of both those that it affects and those that are trying to offer services to them. The Immigration and Asylum Act 1999 was the third major piece of legislation in six years. The Act was a substantial piece of legislation covering the whole system; from arrival, to support, to removal of failed applicants. The following new measures were introduced:

- Changes to immigration controls.
- Increased use of detention, detained asylum seekers were to receive automatic bail hearing and the government to introduce

rules for the management of detention centres.

- Simplification and speeding up of the appeal system.
- The regulation of immigration advisors.
- Immigration officers were granted powers of entry, search and arrest, similar to that of the police.
- The introduction of a new support system for asylum seekers while awaiting a decision on their asylum claim. The main features of this measure was the introduction of dispersal and vouchers instead of cash benefits.

Less than two years into this new system further major changes are yet again in the pipelines. The Home Secretary outlined a series of changes to the asylum system in his speech to the House of Commons on 20th Oct 2001. Although a white paper detailing these changes is not expected until early 2002, the following were amongst the changes that were mentioned in the speech:

- Voucher scheme to be scrapped and replaced by a 'smart card' ID for asylum seekers.
- Setting up of new induction and accommodation centres for newly arriving asylum seekers.
- Increased use of detention for refused asylum seekers.
- Greater reporting requirement for those still awaiting decisions.

Reasons for Unaccompanied Exile

People are generally forced into exile to seek sanctuary when they are experiencing, or are threatened by, persecution. Although children and young people experience similar persecution to the adults in their community, there are unique circumstances that particularly affect them and many children have to flee their countries unaccompanied. Some of the most common causes of the unaccompanied exile of children are:

- Forced recruitment into military service.
- The death of parents or inability to care for them (as a result of conflict in the region).
- Forced re-education.

- Prohibition from participating, or being forced to participate, in religious activities.
- Being forced to give information about the activities of a group or members of their family.
- Pressure to denounce family members.
- Involvement or non-involvement in political groups.

Refugee children are different both in the nature of their persecution and in their circumstances prior to exile. These differences will result in different reactions to the refugee-making process and to life in exile. But different groups, and individuals within groups, may seek refuge for different reasons, and therefore refugee children from the same country may be here for quite different reasons (e.g. two children could be from the same country but from opposing factions or opposing religious sects).

In a recent publication (Kidane, BAAF, 2001), refugee children and young people gave a variety of reasons which resulted in their unaccompanied exile. These accounts are very similar to those appearing elsewhere in the media and other reports (including Home Office country profiles and Refugee Council updates):

My parents are dead and I used to live with my eldest sister and her family together with my little sister. When the war started the police came and took my sister and her husband. I was the eldest of all the children (three of my sister's children and my sister). I told the neighbour's friends what happened and they phoned my other sister in Sweden. She said she would send the money to get us out of the country and until then we should stay at home with the servant and the guard.
   Filmon, a 12-year-old boy from Eritrea.

There was war in my country. Everyone was fleeing, and my family told me I was to join my aunt's family on a journey to Kenya.
   Saadia, a 15-year-old girl from Somalia.

This country is a democratic country and you have rights. Where we come from people have no rights and so it is difficult for us. People think we come to get money from this country, but actually we pay lots of money to come here. Now that doesn't make sense does it?
   Jazmir, a 17-year-old ethnic Albanian boy.

My country is a former communist country where there is war and division at the moment. This means that some of us have problems with the government because of our race, our religion or our occupation.
Besnik, a 16-year-old ethnic Albanian boy.

Refugee Children in Local Authority Care

In its practice guidelines on unaccompanied asylum-seeking and refugee children, the Department of Health Social Services Inspectorate (1995) places their care firmly within the boundaries of childcare legislation as set out in the Children Act 1989, giving unaccompanied children the same rights as all children. More recent practice guidance (BAAF, 2001) also indicates the importance of local authorities complying with existing childcare legislation.

However, a recent Audit Commission survey (Audit Commission, 2000) found that although refugee children have multiple needs because of their experiences of separation, loss and dislocation, many were not in receipt of the same standard of care routinely afforded to indigenous children in need, with whom they share identical legal rights. For example, many local authorities do not offer 16 and 17-year-olds a full needs assessment. Many are routinely supported in temporary accommodation, with over half of children over 16 and 12 per cent of those under 16 in bed and breakfast, hotel and hostel accommodation. The survey also found that only one-third had individual care plans in place.

Difficulty in determining a child's age in the absence of legal documentation appears to be a problem for a number of authorities. Indeed, some authorities indicate that an increasing number of young adults may present themselves as under 18 in the hope of qualifying for better services. Faced with a lack of reliable procedures to confirm age, a number of children are often placed where there is little or no support and no adult carer with parental responsibility.

The shortage of suitable accommodation is another reason given for failure to adequately meet the needs of unaccompanied refugee children. The lack of affordable accommodation and a shortage of foster carers and appropriate residential placements often lead authorities to place children out of borough, affording the placing authority little chance to appropriately supervise the care of the children placed. Although a special grant is available to meet the cost of supporting unaccompanied refugee children, the level of funding and its administration is found to be difficult for local authorities providing support to unaccompanied refugee children.

A survey by Barnardo's policy, planning and research unit (Barnardo's, 2000) found that a number of local authorities are experiencing difficulty in providing unaccompanied refugee children with appropriate accommodation, as a result of either there being no appropriate provision or the high cost of providing residential and foster care. Thus, an alarming number of young people are living in unsuitable accommodation. Barnardo's calls for these issues to be addressed urgently so that these young people will receive the services they are entitled to and are in need of.

Amongst the main areas of concern for the UK section of the separated children in Europe project (Separated Children in the UK, 2001) are the issues of dispersal and after care provisions for unaccompanied children. The Children (Leaving Care) Act was introduced to improve services for young people leaving care and hence improve outcomes for such young people. However, a great majority of unaccompanied asylum seeking children will not benefit from these provisions as they will not qualify for after care provisions, having been provided with section 17 services.

The Audit Commission also indicated that many unaccompanied children face difficulties when leaving care. This is even more so for those who have had earlier traumatic experiences. Such experiences should be taken into consideration upon transfer of 18–21-year-olds to new support arrangements.

Particular Needs of Unaccompanied Refugee and Asylum Seeking Children Leaving Local Authority Care

Unaccompanied refugee children have the same essential needs as all other children. As with other children in need, local authorities have the responsibility to ensure the safety and protection of refugee children as well as the promotion of their welfare, as stated in section 17(1) of the Children Act:

> It shall be the general duty of every local authority ... to safeguard and promote the welfare of children within their area who are in need ... by providing a range and level of services appropriate to those children's needs.

However, it is clear that unaccompanied refugee children constitute a particularly vulnerable group of children in need. Their primary attachment base and most of their networks have been severed suddenly, often unexpectedly and under traumatic circumstances. Their protection is deemed to be achievable only by separation; hence their parents, relatives and friends are forced to seek such protection for them. Therefore unaccompanied refugee young people leaving local authority care are more likely to be in need of extra support than most of their peers.

One of the primary tasks for adolescents is the gradual establishment of an adult identity. This includes the reassessment of the existing relationships with parents and other family members as friends and more intimate personal relationships become more important. While this period of readjustment inevitably requires some moving away from parental influence, for most young people, parents also remain a source of stability, influence and resources. The process of relinquishing parents as primary attachment figures proceeds irregularly, gradually and progressively. For most unaccompanied refugee children these issues are far more complex than for most adolescents as separation from primary attachment figures occurred at a far earlier stage in their life and in traumatic circumstances.

Leaving care therefore makes unaccompanied children particularly vulnerable

to both the continuation, and the addition, of trauma. Inappropriate care arrangements and insufficient resources impact on the young person's basic need to have a sense of belonging that can make a difference at this crucial stage. This is especially so when there is the added pressure of an undecided immigration status. Unsatisfactory care arrangements could also endanger the safety of young people who, in their desperate search for someone to belong to, could fall prey to inappropriate relationships that might exploit their vulnerability. This is particularly true in situations where there is little or no adequate support for the young person.

Unaccompanied refugee children who have left behind any form of stability and who face uncertainty while their immigration status is settled, are faced with an unfamiliar present and an uncertain future. Successful care arrangements and leaving care packages need to be constructed in a way that helps unaccompanied refugee children and young people to form a secure enough base from which they can make the transition from childhood to adulthood. This needs to happen within the context of secure, lasting and appropriate relationships that can be maintained through time and across geographical space enabling the children to experience both permanence and security. Therefore, it is particularly important that wherever possible relationships and support arrangements are stable and enduring over time. This will ensure ample opportunities for appropriate and lasting relationships that, in the absence of other networks (e.g. familial or peer), the young people could rely on for support into adulthood.

Given the needs of these young people, a carefully co-ordinated leaving care service is clearly needed. Without such services backed by appropriate policies it is impossible to provide the stability and security that is crucial for an uprooted young person. Good practice with an unaccompanied refugee child leaving care should be one that supports them to address their past experiences and enable and equip them to make a healthy transition into adulthood as contributing members of society. However, this can only be built on the good practice that should be in place while the young person was in care. Good practice with an unaccompanied refugee child should be one that reduces anxiety by promoting trust, security and certainty for the child. (Kidane, BAAF, 2001). *Tms in not possibl*

All you want to do is do well and make everyone proud of you. That includes your parents even though they are not here. But that is not easy to do when you have so many things worrying you. I think it is very important to get settled to sort out your housing and your education, but you need people to help you with that. It is not easy when you do not know the rules.

Fawzia, a 19-year-old.

When you apply for a job and they ask you for a reference and experience. You need someone who has known you for that and if you are all on your own you have to go to your social worker, and people do not exactly think of that as a good reference do they?

Suleman, 21.

When you leave care and leave your foster carers you feel like you have no family again. Although I know that my foster carers would want to keep in touch with me and would welcome a visit I still feel like it is asking too much, especially when you know that they would be caring for another child who would need their care like I did.

Helen, 20.

I think the most difficult thing is having to cook and eat all by myself, I don't think I have ever eaten alone before. And even if I have learnt how to prepare basic meals I am a very bad cook and when you have to eat it by yourself ...

Michael, 20.

I like living in my own flat, I was looking forward to it and I enjoyed decorating my flat and choosing my furniture. I have to be careful about money though when you have bills to pay and all that but it is all part of growing up isn't it?

Martha, 19.

We have been rejected by the home office and are appealing. We came here when we were 11 and 12 and lived with a foster family until now, we like being together.

Alex, 18, and Josh, 19.

Good Practice for Young Unaccompanied Refugees and Asylum Seekers Leaving Care

Appropriate policies and procedures

Without the existence of appropriate policy and practice framework it is impossible to plan, deliver and review services for any group of children. The special needs and circumstances of unaccompanied children make it even more important for local authorities to have such a framework. Leaving care services should be a continuation of care services provided to children. Needs should be identified and support services and networks put in place in a framework that takes the young person's circumstances and needs into account. A young person who leaves care without their immigration status resolved, will have different needs to one who is appealing against a decision, or one who has exhausted all rights to appeal. However, the local authority has the same responsibility and each of these young people have the same rights as any other child in need.

Preparation for adulthood

The inadequacies of the UK care system in preparing young people for adult life has been pointed out time and time again. This is especially so for young people with particular needs, for example young black people (Page and Clarke, 1977; Black and in Care, 1984; Who Cares? Trust, 1993; Biehal et al., 1995). Any preparation that is given to unaccompanied children should take their experiences and the impacts of these on the young person into consideration. Some young people could look and behave in an exceptionally mature way, it is however important to ensure that this applies to all aspects of their development. The Looking After Children Assessment and Action Records (LAC), which most local authorities have now adopted, provide a good opportunity for ongoing assessment of the young persons' skills and abilities to inform planning for leaving care.

Factors that will affect the young person's entitlements to services and benefits should all be clearly explained and the young person should be supported to access those services to which they are entitled. Young people whose asylum claims remain unresolved and those who are appealing against a decision are not entitled to benefits and are currently supported by a system of vouchers and a small amount of cash (initially £10 raised to £14 following the most recent review of the system). This service is co-ordinated and delivered by a department at the Home Office known as the National Asylum Support Service (NASS). One aspect of NASS support is that recipients are offered accommodation outside areas in the Southeast of England. Asylum seekers who require NASS to provide them with accommodation are usually dispersed (on a 'no choice' basis), however children who have been 'looked after' under section 20 of the Children Act will not be dispersed. Local authorities should work with NASS to find young people suitable accommodation within the areas that they have settled in. Unfortunately, those who were supported under section 17 do not fall into this category and hence could be dispersed upon turning 18 years.

Implications of possible changes that come with the young person's asylum status determination (e.g. the granting of full status or when applications are unsuccessful) should be discussed fully and the young person should be given all the support (emotional and practical) that are required. A young asylum seeker should also be prepared for the possibility of all the outcomes upon determination of asylum application. Depending on the age that young people became unaccompanied they may have a varied level of practical skills and an assessment of their skills would give workers an idea of what is required to supplement the deficit in skills. When you are preparing a young person, for whom there are several outcomes, you have to prepare them for all possibilities. For example, a young man was preparing to go to university if he was granted leave to remain in this country but wanted to study a trade

(carpentry in his case) if his asylum claim was turned down.

Coming from a society where young people leave their parents only to get married I worry about the young people leaving my care, especially for the girls. I try to prepare them for things that the social workers may not ... like looking out for situations that might undermine their reputation.

An Eritrean foster carer.

You see them all excited about their brand new flats and their new independent life but I have seen enough to know that that is when they need the most help and support.

A youth worker.

You accept living by yourself in the same way you accept living in this country, you accept it, you live from day to day and you try and do the best you can.

Martha, 19.

When you are about to leave your foster placement all the uncertainties come back, especially if you are waiting to hear from the home office. Where will I end up? And every thing you prepare for may not happen but it is good to discuss things and know all the options.

Helen, 20.

I never took my social worker seriously when we discussed some of that stuff you just think it is easy and of course you would manage it, what I did not know then is how much other people did for me all my life ... my parent, my foster carer, my social worker. But I am learning and cooking was the first step.

Michael, 20.

When you come here as a refugee you know you are all by yourself and although it is good to have people supporting you the reality is that you have left home when you became an unaccompanied refugee.

Suleman, 21.

Talking to my friends who came here like me and are now living in their own flats helped because they did it and they were able to tell me what to do especially those who live in my estate were very good neighbours.

Josh, 19.

Maintaining existing relationships and initiating and developing new ones

Looking at the list of people that I have the most contact with (people that I call friends) you can say that most are people like me who came here young and alone, you understand each other and since you go through similar situation you can support them and vice versa.

Josh, 19.

Unaccompanied refugee children who lose their family, home and community are amongst the most isolated groups of children in public care. While in care it is important that these children are supported to establish and maintain links with members of their community. Members of the refugee child's own community have the potential of becoming part of an extended family, with positive outcomes for a lone child. Ample opportunities should be provided for the child to participate in appropriate cultural and community activities in order to cultivate such links. Upon leaving care it is imperative that the young person is actively supported and encouraged to maintain existing links and forming new ones. Community centres, youth schemes, religious communities could all be approached to provide such links. To do this the young person's existing sources of informal support and potential to make lasting friendships should be explored. Wherever possible the young person should be actively supported to maintain these relationships, it could be arranged for the young person to live near these contacts and/or travel expenses covered. Young people could also be linked via a specialist group that is set up for the purpose of enabling young people to form support networks:

Even though she does not live with me now I still see her at church most Sundays and she keeps me up to date with her progress at university.

An Eritrean foster carer.

Promoting healthy lifestyle
Physical health

Some unaccompanied children may suffer physical difficulties associated with experiences of torture. Some might exhibit the consequences of war and violent conflict, for example bullet wounds, disfigurement or mutilated limbs resulting from landmines or other forms of violence. They may have had inadequate health care prior to exile, resulting in limited levels of immunisation and undiagnosed and misdiagnosed conditions. Children may have come from areas where some diseases are common and may be affected by those – e.g. malaria, TB, HIV. There may have been food shortages in the areas from which refugee children have come and in the refugee camps that they may have lived in prior to arrival in the UK, resulting in some cases of nutrition-related difficulties. It is very important that any health difficulties are addressed as they are identified. It is also important that the young person is made aware of primary health services and health promotion (leisure activities, sexual health and drugs awareness) as the young person is about to leave care.

Mental health

Unaccompanied refugee children have been uprooted and lost their homes and communities in the attempt to gain safety in a host country. They may consequently suffer a range of emotional and psychological difficulties. These emotional difficulties are exacerbated by the uncertainty they face in exile, hampering their ability to form suitable attachments and make sense of their situation and environment. In cases where there are identified mental health difficulties it is important that the appropriate services are in place and the young person is supported in accessing them. The young person should also be informed about mental health services even when there are no signs of mental ill health at that time.

Employment, training and education

The educational needs of refugee children vary depending on their age and the educational opportunities they had prior to exile. Educational opportunities may have been limited due to various situations including political unrest or social attitudes and expectations. Some children may have been denied education as a result of their parents' socio-political grouping. In particular, girls may not have been allowed or expected to have education beyond a given limit. Some children may have been in an educational system that put them ahead of their age group in the UK system. It is very important that the assessment establishes the educational level of each child, and action is taken to support those who need additional support. This should help to improve the career chances of young unaccompanied people leaving care. There is anecdotal evidence of high levels of achievement among some groups of unaccompanied refugee children. This indicates that where the motivation of young people is matched by support and dedication from carers and professionals young refugees are able to attain the desired educational levels. It is also worth noting that due to gaps in their education refugee children might take longer to attain exam passes, making it important for support to be extended for perhaps a slightly longer period of time.

Education and employment can provide a useful focus and a valuable source of resilience for unaccompanied young refugees. It is very important that young people are encouraged to acquire skills and training that will enable them to gain meaningful employment.

Safe, affordable and supported accommodation

While it is clear that the particular housing needs of unaccompanied young refugees leaving care might be varied, it is important to note that they have left 'home' at least once often under a traumatic set of circumstances. It is crucial that young people are given adequate support and preparation to move on to independent living.

It is also important that they are given a range of options and flexible packages, to reflect their needs. The location of the accommodation also needs to take into account the special needs of unaccompanied young refugees to maintain support networks (formal and informal).

Given the importance of young people to acquire training and meaningful employment it is very important that there is a clear financial plan for the accommodation.

Having a flat was nice until I started going to Uni and had to live on a student grant, I had to work long weekend shifts just to make ends meet.

Saba, 23.

Conclusion

My fear was that I will be all alone again, I thought when you turn 18 that's it you leave the home and have to fend for yourself but I was surprised by the help that you can still get.

Adam, 20.

The mark of a successful leaving care service is in its capacity to enable young people to attain the best possible outcome upon their transition from the care system into adulthood. For unaccompanied young people this is complicated by the particular circumstances of their status as unaccompanied young people. Public authorities have a prime responsibility to meet the needs of these young people on leaving care taking into account their circumstances. It is the mark of a responsible society not to create further hurdles to those that these young people have already overcome in trying to create a secure and productive adult life for themselves.

References

Audit Commission. (2000) *Another Country: Implementing Dispersal Under the Immigration and Asylum Act 1999*, London, Audit Commission.

Ayotte, W. and Williamson, L. (2001) *Separated Children in the UK, An Overview of the Current Situation*, London, Refugee Council/Save the Children.

BAAF/Refugee Council. (2001) *Where are the Children? A Mapping Exercise on Numbers of Unaccompanied Asylum-seeking Children in the UK: September 200–March 2001*, London, BAAF/Refugee Council.

Barnardo's. (2000) *Children First and Foremost: Meeting the Needs of Unaccompanied, Asylum-seeking Children*, Survey findings from local authorities presented at a Barnardo's seminar 4 Jul. London, Barnardo's.

Biehal, N., Clayden, J., Stein, M. and Wade, J. (1995) *Moving on: Young People and Leaving Care Schemes*, London, HMSO.

Children's Legal Centre. (1984) *Black and in Care Conference Report*, London: Children's Legal Centre.

Department of Health Social Services Inspectorate. (1995) *Unaccompanied Asylum Seeking Children: A practice Guide*, London, HMSO.

Kidane, S. (2001) *Food Shelter and Half a Chance: Assessing the Needs of Unaccompanied Asylum-seeking and Refugee Children*, London, BAAF.

Kidane, S. (2001) *I did not Choose to Come Here: Listening to Refugee Children*, London, BAAF.

Page, R. and Clarke, G. (Eds.) (1977) *Who Cares?*, London, National Children's Buereau.

United Nations. (1951) *Convention on Refugees*, New York and Geneva, United Nations.

United Nations. (1989) *Convention on the Rights of the Child*, New York and Geneva, United Nations.

Who Cares? Trust. (1993) *Not Just a Name: The Views of Young People in Foster and Residential Care*, London, National Consumer Council.

15. The Health Needs of Young People Leaving Care

Sue Daniel, Ann Heelas, Catherine Hill and Sue Smith

What do we Know About the Health Needs of Young People Leaving Care? (*Catherine Hill*)

Young care leavers are a diverse group of individuals with a spectrum of strengths as well as vulnerabilities. Nonetheless, they are united by the common experience of corporate parenting, and in many cases of neglectful and abusive pasts. Health may be jeopardised by historical abuse and neglect but may be further damaged within public care (Gallagher, 1999).

What do we know about the health problems and needs of this population? The Social Services Inspectorate report '*When Leaving Home is also Leaving Care*' summarised some disturbing statistics about these young people as below.

- More than 75% of care leavers have no academic qualifications.
- More than 50% of young people leaving care after 16 years of age are unemployed.
- 17% of young women leaving care are pregnant or already mothers.
- 38% of young prisoners have been in care.
- 30% of young single homeless people have been in care.

(Social Services Inspectorate, 1997)

Unemployment, homelessness, offending behaviour and young parenthood result in a population characterised by extreme socio-economic deprivation. Health is powerfully determined by socio-economic status (Acheson, 1998). If health is considered in its broadest sense as 'a complete sense of physical, mental and social wellbeing' (WHO, 1958) the complex nature of the problem is evident. The extent and nature of adverse parenting experiences (family and corporate), and a young person's intrinsic resilience will influence future health more than individual ill health factors. Young people would appear to share this holistic concept of health (Saunders and Broad, 1997). When interviewed by their peers, young care leavers ranked housing, relationships and employment as more important to their health than health service access or health related behaviours such as eating habits and smoking.

Clearly, addressing the health needs of care leavers is far more than disease management or health service provision but requires an approach that recognises the health consequences of deprivation and harnesses multi-dimensional solutions.

There is a lack of research that examines the health problems of a population of care leavers. This alone speaks volumes of the historical lack of continuity of services offered to these young people leaving their corporate homes. A review of the literature of the health of children within the care system gives a clue to the aftermath of care. This research remains patchy and studies have generally been small scale and may not have represented the population. Nonetheless common patterns emerge:

Health neglect

The health of young people in the care system has notoriously been neglected. A number of studies have highlighted common themes of poor immunisation uptake and missed child health surveillance (Hill and Watkins, 2000). Mary Mather in her study of 194 children in Greenwich found that 10% of children were apparently not registered with a GP (Mather et al., 1997). Jackson et al. (2000) compared a group of 119 looked after children with children living in their families. The looked after group fared worse for routine dental care and immunisation status. While these deficiencies of care are unlikely to make local headline news, they can result in a state of chronic sub-optimal health. A young person, for example, who has not had the benefit of regular dental care in childhood takes into adulthood a legacy of dental decay. Furthermore they are doubly penalised as an adult, having to pay expensive dental fees to redress this early neglect. Furthermore, a system of child public health, free to all and a right to all citizens under the UN Convention of the Rights of the Child is denied those most in need.

> *States Parties recognize the right of the child to the enjoyment of the highest attainable standard of health and to facilities for the treatment of illness and rehabilitation of health. States Parties shall strive to ensure that no child is deprived of his or her right of access to such health care services.*
>
> Article 24

Health risk and health threatening behaviour

Young people leave care at a time of vulnerability, that is to say, during their adolescence. Adolescence in recognised by the World Health Authority as *the process of growing up in the period between childhood and maturity encompassing the ages of 11 and 21* and is characteristically a time of risk taking. Adolescence has an important function in the developmental transition from dependent child to independent adult, enabling a process of self-definition through experimentation. Typically the adolescent has a sense of invulnerability. A combination of risk taking and limited life experience inevitably creates casualties, as exemplified by age trends in deaths from injury (Woodruffe et al., 1993). Research with both young people in care and care leavers has highlighted their vulnerability to problematic and persistent risk taking including substance misuse (DoH, 1997a) and risky sexual behaviour (West, 1995; Corlyon and McGuire, 1997). Saunders and Broad (1997) in their peer interview study of 48 care leavers found that 70% used drugs, principally cannabis (94%), also speed, cocaine, ecstasy and LSD. 26% of the study group admitted to drinking alcohol heavily. The vulnerability of young people in and leaving care to teenage pregnancy is recognised by the Teenage Pregnancy Unit as a major concern, and a

practical framework for addressing this issue will be addressed by Sue Smith later in this chapter.

Some behaviour may be more susceptible to risk taking. Evidence from Sweden (Berg-Kelly, 1995) suggests that adolescents are more likely to report risk taking with new 'adult' behaviours such as sex and alcohol intake, than health behaviours already established in childhood, for example healthy eating. This has implications for the timing of health promotion. Earlier integration and normalisation of healthy behaviour models into the pre-adolescent learning may protect against risk behaviour, highlighting the importance of healthy care for all ages. Experimentation takes place within a social context of family and peer influence. Adolescents conform to peer pressure more than younger children or adults (Berk, 1997). The peer group can exert a negative influence on health behaviour if risk is accorded kudos. Equally, it can be successfully exploited to promote health behaviour choices (*The Lancet*, 1994).

The corporate parent has a critical role in supporting and validating health promotion interventions. For example, it is known that adolescents in families promoting autonomous decision making, where parents are supportive and good communicators, tend to delay age of first intercourse (Brooks-Gunn and Furstenberg, 1989). Indeed many successful school based sexual health programmes have harnessed parental involvement (Hubbard et al., 1998).

An individual's risk behaviour is determined by complex influences including societal and cultural values, individual personality, knowledge levels and environment. Behaviour may change over time and be unpredictable. Only with a sound understanding of the normal patterns of teenage risk behaviour can appropriate health promotion interventions be designed and evaluated.

Mental health

Young people in and leaving local authority care are particularly vulnerable to emotional and behavioural and mental health difficulties. Evidence given to the Health Committee suggested that young people in care are four times more likely than young people living at home to have a psychiatric disorder (House of Commons Health Committee, 1998). Other studies are highlighted in the following chapter specifically looking at the mental health needs of care leavers. Some US states with superior health monitoring of 'foster care children' and an enhanced ability to study health care utilisation through Medicaid claims (Simms et al., 2000; Bilaver et al.,1999) have found that this vulnerability to mental health difficulties is independent of socio-economic influences and is unique to the particular situation of the looked after child.

Even if young people are recognised to have difficulties, access to mental health support can be problematic. Young people report dissatisfaction with mental health services, citing issues such as professional dishonesty, lack of trust and not being listened to as the reasons for their lack of engagement (Broad, 1999).

Physical health, mental health and unhealthy behaviours can be separated into convenient categories by authors but not by young people whose life experiences underpin the nature of the difficulties they experience. The reality, of course, is that one problem tends to exacerbate another until often young people are overwhelmed by a complex series of difficulties. It is known, for example, that smoking and alcohol abuse are more common in children and young people with mental health problems (Meltzer et al., 2000). Furthermore, both substance abuse and mental health difficulties are factors that influence sexual health risk behaviours in adolescents. Solutions that address only one aspect of a young person's difficulties are inevitably doomed to failure.

Difficulties are likely to be further exacerbated if young people also live as ethnic minorities within their community or suffer a disability. Ward and Skuse (2001) found a high frequency (6.3–50%) of learning disability across the five local authorities represented in their data. As discussed later, this presents particular challenges to promoting health. Ethnic minority children are more likely to have adverse health experiences (DoH, 1999) and particular needs (Barn, 1999) in care. Data on disabled children is not accurately reported at present in

Government statistics but at least 9% of all looked after children in the UK require care (mostly respite) due to their disability (www.doh.gov.uk). Disabled children and young people with more complex needs may find themselves in the care system because their parents are unable to manage their complex needs. As a population these children are particularly vulnerable to abuse and discrimination.

Policy Context (*Ann Heelas*)

The Children (Leaving Care) Act 2000 which came into force in October 2001 aims to improve the life chances of children leaving care and bring about real change to the sometimes depressing statistics outlined in the previous section. The key to the Act is the extension of responsibility of local authorities in England and Wales to support care leavers to the age of 21 (24 if they are in education). A needs assessment for care leavers should include an assessment of health issues which should be integrated into the pathway plan, supported by regular reviews and a personal advisor. The draft guidance (DoH, 1999) recommended that pathway planning should be based on the guidance shortly expected from the Department of Health on promoting health for looked after children and recommended:

> *... a holistic heath assessment and the maintenance of detailed health records will provide the platform for pathway plans to promote a healthy lifestyle, ensure appropriate use of primary care services, plan access to specialist health and therapeutic services where necessary and promote leisure interest. It is especially important the young people are helped to take responsibility for their own care.*
>
> DoH, 2001.

These recommendations offer new opportunities for improved working between health and social services to promote health for care leavers. Delivery of health assessment that is both of high quality, relevant and acceptable to young people in order to inform the pathway plan remains a challenge. It also offers the opportunity to ensure that health data collated during a young person's period in care is translated into a useful format to inform their future health choices. At the least this should include a written summary of key health information including extended family history (Hill, 2001).

Use of health services

Is a NHS free to all at the point of delivery and accessible to young people not enough? Do young care leavers require anything different? Naomi Eisnestadt, director of Sure Start observed that:

'Services for everybody fail the poor but services for the poor are poor services.

It has long been recognised that looked after children require additional advocacy for health. The statutory health assessment and Looking after Children Action and Assessment Records (LAC) attempt (although frequently fail) to provide targeted health review for these children (Dartington Research Unit, 1995). However, at the age of 16 as the young person reaches independence this fragile safety net vanishes. In the next section Sue Daniel will discuss the theory and practice of achieving appropriate and helpful health assessment for young people leaving care.

Principles of Designing Services to Meet Young People's Needs (*Sue Daniel*)

Studies have shown that teenagers and adolescents do not access a first class service from the primary care sector. Jacobson and colleagues (1994) identified that teenagers of both sexes had shorter consultations with their GP than all other patients This may be due to a number of factors: the difficulties in timing an appointment to fit in with school or college, a reluctance on the part of the family practitioner to engage with young people unaccompanied by an adult or perceptions that the family doctor will report back the conversation to parents and carers. These, exacerbated by limited time allocated to each patient, all lead to poor uptake of services.

In contrast to this many young people leaving the care system may have been used to annual medicals or statutory health reviews. These

ideally bring both time for, and expertise in, communicating with adolescents. Young care leavers may have used them as a time to ask questions and explore the wider issues around good health, or, in contrast they may have found them intrusive and view contact with a doctor or nurse as something to be avoided. For the health professional working with looked after children there is an important role in supporting young care leavers in their transition from specialist to primary care services. The Social Services Inspectorate (1997) reported that there was generally no difficulty in accessing primary care services but young people did not know how to get advice about healthy living, safe sex and emotional development. They also identified particular problems for this group in accessing mental health services.

Research shows that young people leaving care have not only all the usual problems of adolescents, but as described in the preceding sections have higher levels of mental, emotional and physical ill health. Dealing with emotional or mental health issues is time consuming and not usually managed in a one-off contact, wider issues need to be explored and this can often be done within the context of a health assessment. This is not a one-off event but rather an ongoing process which can be used to plan provision of future care, identify any unmet needs and promote good health.

Prior to leaving care all young people should be offered a health assessment to inform their pathway plan. This is an opportunity to ensure there are no unmet physical needs, and can be supportive for a young person moving into independent living. A survey, by Oppong-Odeiseng and Heycock (1997), of 14 and 15-year-olds found the preferred source of advice for health related care was adult family members, and for relationship problems was peers or siblings. For young care leavers many of these supports are absent. Information, both verbal and in a suitably written format, should be provided for young people about how and when to access sexual health services, dental care, general practitioner, opticians and hospital services.

In Southampton we are fortunate in being able to use health facilities sited in a leisure centre to run a clinic for teenagers in care and those leaving care. The Quay to Health has proved very popular with all ages but in particular young people where other more traditional venues may not be acceptable. Running alongside health assessments are sexual health advisors, substance misuse counsellors, youth offending team, education and youth workers, arts and drama, swimming and use of the gym. Consultation with the young people attending the clinic in Southampton identified that the most important features of the clinic were 'time to talk to a health professional who would listen,' and 'the availability of other services on site'. Teenagers have reported poor interaction with their GPs whom they find patronising and judgmental (Donovan et al., 1997). Health workers must be aware of normal adolescent development, the need to develop independence and to engage in risk taking activities. Failure to acknowledge this will mean the young person quickly becomes disenchanted and will not openly discuss the very issues most likely to affect their health. Alternative lifestyle choices may need to be explored. This may take some time, may not initially be acceptable to the young person and the need for ongoing support must be recognised.

Identifying a suitable venue is important but attention must also be paid to timing appointments to fit in with college or school, as this can be a common reason for failure to attend. Another feature of adolescents is the need for instant service provision. Young people generally are not particularly well organised at planning ahead (ask any parent) and appreciate a service where they feel able to drop in for advice. As advice given when asked for is likely to be more effective, drop in services for young people have been developed across the country, these may be in clinics, leisure centres or at schools. Young people leaving care need particular help in developing confidence to use these services.

Given the opportunity, young people are the best at obtaining the views of their peer group. Work done by Saunders and Broad (1997) used young people in assessing the health needs of their peer group. Young people showed a holistic approach to health and health determinants which identified the need for co-operative interagency strategies in planning

for the best outcomes. Broad concluded that young people should be more involved in the decision-making processes.

Young people who have been in local authority care are often mistrustful of sharing information that may be circulated without their consent. All too often they report that previously their personal thoughts, health status and family details were shared by many agencies. At a time in their life when there is an increasing need for privacy they may be reluctant to seek advice particularly for sexual, emotional or mental health issues. It is good practice to display a confidentiality statement when seeing all young people and to explain its meaning at the time of contact. Health care plans following assessment should be developed with the young person's agreement and the content negotiated. Young people should be able to decide who will receive a copy of the plan and should always receive a copy themselves. Information in the form of leaflets may be given to back up health messages and should be in appropriate language for the young person to understand. The use of a health fax or personal health record can be usefully promoted. In this the young person may document ongoing health care plans, family health information and details about early childhood immunisations and illnesses etc. Each health fax should have a section detailing how to access services locally with contact phone numbers for phone advice. The health fax should ideally be issued to all young people who are expected to remain in the care system from about the age of twelve years and become their main health document. These young people do not always have family members to remind them of early life events and may be at risk from familial genetic health problems of which they have no knowledge (Hill, 2001).

Engaging young people at the end of their care experience can be difficult. Teenagers who are most at risk of poor health outcomes are those who have been poor school attenders and they are the least likely to attend for health advice. It is important that the social worker and health professional work together to promote the advantages of health assessments and that young people are encouraged and supported in attending. Invitations that are easily understood, attractive and sent directly to the young person can be effective in overcoming pre-conceived ideas about 'medicals'.

Health professionals must be aware of the important role of advocates in seeking to promote better services and a more holistic approach to good health on behalf of a traditionally socially excluded and disadvantaged group in society.

Health cannot be viewed in isolation and there is a continuing need to further develop the links between education, leisure, social services and health. Professional sensitivities must not be allowed to impede the development of services to meet the ever-changing needs of these young people.

One of the strengths of the drop in sessions at the Quay to Health is the sexual health project. Sue Smith explains in the next section the background to her work and outlines the approach that is used in practice.

Sexual Health: Addressing the Needs of Young People in and Leaving the Care System (*Sue Smith*)

Sexual Health is defined by the World Health Organisation as:

The integration of the physical, emotional, intellectual and social aspects of sexual being in ways that are enriching and that enhance personality, communication and love.'

And in 1988 WHO defined three principal elements to sexual health as:

- A capacity to enjoy and encounter sexual and reproductive behaviour in accordance with a social and personal ethic.
- Freedom from fear, shame, guilt, false belief and other psychological factors, inhibiting sexual response and impairing sexual relationships.
- Freedom from organic disorders, disease and deficiencies that interfere with sexual and reproductive fulfilment.

The LSI (Love, Sex, Intelligence) Report on the sexual health needs of young people in Southampton and South West Hampshire (Lynch, 1995) gathered the views of over 600 young people in the area. Priority was given to potentially vulnerable young people who may not easily access health services, including young people leaving care.

Those who had been, or were still looked after by the local authority showed significant differences compared to other groups of young people.

Results showed that they had:

- The lowest age of first sexual experience.
- Least access to sexual health information.
- First sexual information primarily gained from sexual partners.
- No access to information on lesbian, gay or bisexual identity.
- Lowest condom use. In survey – 68% never used condoms.
- Least access to services for fear of judgement and lack of confidentiality.

Results from a survey of 139 young people aged 15–17 which included care leavers (University of Southampton, 2002 in publication) highlighted many differences in the expectations and knowledge of the young people.

Sexual health information and support should be part of a package for young people in, or who have left, care, and at the centre of any planning. It should also be part of the assessment process. The individual plan needs to be implemented in a positive way and with realistic expectations both for a young person and the service provider. It must be monitored and evaluated and assessed regularly – is it working? It must also be flexible. All necessary changes should be made in the light of the young person's changing needs. All sexual health assessments must be confidential and non-judgemental and take into account the young person's ethnic origin and learning abilities.

A sexual health plan needs to contain ways to assist a young person so that they can be supported to use mainstream services as any other young person might who is living at home. As a young person moves on, they need to feel confident and have the skills to walk into a GP surgery for example, to ask to see a doctor and to be able to say what they want and what their needs are. Young people need to know they can return to whoever has supported them if they need to.

A sexual health clinic, for example, can provide practical help e.g. contraception, but young people need to have life skills, a positive attitude and need to know what to do if things go wrong. It is about young people avoiding situations, making decisions, about whether to have sex or not and about making choices. Young people may sometimes have the information to make an informed choice but do not always know how to take that step.

The personal attitude of carers and professionals to sexual health issues and the language they use is important. Using medical terms may not be appropriate whereas using 'street slang' may not be right either. We need to find a common ground. This is not just relevant to medical professionals, but carers and social workers too. Conversely, if a foster carer for example is uncomfortable about talking to a young person about sexual health issues then they need to know where they can refer a young person to for information and advice. Everyone working in the field needs to have the confidence and skills to meet the sexual health education needs of these young people.

It is important to create an atmosphere and environment where a carer or social worker is relaxed enough to answer a young person's questions. People are often uncomfortable discussing issues around sex. If a parent didn't know something or know about an appropriate service they would find out. Carers and social workers should do the same. Young people need to feel comfortable within their peer groups and it is important to find ways to help them achieve that.

So how can we help young people?

Many young people within the care system will have moved school many times or may not be in school. As a result they often miss out on their Personal, Social and Health Education (PSHE) lessons. An effective assessment package will identify the young person's sexual health education needs.

Some of the difficulties around sexual health issues may relate to a young person's previous life experience and they may need the services of the mental health team. Sometimes young people need specialist counselling. This should

be offered as an ongoing service for the young person – needs led rather than time-limited because of funding. It is also important that there is support available after counselling sessions as sometimes very sensitive and upsetting issues are reawakened in a young person.

Young people in care, and leaving care, may benefit from the opportunity to meet with other young people in similar circumstances. Health promoting activities encourage groups of young people to learn about themselves, share concerns in a safe environment and meet with other professionals who can offer them further support. An example of this is a project at the *Quay to Health* in Southampton's swimming and diving complex mentioned earlier in this chapter. The aim is to boost a young person's self-esteem and encourage them to develop essential life skills including choices concerning their sexual health. Other agencies, such as Connexions personal advisors, leaving care mentors, social services, residential workers, foster carers, education and voluntary workers may refer young people to the project as part of a leaving care package.

Children in care often have different, diverse and complex needs compared to say, 20 years ago. It is important that attitudes and awareness keep abreast with these changes and that young people are given advice and support from whoever they choose to be the most appropriate person at the time. This advice must be honest and accurate and offer practical support on all issues of sexual health including sexual orientation, emotional and physical development and personal relationships.

Conclusion

Care leavers remain the most socially excluded of our young people who have historically suffered the inverse care law (Webb, 1998). The legislation within the Children (Leaving Care) Act 2000 and the burgeoning examples of good practice in the field of interagency working create a real future possibility of health equality. In order to achieve this equality the complex nature of health must be recognised and agencies need to work collaboratively to advocate for improvements in all aspects of healthy living for these young people. Health services do have a part to play but must work flexibly, often outside the traditional models of care if they are to achieve success.

References

Acheson, D. (1998) *Independent Inquiry Into Inequalities in Health*, London, Stationery Office.

Barn, R. (Ed.) (1999) *Working with Black Children and Adolescents in Need*, London, BAAF.

Berg-Kelly, K. (1995) Normative Developmental Behaviour with Implications for Health and Health Promotion Among Adolescents: A Swedish Cross-sectional Survey. *Acta Paediatr* 84: 278–88.

Berk, L. (1997) Peers, Media and Schooling. *Child Development*, 579–625.

Bilaver, L., Jaudes, P., Koepke, D. et al. (1999) The Health of Children in Foster Care. *Social Service Review*. The University of Chicago.

Broad, B. (1999) Improving the Health of Children and Young People Leaving Care. *Adoption and Fostering* 23: 1, 40–8.

Brooks-Gunn, J. and Furstenberg, F. F. (1989) Adolescent Sexual Behavior, *American Psychologist* 44: 249–57.

Children (Leaving Care) Act: Draft Regulations and Guidance. (2001). Department of Health.

Corlyon, J. and McGuire, C. (1997) *Young Parents in Public Care: Pregnancy and Parenthood Among Young People Looked After by Local Authorities*. National Children's Bureau.

Dartington Research Unit. (1995). *Looking after Children: Assessment and Action Records*, (revised version) London, HMSO.

Department of Health. (1997a) *Substance Misuse and Young People: The Social Services Response*. A Social Services Inspectorate study of young people looked after by local authorities, DoH.

Department of Health. (1999) *Promoting Health for Looked After Children*. Consultation document. Department of Health, HMSO.

Donovan, C., Mellanby, A. and Jacobson, L. (1997) Teenagers' Views on the GP Consultation and Their Provision of Contraception, *British Journal of General Practice* 47: 715–8.

Gallagher, B. (1999) The Abuse of Children in Public Care, *Child Abuse Review* 8: 357–65.

Hill, C. M. (2001) Family History: The Importance of Health Inheritance of Children in Public Care, *Adoption and Fostering* 25: 1, 75–7.

Hill, C. M. and Watkins, J. (2000) *Does the Statutory Medical Review Offered to Children Looked After by Southampton City Council Provide an Effective Means of Health Assessment?* Report, SE Regional NHSE. *http://www.doh.gov.uk/public/stats1.htm*

Hubbard, B. M., Giese, M. L. and Rainey, J. (1998) A Replication Study of Reducing the Risk, a Theory-based Sexuality Curriculum for Adolescents, *Journal of School Health* 68: 243–7.

Jackson, S., Williams, J., Maddocks, A., Love, A., Chung, W. and Hutchings, H. (2000) *The Health Needs and Health Care of School Aged Children Looked After by Local Authorities*. Final report to the Wales office of research and development. Swansea, University of Wales.

Jacobon, L., Wilkinson, C. and Owen, P. (1994) Is the Potential of Teenage Consultations Being Missed? A Study of Consultation Time in Primary Care. *Family Practitioner* 11: 296–9.

Lynch, J. et al. (1999) *Barnardo's and Southampton City Council Social Services Sexual Health Education Policy*, Barnardo's.

Mather, M., Humphrey, J. and Robson, J. (1997) The Statutory Medical and Health Needs of Looked After Children. Time for a Radical Review? *Adoption and Fostering* 21: 2, 36–40.

Meltzer, H., Gatward, R., Goodman, R. and Ford, T. (2000) *The Mental Health of Children and Adolescents in Great Britain*. London, Office for National Statistics, The Stationery Office.

Oppong-Odiseng, A. C. K. and Heycock, E. G. (1997) Adolescent Health Services: Through Their Eyes, *Archives of Disease in Childhood* 77: 2, 115–9.

Quality Protects Newsletter (2000) *A Dedicated Centralised Service for Looked After Children*. Dec.

Saunders, L. and Broad, B. (1997) *The Health Needs of Young People Leaving Care*, Leicester, de Montfort University.

Simms, M. D., Dubowitz, H and Szilgyi, M. (2000). Health Care Needs of Children in the Foster Care System, *Pediatrics* 106: 4, 909–18.

Social Services Inspectorate (1997) *When Leaving Home is also Leaving Care*, Department of Health, CI (97, 4).

The House of Commons Health Committee (1998) *Children Looked after by the Local Authority*. The House of Commons Health Committee.

The Lancet. (1994) Sex Education in Schools: Peers to the Rescue, *The Lancet* 344: 899–900.

Webb, E. (1998) Children and the Inverse Care Law, *BMJ* 316: 1588–90.

West, A. (1995) *You're on Your Own: Young People's Research on Leaving Care*, London, Save The Children.

Woodruffe, C., Glickman, M. and Barker, M. et al. (1993) *Children, Teenagers and Health. The Key Data*. Open University Press.

16. The Mental Health Needs of Young People who are Leaving Public Care

Ciaran Kelly

This chapter looks at the mental health needs of young people leaving care. It defines mental health and then looks at some of the services available to these young people. It then moves on to look at specific needs of care leavers in comparison to other adolescents and the need for a network approach. It concludes by making a series of suggestions for developing specialist mental health services for young people leaving care.

What is Mental Health?

There is a need to consider the definition of mental health before writing about the mental health needs of young people who are leaving care. As one young person recently told me, mental health is: 'When I feel good about my life and my friends, when I know where I'm going and what I want to do'. The mental health of young people is essentially about their emotional wellbeing and level of adjustment within society, not just specifically about their happiness, or about an absence of formal mental illness.

For all of us when we talk about being mentally healthy we are talking about our minds, about how we feel, think, understand the world around us, anticipate our futures and remember our past. This definition is hopefully applicable to everybody and allows for individual and cultural differences. It allows for recognition that adolescents are dealing with many different challenges including bodily changes, establishing their identity and changing relationships with adults. 'Leaving Care' is a process rather than an event and as such it is a time of frequent changes and transitions; a combination of new exciting challenges as well as losses, uncertainty and the disruption of fragile but important attachments.

We all have a responsibility as corporate parents to help young people through the process of leaving care whilst recognising that the mental health of a young person is indicated by their:

- Capacity to learn and work.
- Appreciation of themselves and others.
- Ability to form significant relationships.
- Readiness to meet a challenge.
- Sense of hope.
- Freedom from serious emotional and behavioural problems.

The Prevalence of Mental Health Problems

Any assessment of the prevalence of mental health problems will depend on the nature of the population studied, the definition of mental health problems and the method used to study the population. Studies of the prevalence of mental health problems have been done for samples of young people in the general population as well as for looked after children. There was an important study undertaken in 1999 by the office for National Statistics (Meltzer et al., ONS, 2000) to examine the prevalence of mental health disorders in the general population and to identify the main risk factors. The survey used the diagnostic criteria of the international classification of diseases, which specifies the level of functional impairment for these disorders. Overall, 10% of the population of children aged 5–15 years were diagnosed with a mental disorder. 5% had clinically significant conduct disorders, 4% were assessed as having emotional disorders, particularly anxiety and depression, and 1% were rated as hyperactive. Among the 10,438 children studied, 10% of boys and 6% of girls between the ages of 5–10 years had a mental disorder. In the older age group of those aged 11–15 years, the proportion of children with diagnosed mental disorders was 13% for boys and 10% for girls.

The prevalence rates of mental disorders were greater among children in the following higher risk groups:

- In lone parent compared with two parent families (16% versus 8%).
- In reconstituted families rather than those with no step children (15% versus 9%).
- In families with five or more children compared with two children (18% versus 8%).
- If the interviewed parent had no educational qualifications compared with a degree level or equivalent qualification (15% versus 6%).
- In families with neither parent working compared with both parents working (20% versus 8%).
- In families with gross weekly household incomes of less than £200 compared with £500 or more (16% versus 6%).
- In families of social class 5 compared with social class 1 (14% versus 5%).
- Whose parents are social sector tenants compared with owner occupiers (17% versus 6%).
- In houses with a striving rather than thriving geo-demographic classification (13% versus 5%).

It is clear to see that children and young people who are looked after are likely to have experienced, and to continue experiencing, many more of the identified risk factors for mental illness. It is widely acknowledged that there is a high prevalence of looked after children who experience mental health problems.

Looked after children, especially those in residential care, are identified as a group whose mental health needs are known to be greater than those of the general population of the same age.

Utting et al., 1997.

The Utting Report was based on the study by McCann et al., which systematically examined the prevalence of psychiatric disorders amongst adolescents looked after by Oxfordshire local authority (McCann et al., 1996). The overall prevalence rate of psychiatric disorders for this group was 67%, compared with 15% in a comparison group. 96% of the adolescents in residential units had formally diagnosed disorders compared with 57% in foster care. The most common diagnosis was one of conduct disorder which was applicable to 28% of those studied, 26% were experiencing an anxiety disorder, 23% suffered from a major depressive disorder, and 8% were diagnosed as having an un-specified functional psychosis. Many of the young people studied had two or more diagnosis. The authors emphasised their concern that a significant number were suffering from severe and potentially treatable disorders which had gone undetected.

Particular Mental Health Problems Experienced by Young People who are Leaving Public Care

There is a dearth of research examining the mental health problems experienced by young people leaving public care. However, conclusions can be drawn from the available research which has studied the prevalence of mental health problems among young people entering local authority care, those problems experienced whilst being looked after, and follow up studies which have considered the outcomes. It seems likely that care leavers have even higher levels of emotional difficulties and psychiatric problems than most looked after children. Research from the Department of Health indicates that approximately 40% of looked after children return home after less than eight weeks and more than half will have gone home within six months. 70% of children who start from being looked after return home within a year (DoH, 2000a). These findings indicate that it is likely to be young people with more extreme difficulties and complex needs that remain in care until they are 16 or 17-years-old and become care leavers.

Experience suggests that young people who are leaving public care are more likely to experience particular difficulties with:

- Serious depression and self-harm.
- Chronically low mood and poor self-esteem.
- Conduct disorders and aggression.
- Attention problems including Attention Deficit Hyperactivity Disorder.
- Substance misuse or dependency.
- Eating disorders.

There will also be a small proportion (approximately 1–2%) of young people who will begin to develop a serious long-term mental illness such as either schizophrenia or manic depressive psychosis (Bi-polar mood disorder). Typically these disorders become apparent during later adolescence or early adult life. Unfortunately, there is very commonly a period of gradual decline in the young person's social functioning, peer relationships and mental health for some time before a positive diagnosis is made and the provision of appropriate services and treatment.

Mental health problems cannot be considered in isolation but need to be understood in the context of social and peer group influences. Many young people who are leaving care will be experiencing major anxieties related to disruptive peer group influences, relationship difficulties, and uncertainties about their future education, housing, family relationships and social support.

A study by Dimigen et al. (1999) assessed the prevalence of mental health problems amongst adolescents at the time they entered local authority care. 70 young people completed questionnaires, 26 from residential units and 44 from foster care. As with McCann's study the most common mental health problems were conduct disorder and depression. Very severe levels of depression were identified particularly among children in residential establishments. 21 of the young people had severe attention difficulties and 18 had profound difficulties with communication skills and showed an impaired ability to form any significant relationships. Again, as with McCann's study, there were high levels of young people diagnosed with more than one mental health problem and worryingly high numbers of young people with serious psychiatric disorders who had not accessed psychological help.

Cheung and Buchanan (1997) have examined the mental health and psychosocial adjustment of adults who have previously been in care. Their study compared young adults who had been looked after with other people who had experienced 'severe social disadvantage'. Their results indicate that the experience of being looked after increases the risk for depression in adult life. There were differences between genders with women being significantly more likely to score highly for depression, but the risk of depression lessened for women as they grew older. The reverse was true for men who had been looked after with the risk of depression growing as they grew older.

Why do Looked After Children have Greater Mental Health Problems?

Children become looked after at a wide range of ages and remain looked after for varying amounts of time. There are also a wide range of issues contributing to the reason why children and adolescents become looked after, almost invariably there is a complex interaction of family and social problems which are further compounded by health and educational difficulties experienced by the child and young people. The single factor most highly correlated with becoming looked after is the child or young person having parents who are separated or divorced (Bebbington and Miles, 1989). The early developmental experiences of children who become looked after include exposure to many of the identified risks of childhood psychiatric problems. Bebbington and Miles (1989) found that of children who become looked after 25% had previously lived with both parents, 75% of the families received income support, more than 50% were living in disadvantaged neighbourhoods and only one in five lived in owner occupied housing. The risk of becoming looked after was increased by over crowding, a large number of siblings, and young parenthood.

The House of Commons Health Committee Report (1998) identified the experience of abuse or neglect as being the main reason for becoming looked after amongst 20% of children in 1999. Historically there has been inadequate attention paid to the prevalence of having been sexually abused amongst this group though there is increased recognition given to the importance of early attachment relationships and the long lasting detrimental effects of a history of disrupted attachment. It is also relevant to consider the child's genetic inheritance, which may well result in a greater vulnerability to mental health problems. Such vulnerable children, who experience and are then exposed to environmental adversities, are understandably much more likely to develop significant emotional and behavioural problems as well as social and educational difficulties. The pre-existing vulnerability and problems young people have at the time they become looked after are frequently compounded by negative experiences in residential and foster care.

Outcomes for Young People who have Been Looked After

Young people who have been looked after leave the care of local authorities when they are aged 16–17 years, and this is in contrast with the general population where the average age of leaving home is 22 years (DoH, 1999). It is recognised that there are high levels of early parenthood, mental health problems, social isolation and risk taking behaviours amongst the population of young people who are leaving care. Bob Broad (1998) has identified that half of this group become unemployed and 20% experience homelessness within two years of leaving care. Data from the DoH (1999) indicates that 25% of young people leaving care have a disability and 25%–30% are teenage parents.

Saunders and Broad (1997) studied a sample of 48 care leavers, of whom 17% had long term mental illness including depression, eating disorders and phobias. 35% had engaged in repeated acts of deliberate self-harm and 60% of the total had suicidal thoughts, four of the young people had made very significant suicide attempts. It is very concerning that of the 31% who had access to mental health services 77% had not found the service useful.

The educational outcomes for young people who have been looked after also give cause for serious concern and are well documented. The rate of permanent exclusion from school amongst looked after children is ten times higher than average and many estimate that up to 30% of looked after children are effectively out of education at any one time. There are likely to be many interacting factors relevant to the poor educational outcome for looked after children, not least the fact that so many young

people experience disrupted education following placement breakdown. Morgan has reported that 80% of looked after children who experience placement breakdown also have to change school. These young people then experience difficulties coping with curriculum changes as well as the upheaval of changing schools and placement breakdowns (Morgan, 1999).

The rate of looked after young people's involvement with the criminal justice system is equally alarming with up to 35% of young prisoners having been looked after. Young people with criminal convictions are well recognised to have significantly higher rates of mental health problems, particularly attention difficulties, depressive disorders and psychotic illnesses (Rutter et al., 1998). A study of 'persistent' young offenders by Hagell and Newburn (1994) identified higher rates of involvement from social services particularly related to the use of secure accommodation orders.

It is important to balance the risk factors for mental health problems in young people with protective factors that have been identified. Ann Buchanan has studied life satisfaction of adults who have previously been looked after children (Buchanan, 1999). Whilst the study identified a significant risk of psychological problems at sixteen and depression by the age of thirty-three, it was noted that 75% did not have psychological problems at aged sixteen and 80% were not depressed at age thirty-three. It seems that the most important protective factor is stability and continuity of care. Dumaret concludes that accommodation or placement stability can be improved by specialist support from a dedicated fostering agency (Dumaret et al., 1997). The stability of placement also appears to be related to more positive educational achievements, relationship skills and employment outcomes (Koprowska and Stein, 2000). Biehal et al. (1995) found that if young people have the opportunity to explore their own personal history they were more likely to have a higher self-esteem than other young people who remained confused about their family and past history.

Difficulties Accessing Mental Health Services for Care Leavers

The high prevalence of mental health problems amongst looked after children and the high proportion not accessing mental health services has been well documented in recent research (McCann et al., 1996; Dimigen et al., 1999; Arcelus et al., 1999). Young people who are leaving care are likely to experience even greater difficulties accessing appropriate mental health services. The difficulty that young people have accessing these services is likely to be further compounded by the many transitions relevant to leaving care. As they leave care they are also likely to move geographically and may well move from one health authority to another which increases the risk of discontinuity of care. With long waiting lists in many areas it is very possible that even when a young person has been well engaged with therapeutic services there may be an unhelpful interruption of services because of the transitions involved in the process of leaving care.

There is frequently a gap in the provision of services for young people between the ages of 16 and 18 years (Young Minds, 2001). Many child and adolescent mental health services (CAMHS) have been set up to provide services up until the age of 16 years and in the same area adult mental health services see people aged 18 years and over. This potential gap in CAMHS provision is being increasingly recognised. In 1995 the Health Advisory Service found that whilst 80% of health authorities had identified services for children and adolescents with mental health problems, only 18% had specific CAMHS services for looked after children. My enquiries with colleagues indicate that nationally there are few CAMHS services specifically targeting young people who are leaving care. There are however individual areas of good practice such as Bury, Sheffield, Glasgow and Tower Hamlets and Lewisham in London. There are wide local variations in the organisation and quality of services for care leavers which in effect results in a postcode lottery.

There are very significant issues concerning the ability of traditionally organised child and adolescent mental health services to meet the needs of young people who are leaving care. Many of the mental health difficulties commonly encountered do not fall neatly into the diagnostic criteria for mental disorders. In particular there is the challenge to the mental health services of providing effective interventions for conduct disorder, aggression and delinquency. Care leavers who present conduct-disordered behaviour very commonly have other mental health diagnosis and/or learning difficulties. The limited availability of CAMHS and the 'non-medical' nature of conduct disorder has led to influential advice that conduct disorder should not be a core responsibility for CAMHS and psychiatrists in particular (Goodman, 1997). There is, however, good evidence of positive outcomes when adolescents with conduct disorder receive intensive and co-ordinated interventions that address multiple social systems which sustain the behavioural difficulties (Kazdin, 1997; Hengeller, 1999). The complex difficulties presented by these young people require intensive interventions, which ideally should be co-ordinated by a network of multi-agency professionals.

A proportion of young people who leave care will lurch from crisis to crisis and CAMHS services need to be able to provide an emergency response. The ability of CAMHS to provide an emergency response requires flexibility and time which can be practically difficult to organise because of the relentless pressure experienced by mental health services. Adolescents may also feel stigmatised by having to attend a clinic based mental health service. Ideally, mental health services should be provided in a range of settings and should include an outreach service so young people can be seen on their 'own territory'. Alternatively, adolescents may well be more inclined to use a 'drop in' service rather than adhering to appointments which have been arranged in the traditional medical model.

The communication skills of CAMHS professionals are crucial to the process of engagement with adolescents. Equally important is the issue of confidentiality, and many young people will be understandably anxious about confidentiality issues which need to be openly discussed at an early stage of the engagement process. Adolescents will need to know who will be informed about their consultation or if indeed anybody needs to be informed. They will also need to know which details will be related to which other people. These issues of confidentiality will be particularly relevant for young people who have concerns about sexual health or abuse, drug or alcohol misuse or criminal involvement. Adolescents may welcome the opportunity of discussing the content of any correspondence concerning them before it is sent. This process can usefully generate a therapeutic dialogue about mutual perspectives and can facilitate self-reflection.

The Need for a Network Approach

The mental health difficulties of young people should never be considered in isolation; they must be understood within the social, family, peer group and educational context. There is increasing recognition that a comprehensive needs assessment can usefully inform the young person's overall management plan. The *'Framework for Assessment'* very helpfully adopts this needs-based model of assessment and intervention and should be increasingly used by health, education and social services. The need for a holistic multi-faceted approach is perhaps particularly relevant to care leavers.

A comprehensive assessment of need will inevitably identify not only mental health problems but will also identify equally relevant issues in the young person's social care, education, peer and family relationships. For most young people leaving care it will be important to systemically consider how each of these needs is addressed. This can be done by convening network meetings involving the social worker, family member or carer, key education representatives and possibly also input from voluntary agencies in addition to the CAMHS professional. Such network meetings operate most effectively when there is broad agreement of each professionals role and responsibilities within the needs lead management plan. Within such networks it is important for each professional to have been directly involved in the assessment of the young person's needs in their particular area of responsibility.

The Behaviour Resource Service (BRS) in Southampton has developed this networking approach by providing intensive multi-agency assessments and co-ordinated packages of care for young people who present the most extreme challenges to professionals and society. The BRS is one of 24 projects nationally to have been funded by the Department of Health (DoH), CAMHS Innovation Grant (www.youngminds.org.uk). These 24 projects all target the most vulnerable young people by providing more integrated services through mental health services working in collaboration with social services.

The BRS has been jointly planned and is staffed, managed and funded by health, social services and education. Young people can access the BRS if they have extreme mental health problems, social care and education needs. The service accepts referrals of young people who present serious behavioural problems, highly risky behaviour, are experiencing family or placement breakdown and educational exclusion. The BRS operates in partnership with existing specialist services within CAMHS, social services and education by the development and co-ordination of networks working together to address the range of identified needs. It has proved important to the service to also work in partnership with local voluntary agencies, community projects, adult mental health and the police. Our experience underlines the importance of assessments and proposed interventions being owned by the relevant professional and fully agreed by all participants including the young person. It has proved important for all decisions to be clearly documented with individuals and time scales clearly identified. These network meetings need to be re-convened on a regular basis to feed back and evaluate the effectiveness of interventions and to review the young person's progress. The management or care plan can then be accordingly modified.

The treatment or care plans for young people should not have a restricted focus on the management of mental health or behavioural problems but should include more positive aspects of the young person's developmental needs. For young people leaving care attention will be paid to the future accommodation and educational needs. It can also be very relevant to consider family and peer group relationships during the process of leaving care. Many care leavers feel very vulnerable with the prospect of future independence and self-reliance. Understandably, such anxiety and a sense of insecurity is likely to influence the young person's relationship with their birth parents and siblings. There can be many possible benefits as well as risks associated with these changing dynamics. Perhaps equally important is the need for young people to develop pro-social community based activities including sports and leisure. For the most disadvantaged and disillusioned adolescents this can require determined efforts by key professionals to engage the young person. The prevention of anti-social peer group influences can prove particularly important in the management of young people who have conduct disorder as well as being a relevant consideration for almost all adolescents. Community support workers and youth workers are often best placed to provide specialist advice and can help the young person link in with appropriate activities.

The Leaving Care Act 2000 and the Provision of Mental Health Services

The Leaving Care Act clearly has significant implications for the provision of mental health services to care leavers. The Act has the following main aims:

- To delay young peoples discharge from care until they are prepared and ready for independence.
- To improve the assessment, preparation and planning for leaving care.
- To provide better personal support for young people after leaving care.
- To improve the financial arrangements for care leavers.
- To promote contintinuity and consistency through the 'looked after' experience.

The young people who qualify for the new arrangements are entitled to a personal advisor and a pathway plan at the very least. Certain groups of young people are also eligible to receive a needs assessment, accommodation and maintenance depending if they are 'eligible' or 'relevant' children.

The personal advisor does not necessarily have to be the young person's primary support but is, in any case, responsible for building a network of support. This network of support may well need to include mental health professionals. The main aims of the Act are very broadly defined and should always include consideration of the young person's psychological well-being and mental health needs. The personal advisor is expected to ensure that the young person accesses the services that have been identified in their needs assessment and pathway plan. Personal advisors are expected to ensure that the young person is well engaged in the process, and by co-ordinating the agencies and individuals involved ensure that services are delivered appropriately and at the right time.

Many questions remain about the future development of services for looked after children. Different local authorities throughout the country are at very different stages of developing services. It appears that the majority of local authorities have developed a dedicated leaving care team, but, however, many continue to employ social workers to undertake the role of personal advisors whilst not being named as such. There should be opportunities for a wide range of professionals to become personal advisors. Young people have a right to express their view about who their personal advisor will be, and potentially the personal advisor could be any adult who the young person trusts, respects or likes.

Within the wide remit of the Leaving Care Act it is likely that personal advisors will be working with psychological and mental health issues on a daily basis. However, it appears quite improbable that any significant proportion of personal advisors will come from a mental health background. It remains unclear how personal advisors will be recruited and how some knowledge and training in mental health issues can be ensured. There are also questions about the most appropriate arrangements for the management and supervision of personal advisors. The role of the Connexions service and personal advisors is discussed in Chapter 20 but there is still much debate about how the service will operate in practice.

Suggestions for Developing Specialist Mental Health Services for Young People Leaving Care

Listed below are suggestions to promote the development of specialist mental health services for young people who are leaving care. Different primary care trusts and local authorities will have a wide range of different local factors and influences, which need to be taken into account when considering strategic developments. The points below are however generic and should be applicable to most locations:

1. A multi-agency mapping exercise should be undertaken to identify the role of different agencies, professionals and voluntary groups in meeting the mental health needs of young people leaving care.
2. Social service departments should consider the establishment of specialist leaving care teams if they have not already been developed.
3. Social services/leaving care teams should develop a clear strategy for meeting the mental health needs for young people leaving care.
4. Specific attention should be given to the accessibility of specialist mental health services for 16–18-year-olds.
5. Adolescent mental health service providers may need to reconsider and improve the accessibility of in-patient psychiatry beds specifically for looked after children and care leavers.
6. The accessibility and 'user friendliness' of mental health services for looked after children and young people leaving care should be reviewed and the views of service users sought.
7. Consideration should be given to the ability of mental health services to provide an emergency response and an outreach model of service delivery.
8. Specialist mental health professionals should be available for consultation to professionals and workers in leaving care teams and voluntary agencies.
9. Specialist mental health teams and leaving care teams should together develop a strategy to address mental health training and supervision needs.
10. Specialist mental health teams and foster care services should together develop a strategy to address the mental health training and supervision needs of foster carers.
11. Specialist mental health teams and residential teams should together develop a strategy to address the mental health training and supervision needs of residential social workers and practitioners.
12. Local authorities should develop a strategy for developing the role of personal advisors, with particular attention paid to their role in the management of mental health problems.

References

Arcelus, J., Bellerby, T. and Vostanis, P. (1999) A Mental Health Service for Young People in the Care of the Local Authority, *Clinical Child Psychology and Psychiatry* 4: 2, 233–45.

Bebbington, A. and Miles, J. (1989) The Background of Children Who Enter Local Authority Care, *British Journal of Social Work* 19: 349–68.

Biehal, N., Clayden, J., Stein, M., et al. (1995) *Moving on: Young People and Leaving Care Schemes*. London, The Stationery Office.

Broad, B. (1998) *Young People Leaving Care: Life After the Children Act 1989*, London, Jessica Kingsley.

Buchanan, A. (1999) Are Care Leavers Significantly Dissatisfied and Depressed in Adult Life? *Adoption and Fostering* 23: 35–40.

Cheung, S. Y. and Buchanan, A. (1997) Malaise Scores in Adulthood of Children and Young People Who Have Been in Care, *Journal of Child Psychology and Psychiatry* 38: 575–80.

The Stationery Office. (1998) *Children Looked After by Local Authorities*, London, The Stationery Office.

Department of Health. (1998) *The Quality Protects Programme: Transforming Children's Services*. London, Department of Health.

Department of Health. (1999) *Framework for the Assessment of Children in Need and their Families*, Consultation draft. London, Department of Health.

Department of Health. (2000) *Children Looked After in England: 1999–2000*. Bulletin 2000/24. London, Department of Health.

Dimigen, G., Del Priore, C., Butler, S., et al. (1999) Psychiatric Disorder Among Children at Time of Entering Local Authority Care: Questionnaire Survey, *British Medical Journal* 319: 675.

Dumaret, A., Coppel-Batsch, M. and Couraud, S. (1997) Adult Outcome of Children Reared for Long-term Periods in Foster Families, *Child Abuse and Neglect* 21: 911–27.

Goodman, R. (1997) Child Mental Health: An Overextended Remit, *British Medical Journal* 314: 813–4.

Garrett, L. (1992) *Leaving Care and After*. London, National Children's Bureau.

Hagell, A. and Newburn, T. (1994) *Persistent Young Offenders*, London, Policy Studies Institute.

Hengeller, S. W. (1999) Multisystemic Therapy: An Overview of Clinical Procedures, Outcomes, and Policy Implications, *Child Psychology and Psychiatry Review* 4: 1, 2–10.

Kazdin, A. E. (1997) Practitioner Review: Psychological Treatments for Conduct Disorder in Children, *Journal of Child Psychology and Psychiatry* 38: 161–78.

Koprowska, J. and Stein, M. (2000) The Mental Health of 'Looked After' Young People, in Aggleton, P., Hurry, J. and Warwick, I. (Eds.) *Young People and Mental Health*. London, John Wiley & Sons Ltd.

McCann, J. B., James, A., Wilson, S., et al. (1996) Prevalence of Psychiatric Disorders in Young People in the Care System. *British Medical Journal* 313: 1529–30.

Meltzer, H., Gatward, R., Goodman, R. and Ford, T. (2000) *The Mental Health of Children and Adolescents in Great Britain*. London, Office for National Statistics, The Stationery Office.

Morgan, S. (1999) *Care about Education: A Joint Training Curriculum for Supporting Children in Public Care*, London, National Children's Bureau.

Phillips, J. (1997) Meeting the Psychiatric Needs of Children in Foster Care: Social Workers' Views, *Psychiatric Bulletin* 21: 609–11.

Richardson, J. and Joughin, C. (2000) *The Mental Health Needs of Looked After Children*. London, Gaskell.

Rutter, M., Giller, H. and Haggell, A. (1998) *Antisocial Behaviour by Young People*, Cambridge, Cambridge University Press.

Saunders, L., and Broad, B. (1997) *The Health Needs of Young People Leaving Care*, Leicester, De Montfort University.

Utting, W., Baines, C., Stuart, M., et al. (1997). *People Like Us: The Report of the Review of the Safeguards for Children Living Away from Home*, London, The Stationery Office.

Street, C. (2000) *Whose Crisis? Meeting the Needs of Children and Young People With Serious Mental Health Problems*, London, Young Minds.

17. Enabled by the Act? The Reframing of Aftercare Services for Young Disabled People

Julie Harris, Parveneh Rabiee and Mark Priestley

This chapter aims to explore some of the historical contributors to the current situation with regard to the provision of after care services for young disabled people, and draws out some of the service implications of the Children (Leaving Care) Act. It calls for a joined up approach to policy and planning that will facilitate the development of integrated and specialist services to a group of young people who face many barriers to social inclusion. It is written primarily for aftercare service providers who, for the first time, are facing the challenge of assisting in the removal of those barriers.

This chapter draws substantially on the views and experiences of young disabled people who participated in the 'Whatever Next? Young Disabled People Leaving Care' project – a research collaboration between the First Key, the Centre for Disability Studies at the University of Leeds and Bradford Local Authority Social Services.

Introduction

The implementation of the Children (Leaving Care) Act 2000 in October of this year marks the culmination of over 20 years of campaigning and lobbying activity by the 'leaving care world', calling for the tightening of local authority responsibility towards those young people leaving public care. Research undertaken from the 1970s onwards, though small scale and qualitative, has consistently identified the poor outcomes of this group of young people in comparison with those of the general population, raising the profile of these issues and contributing substantially to national information and debate.

The necessity for such research is underlined by Broad (1998) who notes its contribution in identifying policy and practice issues, in enabling at least loose comparison of service provision on a national basis and in the production of reliable data that can contribute to national statistics, management information and subsequent service planning.

Amongst the voices that have contributed to the debate over these three decades are politicians, policy makers, practitioners in the public and voluntary sectors, social researchers and not least, the young people themselves who have effectively made themselves heard through campaigning organisations such as the National Association for Young People in Care (NAYPIC) and more recently, A National Voice. Many young people have contributed their personal stories to the wealth of local research information that cumulatively gives us the bigger picture.

The same cannot be said, however, for the significant group of young disabled people 'looked after' by local authorities. Despite representing some 25% of the 'looked after' population young disabled people are seldom referred to in the context of leaving care. In comparison to other young people looked after, we know virtually nothing about these young people, where they are or what happens to them. Morris (1995) highlights the failure of researchers, lobbyists and campaigners to focus on a group of young people who may spend a significant proportion of their childhood and adolescence being cared for away from the family home. It is estimated that of the 360,000 disabled children in the UK, 46,000 are 'looked after'.

There may be a number of explanations for the paucity of information, not the least of which is the tendency for local authorities to categorise young people 'looked after' and young disabled people as distinct service user groups. Historically, disability services have been segregated and located 'offside' the mainstream children's service, albeit with the intention of ensuring the dedication and protection of resources. An absence of 'joined up' thinking however has resulted in an either or approach to service delivery and a mutual exclusivity that has left aftercare services inaccessible to most young disabled people. In some instances this has resulted in young people, particularly those with learning difficulties, being swallowed by the gap between the two.

There is evidence that this segregation has also left young disabled people in receipt of services that are not subject to the usual checks and scrutiny put in place by the Children Act 1989. Drawing on research undertaken by the Who Cares? Trust the 1998 Commons Health Committee reports:

> *Some disabled children were spending time away from home in short term placements without any knowledge or involvement of social services, and some on long term placements were not being accorded the protection of the Children Act. There was little evidence of disabled children's 'wishes and feelings' about their placements being 'ascertained' (as required by the Act) and reviews of placements were overdue in a significant number of cases. There was a lack of information about disabled children receiving short- and long-term care away from home, about the services they were receiving and whether the services met their needs.*
>
> House of Commons, 1998, para 260.

Research undertaken by the Joseph Rowntree Foundation exploring the experience of disabled children at residential schools found that most education departments were unaware of their statutory responsibility under the Children Act 1989 to inform social services of any child taking up a residential placement for a period of three months or more (Abbott, Morris, and Ward, 2000).

This flags up an equally concerning implication with regard to management information and suggests that many young disabled people may be 'invisible' to mainstream children's services; they will almost certainly not have been included in the data used to calculate spend within the ringfenced budget allocated under the Children (Leaving Care) Act. The '*Whatever Next?*' report (Rabiee,

Priestley and Knowles, 2001) describes the difficulty of the researchers in identifying young disabled people who were looked after in the research population area. It seems likely that this particular local authority area is not unique in this respect and that many local authorities would need to manually collate information relating to young disabled people 'in care.' The evidence suggests that monitoring systems can rarely boast the level of sophistication necessary to identify disabled people becoming eligible for aftercare services.

That the planning and implementation of the Children (Leaving Care) Act has thrown up a corresponding gap in current service provision is perhaps unsurprising then. It seems possible, ironically, that the exclusion of some groups of young disabled people from the new arrangements (see *eligibility* below) has in fact served to highlight the eligibility of others. Historically of course, young disabled people have always been entitled to aftercare services under Section 24 of the Children Act 1989, though there is little evidence that in reality these have been delivered. The National Standards in Leaving Care produced by First Key in 1996, omit service criteria for young disabled people simply because there was insufficient information to be able to identify good practice.

For the purposes of the new legislation, children and young people are identified as disabled as defined by the Children Act 1989 (section 17 (11)). This definition, based upon the medical model of disability, is in urgent need of revision. It focuses on impairment, locating the 'problem' with the person rather than, as in the social model of disability, with the environment and social attitudes, which serve to disable the person. Morris (1998) illustrates how this definition has in effect undermined the agenda of the Children Act 1989 i.e. that of social inclusion. Section 17(10) offers three definitions of children 'in need'. The first two definitions focus on the provision of services to children that ensure a 'reasonable standard of health or development' thus encouraging a wide, needs-led approach to service provision. The third however, says simply that a young person is 'in need' if they are disabled. Section 17(11) then goes on to say:

... a child is disabled if he is blind, deaf or dumb or suffers from mental disorder of any kind or is substantially and permanently handicapped by illness, injury or congenital deformity or such other disability as may be prescribed ...

When a child falls into this category of 'in need' the emphasis is on the impairment, which qualifies them for a service, rather than on the range of needs vital to social and emotional development and well-being. This necessarily impacts on the nature of the service given resulting in a focus on the perceived difficulties caused by the impairment, rather than on the needs of the child as a developing individual and the overcoming of barriers to their social inclusion and integration. Morris illustrates how this definition has led to local authorities developing rigid service qualification criteria, based upon the level and type of impairment, and the subsequent segregation of services and social exclusion of the young people using them.

This is also the cause of the 'gap' between services where young people referred to as having 'mild to moderate learning difficulties' can often find themselves stranded between the mainstream service that is not able to provide them with the level of support they need, and specialist disability services whose definition of 'disability' does not admit them to the service.

In terms of leaving and aftercare support, the case is well made by disability services that, as part of the drive towards social inclusion and the development of effective community support mechanisms, these young people should access mainstream services rather than be further marginalised as adult service users. Mainstream services however clearly feel they have neither the expertise nor resource to provide such intensive support. The *'Whatever Next?'* report identified that this had resulted in some young people being sent to out-of-authority residential placements because of an inability to meet need locally, or inadequate knowledge of the local resources available. Clearly both service streams need to take responsibility and initiative in defining the intersection that spans the two, to proactively create that safety net.

It is clear to see how the service-led approach as promoted by the Section 17 (11) definition has translated into an absence of aftercare support to young disabled people. It is also clear that if meaningful and effective aftercare support services are to be provided in the future they must be needs led and aspirational for disabled young people as for their non-disabled peers. They must be based on the fundamental premise that all young people leaving care have the right of equal access to education, information, employment, leisure, housing etc. and to the life chances and opportunities that will enable them to fulfil their personal potential as human beings. A good aftercare service is one that focuses on breaking down the barriers that prevent them from doing so.

The Children (Leaving Care) Act 2000 and the Disability Discrimination Act compel the provision of equal access to services and the development of effective aftercare support mechanisms. The following section calls for a fundamental shift in our approach to providing aftercare services to young disabled people whose needs '... will not suddenly and fundamentally cease when they do leave care' (Regulations and Guidance Ch.4(30)) and suggests that what is called for is a re-framing of aftercare services in providing integrated and specialist services with the necessary flexibility to effectively meet need.

Re-framing the Service

Although young disabled people in a variety of circumstances have been eligible in the past for Section 24 support, these services have rarely been forthcoming and it is fair to say that in the leaving care world, aftercare services have not, in general, been developed to meet the needs of these young people to a satisfactory level. The Children (Leaving Care) Act 2000 therefore presents these services with a considerable challenge, not just in terms of the range of supports they offer but also in terms of their location, level of inter-agency collaboration and other such management issues.

The following headings highlight some of the strategic implications for service managers and suggest guidelines that may be taken into consideration when devising new frameworks for services that can meet the diversity of need.

Management and location

Recent research (Stein, 1997; Broad, 1998) in conjunction with Department of Health information demonstrates the enormous range in levels of aftercare service provision across the country. The model of service delivery likewise differs from one local authority to another and these variables, combined with the alternative arrangements for the support of young disabled people, set limits to the degree to which it is possible to prescribe a joint service framework.

Any such development should however take into consideration the structural location of the two services in relation to each other and the potential area of intersection between them. Aftercare services, if delivered in-house, range from integrated services attached to mainstream fieldwork teams (particularly in large county authorities) to centrally based and independent aftercare teams. In some cases these may provide a 16 plus social work service with case management responsibility, and in others a more specialist role providing a holistic range of support services. If contracted out to the voluntary sector the service is again likely to be comprised of a team. Some local authorities have developed multi-agency teams along similar lines to the youth offending teams.

The implementation of the Children (Leaving Care) Act presents a prime opportunity to develop services that are increasingly reflective of need and many local authorities are doing so through a combination of Quality Protects funding and the Children (Leaving Care) Act ring fenced budget. This may be achieved either through the creation of a dedicated post and active recruitment of staff with a background in disability and transition or through joint working and the development of rolling secondment arrangements, for example. In this sense it is at the discretion of the local authority to use flexibility and creativity in developing arrangements that are realistic for the population, geographical area and existing service structure.

Needless to say there is a training need for all staff working within the aftercare field regardless of any arrangements to provide a dedicated resource. The *'Whatever Next?'* report identified that many staff working within the field felt uncomfortable about working with young disabled people and unsuitably qualified to provide effective support (p74). It is essential that staff receive disability equality training to raise their understanding of the barriers that young disabled people are facing so that they will have confidence in supporting them to overcome them.

Consideration should also be given to the geographical location of aftercare services in ensuring that they are accessible by public transport and in areas that young people perceive as safe. The accessibility of buildings may also be an issue and services should ensure that adapted equipment is available.

A multi-agency approach

The Children (Leaving Care) Act places renewed emphasis on the responsibility of the local authority as a whole to develop an effective response to the needs of care leavers. In order to ensure that social services are able to access the comprehensive range of supports required it is essential that a corporate and multi-agency strategy be developed, initiated at committee level, and declared through a clear philosophical commitment within the children's service plan. This should include a statement relating to the support of young people with different needs including young disabled people and should reflect the duties that many of the statutory services have with regard to this group.

Any such multi-agency strategy should be inclusive of providers of services to young disabled people including in-house children with disabilities teams, transitions teams and adult teams and any voluntary sector service providers or community organisations.

The Regulations and Guidance to the Act (Ch.3 (11)) places a particular emphasis on the importance of good links between voluntary and statutory agencies and the clear signposting of services for young people. Voluntary services may have a specialist role to play in providing young disabled people with the advice, information and support that they need.

Policy and procedures

Likewise, all aftercare policies need to contain a separate section describing arrangements for the support of young disabled people. Any local qualification criteria should be mutually determined by the relevant services and cover a range of impairment recognising the tendency for some young people, especially those with mild to moderate learning difficulties to fall through the support net.

Policy and procedures should include:

- Arrangements for the management of information between services.
- Arrangements for the allocation of (leaving care) personal advisors.
- The arrangements for transfer to adult services.
- Clarity around how the assessment of need and pathway planning process coincides with the transitional review process.
- Arrangements for working with schools (given that young disabled people will often remain in school until they are 19).
- Arrangements with housing and other local accommodation providers to ensure the availability of a choice of safe, appropriate and affordable accommodation.
- Arrangement with the Connexions and careers services.
- Arrangements with further education, training providers and local employers to provide real opportunities for educational and vocational career development.
- Inter-authority agreements that clarify arrangements for young people placed out of authority, including those relating to health.

Roles, responsibilities and process must be very clearly defined between aftercare and the mainstream children's service, children with disabilities teams, transitions services, adult teams, health, education, housing, etc.

Protocols should also be developed with private service providers to ensure that arrangements for aftercare support are in place and there is a system to alert the mainstream service as to the existence of these young people.

Management information – monitoring and evaluation

In theory the aftercare service should be aware of all young people becoming eligible under the Act at 16 or over and this must be no different for young disabled people, regardless of any plans for them post 18. This will require the development of information systems in conjunction with children's disability teams and/or transitions teams and the mainstream children's service.

As well as these systems identifying the disabled young people looked after population who will become eligible for services there will be other groups about whom information will need to be gathered. Systems need to be capable of monitoring, for example, the level of respite use, and identifying those young people who become eligible by exceeding one month's continuous service use (Regulation 3; 2(a)). Young people in out-of-authority placements who become eligible or relevant must also be clearly identified. There are also those young people who will qualify for support under Section 24 who may be using respite services (and qualify via Section 22) or those accommodated by a health or education authority.

Management information systems are a necessity in monitoring the level of service use, thus enabling accurate forecasting of future service requirements. All such systems should be able to record important information such as young people's ethnic origin, and any particular religious or cultural requirements that the service will need to take account of. Young disabled people who are parents, on remand or asylum seekers are likely to face additional barriers and require support. The ongoing collation and monitoring of this information will enable the service to finely tune itself in being genuinely responsive to need.

There are, of course, requirements to monitor outcomes for young disabled people under Quality Protects in terms of education, employment and accommodation outcomes, also 19th year contacts, as there are for other young people. Protocols with other statutory providers for the sharing of information will obviously be required as for any other young person leaving care. There may be other outcomes in addition that services may wish to monitor, such as the take up of direct payments where such schemes are in place (Regulations and Guidance Ch.4 (26)).

Monitoring is an essential component of effective service evaluation, another being that of young people's assessment of services received. Young disabled people should therefore be involved in regular evaluation and consultation exercises, and their views fed through into service development.

The Children (Leaving Care) Act 2001

Eligibility

Young disabled people are entitled, as any other young people, to the provisions of the Act regardless of any other status (Regulations and Guidance Ch.2 (4). This includes young disabled people who have been placed out of area in a special education residential placement (see below), and young people who would have qualified for support on their 16th birthday but are in hospital, who will be considered as relevant (regulation 4).

A transition from children's to adult services at 18 should not affect a young disabled person's entitlement under the new Act. The young person will, in any case, have been in receipt of assessment, pathway planning, and personal advisor services etc from the age of 16. It follows that their status will change to former relevant, as for other young people, on leaving children's services.

It should be noted here that *relevant* young people who are defined as disabled under the Income Support (General) Regulations 1987 *will not* be subject to the exemption from benefits rule and will still therefore be entitled to Income Support or Jobseekers Allowance and any relevant premiums. They will not however be entitled to Housing Benefit. Any amount claimed in benefits will therefore be taken into account when assessing their financial support needs as part of the pathway planning process, within which they are still entitled to financial assistance as appropriate, with education, training, employment, accommodation and general welfare (Section 23B(8) and Regulation 11).

Qualifying young people

Although the personal circumstance of many young disabled people may disqualify them from entitlements under the Children (Leaving Care) Act, Section 24 of the Children Act 1989 may still be used to offer discretionary support. This may include young people aged 16 or above, whose respite service use has not exceeded one month (continuous) but who qualify as 'looked after' young people under Section 22 (Children Act 1989); those young people accommodated by a health or education authority for three months or more on or after their sixteenth birthday; and those who left care before October 2001 who would otherwise have been eligible.

It should be noted that there are additional responsibilities on local authorities under Section 24. These are:

- To keep in touch with local authority care leavers as appropriate in order to discharge the functions under 24A and 24B.
- To provide assistance with education and training up to the age of 24.
- To provide accommodation in the vacation for higher education courses or residential further education courses, where necessary (Section 24B (5)).

Who misses out?

The 'respite rule' may exclude some young disabled people who have a genuine need for the support offered by the Act. Those young disabled people who are regular users of short break or respite services for periods of time 'none of which individually exceeds four weeks,' and who return to their parents or person with parental responsibility after each placement will not be entitled to the new provisions (Regulation 3; 2(a)). This is based on the premise that these young people remain the responsibility of the parent or person with parental responsibility, rather than the local authority. This raises concerns however, for the young people that are very heavy short break service users to the point that they are in effect 'looked after' outside of the family home for the significant majority of their time. In this situation there may be a question mark as to where the responsibility for assisting that young person in their preparation for adult life lies in practice; the parent may spend so little time with them as to make this role implausible and currently there is no responsibility with service providers to fulfil such a role. In many cases these young people will not have an allocated social worker as additional services (to respite), may not have been required.

There is also an issue around the co-ordination of services for those young people who use more than one service, but who are unlikely to have a key figure with an overview of their pattern of service use. The *'Whatever Next?'* research discovered some young disabled people living in respite care full time. Without management information, these young people are effectively 'invisible' to the system and will almost certainly not be accounted for within the 'looked after' figures for the purposes of calculation of spend within the ringfenced budget.

The new legislation fails to acknowledge that while transitions for young people leaving care, in general, may be premature, the opposite may be true for young disabled people who are likely to remain 'looked after' until a much later age. This may have implications for young disabled people currently continuing to be accommodated by social services after the age of 18 however who will lose their 'looked after' status and ostensibly, their eligibility under the Act. This seems nonsensical, especially given the fact that many young disabled people actually remain at school until they are 19. It can be argued that the local authority still has the power to assist under Section 24 of the Children Act but in an environment of stretched resources this is a discretionary responsibility unlikely to be fulfilled.

Delivering the Service

Whilst the Regulations and Guidance include a fairly comprehensive section (Chapter 4) in relation to young disabled people and detail specific arrangements where appropriate, the new Act is primarily written and aimed at developing supports for young non-disabled people leaving care. One of the key findings of the *'Whatever Next?'* research was that

although there may be a great deal of shared experience between young disabled people and other care leavers, the issues that arise for them may be substantially different or do so with different emphasis. Unless care is taken, implementation may inadvertently discriminate in failing to take account of their particular needs. It is therefore vital that disabled young people's views and experiences fundamentally inform service development.

This last section, rather than following the prescriptions of the new Act, identifies areas that young disabled people and their parents or carers have flagged up as being of particular significance or that are likely to throw up different practice implications that will need to be taken account of in planning. Quotes are taken from the text of *'Whatever Next?'* and illustrate some young people's and carers' views.

Assessment and pathway planning

They didn't tell me I was going to have a review. They just did it without me knowing. I'd get to know on the last day ... If they'd put it, to what it was all about, I'd have gone with them, sat down and listened to them.

Harry, young person.

It will not take time [the transition meeting]. All they want is my signature.

Parent.

Anyone who has worked in supporting young disabled people through transition, and any young person who has been in receipt of services, will be aware of the nightmarish complexity that characterises assessment and transition planning. Add to this the new duty to undertake a full assessment of need (Schedule 2 Paragraph 19B(4) and section 23B (3)) and the requirements of pathway planning, and duplication and bureaucracy threaten to overwhelm the system completely. It is vital therefore that transition policies be developed between the relevant services that steer a clear path through the minefield both for service providers and recipients. Where transitions policies are already in existence they are likely to require substantial revision to reflect the new legislative duties and the anticipated roles of a variety of services in fulfilling them.

The real challenge however will be in ensuring the full and meaningful participation of young disabled people in this process. Regulation 6 clearly places the young person at the centre of this process, stressing the requirement that their wishes and feelings be taken into account. This may be no easy task given that young people have historically struggled with a review system they find to be disempowering and irrelevant.

Very specific consideration will need to be given to the facilitation of young disabled people's involvement in this process. This will include ensuring that any physical barriers to the young person's participation are overcome by providing appropriate travel and access, ensuring that communication aids are available or enlisting the support of an interpreter, etc. The guidance requires that '... at least one person involved in the needs assessment has a clear understanding of how he (the young person) expresses his wishes and feelings'.

Not all considerations are of a practical nature however; for some young people (particularly those with a complex impairment label) there may be other barriers to be overcome including others low expectations of their ability to participate. Training must be provided to practitioners involved in planning to ensure that attitudes never impede participation.

Providing young disabled people with a record of their assessment and pathway plan may not be as straightforward as giving them a written copy. Consideration should be given to methods of recording information such as parallel text, Braille, symbols, audio or videotape etc.

The success of the assessment and pathway planning processes will greatly depend on the level of involvement the young person has in this process. This should reflect a developing autonomy, increased choice and responsibility and enable young people to experience a growing control and self determination in the decision making process. The pathway plan is essentially the young person's plan for the future, not that of social services, the parents' or their carers', and should identify their goals and aspirations. These may include very personal goals and will certainly vary with each individual. For some young disabled people the goal may not be ultimate independence in their living situation, but rather the achievement of inter-dependence or the use of direct payments, for example (Carers and Disabled Children Act 2000, and Community Care (Direct Payments) Act 1996).

It is important that the pathway planning process for young disabled people should place a particular emphasis on the removal of disabling barriers that may differ from those experienced by other young people leaving care, and may be found in every area of their lives: leisure and social opportunities, education, training, employment and accommodation. For some young people their pathway plan may identify a transition to adult services, a move that can be a source of anxiety and uncertainty if not planned carefully and in good time (Rabiee, Priestley, and Knowles, 2001). An important element of this support will be the provision of accessible and comprehensive information affording young disabled people the benefit of informed choice. This will include ensuring that young disabled people are confident in the appeal process should they not be satisfied with an assessment or planning outcome (Regulation 5).

Personal support

The role of the personal advisor is pivotal to the success of the transition to adulthood as envisaged by the Act. The Regulations and Guidance emphasise the importance of choice for young people in providing them with a range of advisors able to meet individual need, and also a commitment to the serious consideration of young people's preferences. The young people who participated in the '*Whatever Next?*' project were able to be very specific about some of the qualities they would look for in a personal advisor:

The participants in our project thought that it was very important for a personal advisor to be the right kind of person, with the right kind of experience and skills for the job:

- *A good advisor should have some similar experiences to the young person they are helping.*
- *An advisor should not be too old (maybe in their mid 20s).*

- *They might need to be someone of the same sex, if you wanted to talk about personal things.*
- *Some people would prefer to have an advisor who was also a disabled person.*
- *They should always be there for you (especially in an emergency).*
- *You should be able to contact them easily.*
- *They should be someone you can talk to in private and who understands.*
- *Once they are your advisor they should stay (and not be swapped or changed about).*
- *They should have a good personality (happy, cheerful and friendly).*
- *They should be a good listener.*
- *They should be easy to get on with and easy to talk to.*
- *They should be trustworthy and reliable.*
- *They should be unselfish and put you first.*
- *They should keep their promises.*

p66.

There will of course be practical considerations in ensuring that young people are offered an appropriate choice of advisor, and candidates may need to possess specific language or signing skills and a willingness to invest time in familiarising themselves with a young person's method of communication.

For young disabled people, as for other young people in or leaving care, consistency and the importance of individual relationships arises as an issue, again and again:

> *It takes the piss when you're with someone and they change over to the next person. It takes the piss.*
>
> Steering group member.

The personal advisor role should help to ensure more consistency but it is important that it does not overwhelm other significant relationships and supports. '*Whatever Next?*' discovered that parents, family members, and carers can often act as good advocates and can help young people access the right information and make choices (p32–3):

> *If Chris does get a place at college it would be all due to his parents working so hard to get him a place. He would otherwise be sent to a day centre or a resource centre.*
>
> Teacher.

Many of the young people talked about the importance of friendships, which were often formed through using the same services. One young man in particular, Stephen, relied on his friend Charles to help him communicate with others (p37). Leaving school and moving to college meant that Stephen was going to lose not only his best friend but also his interpreter, yet this highly significant change was not acknowledged within the planning for Stephen's future. If pathway planning and transitional support is to be effective under the Act, it must recognise the significance of such relationships to young people and definitively place young people's needs at the centre of the process. It follows that the personal advisor role should complement rather than supplant existing sources of support.

Accommodation

> *He'd have slipped through that net and ended up in a flat with no provisions. He could end up homeless on the street selling the Big Issue if he was stuck in something that wasn't appropriate.*
>
> Foster carer.

> *You can't send him out into a room in the community because he won't have enough skill ... there should be something other than a group home that has four people in it in the middle of a council estate.*
>
> Teacher.

For most non-disabled young people leaving care the most significant aspirations of the pathway planning process are likely to include independence of living situation – a young person ultimately moving into their own accommodation. Indeed the emphasis on housing issues has historically eclipsed the wealth of issues that accompany the transition to adult life. One of the challenges faced by the campaigning movement and addressed within the new legislation is the attempt to reverse the culture of premature independence.

Young disabled people moving towards adulthood may face a very different set of issues with regard to their living situation however. '*Whatever Next?*' found young people living in a range of accommodation from independent flats to full time residential placements. Young people were often placed according to the resources available rather than their needs as individuals. Examples would include Nathan who at 15 was living full time in a child respite unit and Dawn, an 18-year-old who was living in a residential home for older people (p40–1). This was also illustrated by the experience of young people placed in residential education not to fulfil identified educational needs but to solve an accommodation problem. Some young disabled people may remain indefinitely in fostering simply because no other option has ever been offered to them (p40).

The research also found that sometimes the 'disabled' label acts to limit choice and means that other factors are not taken into account when finding suitable accommodation. Beth, for example, was given a ground floor flat to ensure accessibility but was very anxious about security and felt vulnerable (p38).

An absence of, or poor, information can also limit choice and this is equally applicable to those who are making the decisions in individual care planning. The research found that a lack of knowledge of the different independent living options on behalf of childcare social workers could lead to young people being placed in specialist residential care unnecessarily (p40). This can have a tremendous impact on their lives, particularly where that placement is out of the local authority area, as was the case of Gordon who was moved against his wishes. He felt that rather than move away from his home, he wanted to try out a supported accommodation option.

'Whatever Next?' clearly identified a disturbing gap between the mainstream and specialist services that offers little middle ground for young people, particularly those with learning difficulties who were able to live independently if given adequate support. Mainstream services will need to draw substantially on the expertise and skills of the voluntary sector including the disabled people's independent living movement, in order to provide that choice of safe and appropriate accommodation.

As other care leavers, young disabled people need to be given options and choice. If this is to be meaningful they must also be provided with time and preparation. One characteristic of the transition period appears to be its rushed nature, often no doubt due to the pressure of resources. Recent research (National Foster Care Association, 2000) exploring the experiences of young people with learning difficulties flags up that ' ... the division between ... children's and adults' services is often hard and fast ... This funding and structure can act as a straitjacket, demanding long-term decisions, and sometimes enforcing changes in living arrangements, at what may be highly inappropriate times.' The impact for someone like Tariq ('*Whatever Next?*'), who was moved very abruptly to an adult unit whilst in the process of planning for transition, can be far reaching (p39) and discourage people from using services altogether:

Nobody wants me ... I was moved ... [I want] to talk to people my age ... I'd love to go [back] again.

Tariq.

All young people will need to make changes in their own time and pace and will have their own personal goals and aspirations. It is important that this is reflected in a planning process that is responsive to individual need and identifies contingency arrangements, allowing young people to experiment, make mistakes and change their minds – something that is now increasingly recognised when supporting young people not carrying the disability label, within mainstream services.

Education, training, and employment

If it weren't for me picking up that leaflet by mistake I'd still be without education to tell you the truth, because I wouldn't have known about it.

Beth.

Going to school and going to day centre is exactly the same, the only difference is the name ... she can pass the time and it will be a relief to the parents for at least eight hours ...

Father.

The consultation document *'Me, Survive Out There?'* that preceded the Children (Leaving Care) Act placed a heavy emphasis on the importance of improving educational outcomes for young people leaving care. This was accompanied by the setting of targets through the Quality Protects Programme. The guidance (Quality Protects: Transforming Children's Services (1999)) states that 'All the Governments objectives and sub-objectives apply to disabled children just as much as to non-disabled' yet the reality of the situation for young disabled people looks very different and it is likely that the targets will prove to be unattainable or irrelevant for some young people amongst this group. Some, because they have been expected to survive within the mainstream education and training services with inadequate support, and others because they have been removed from it altogether. Similarly, there are issues around the targets set for training, employment and accommodation outcomes.

The young people's experience of education seemed to vary widely. For some young people the transition to adult life was delayed and extended by staying at school until the age of 19 and was a process co-ordinated through education and the post 14 transitional planning system. It is clear that in order for the new local authority responsibilities under the Children (Leaving Care) Act to be fulfilled, greater co-ordination and coherence will need to be achieved between the relevant agencies in developing an integrated planning cycle that minimises duplication.

The research uncovered young people who had 'fallen out' of mainstream education and hence missed a great deal of their schooling and perhaps wanted to return to education later but had been unsure as to how this could happen (p47). For other young people in specialist provision there appeared to be little to distinguish education from social care. This lack of differentiation could continue at times through to the college experience with adults and carers referring to colleges as care services (as illustrated by the father's comments above).

Upon leaving school many young people found the only alternative to a day care centre was college though in reality it appeared that many further education specialist facilities in colleges duplicated the non-educational day centre function. The source or level of funding available, rather than the needs of the individual, often determined placement decisions and for some these entailed having to move away from family and friends to a different local authority area. In some cases this had led on to later disputes between local authorities as to responsibility. One foster carer told researchers:

> *[The authority] are sort of saying well he's been in another county for eight years ... when is he going to be a resident ... I don't think they know between the counties ... so I don't know what is going to happen.*

This is an issue that will be resolved through the new 'responsible local authority' role prescribed by the Act, which places responsibility firmly with the authority which last 'looked after' the young person.

This blurring between 'care' and further education unsurprisingly resulted in many young disabled people being left unable to complete or comprehend the links between education, vocational training, and employment. This was reinforced for some by their experience of attending training courses purely in order to be able to claim benefits with little prospect or expectation of future employment. Michelle had been sent on the same training course four times and lost her benefit claim when she refused to attend again:

> *I don't like doing training courses ... I'm sick of doing them, that's all I ever do ... They give you the same training course. I've already done that and I'm not doing it again ... I won't do it again. I told them I won't. They can stop my money, I don't care.*
>
> Michelle.

For some young people this sense of low expectation on the behalf of adults translated directly to their experience of trying to get work with employers:

> *Some employers won't employ you if you've got certain disabilities. You know what I mean, some employers just won't, you're an honest hard working person but if you've got*

a disability and you can't meet their standards its hard to get work these days.

                                            Beth.

They [employers] talk as though they [people with learning difficulties] could do those jobs, but they don't take them on.

                                    Foster carer.

The young people's experience, in general, was characterised by an absence of information, advice, expectation, or support with the practical challenges such as travel (p50–1). It is hoped that the personal advisor role encapsulating the Connexions function will greatly improve this situation, though meaningful pathway planning will prove elusive if greater flexibility in funding and the range of options and opportunities for these young people is not achieved.

Conclusion

Where do I go from here? I haven't got a clue what it's about or anything really, no information on it at all … I'd like to know what rights I've got now I'm nearly eighteen … that isn't clear at the moment.

                                            Beth.

When they are young and go to school … you always get … lots of information … once they get to adulthood it is like getting to the end of a cliff and there is nothing. You are just cut off and that's it.

                                           Mother.

These two quotes taken from '*Whatever Next?*' betray an experience of 'leaving care' that is characterised by poor information giving, disempowerment and the minimal involvement of young disabled people in either influencing their own life paths or the services that are offered to them. There is, however, little evidence to support this conjecture because minimal research has been undertaken investigating the outcomes of this highly marginalised group.

Broad (1998) explains the crucial necessity for national research information with respect to local/good practice in services provided for young people in general leaving the care system:

It matters to the young people because they lack national data to compare their situation with others elsewhere and how they are treated. It matters locally, for example, about how many young people leave care from such and such local authority because otherwise how do we know who they are and where they are? How are they to be assessed and helped? It matters because the absence of national reliable data leads to uninformed debates about national statistics. It matters ultimately because knowledge is power and the lack of one leads to denial of the other. Finally, and perhaps most important of all, it matters because the treatment of young people leaving care (and in care) is a political and social scandal, at least as much as it is a professional policy and practice issue.

It is a troubling thought that the 'scandal' that is the 'disabled' leaving care experience has yet to be revealed, much less acknowledged on a national level.

That the system finds ways to listen to the views and experiences of these young people must surely be the starting point. The consultation process is easily rendered meaningless if the preparedness to listen is not mirrored in individual care. The '*Whatever Next?*' report concludes that:

The involvement of young people in transitional planning is a key element of good practice, yet many young disabled people are not adequately supported to contribute. It must always be considered unacceptable to conclude that a young person cannot be involved in making choices and expressing preferences (whatever their perceived level of impairment).

The contribution of the young people to this report amply demonstrates not only their willingness but also ability to help effect change through balanced and constructive involvement:

The report should include both the good things and the bad things.

                            Steering group member.

… and also the sense of empowerment they can gain from simply being asked their view

They weren't there for me when I was young ... They won't like us talking about them. They'll probably buck their ideas up ... They will listen if they read this book ...

Helen.

The Children (Leaving Care) Act provides the means to create meaningful pathways, not just to leaving care, but also through to adult life for all 'looked after' young people. It is the duty of those with responsibility for these young people to ensure that, in the absence of prescription within the legislation, young disabled people are supported fairly and equitably and provided with the same opportunities for developing and achieving their individual potential as their non-disabled peers. The challenge to mainstream, aftercare and disability services alike, is to ensure these young people do not get left behind again.

Footnote: this chapter arises from a one-year research project by First Key (the UK National Leaving Care Advisory Service), with funding from the National Lottery Charities Board (award number RB217887) and the Economic and Social Research Council (award number R000271078).

References

Abbott, D., Morris, J. and Ward, L. (2000) *Disabled Children and Residential Schools: A Study of Local Authority Policy and Practice*, Norah Fry Research Centre.

Broad, B. (1998) *Young People Leaving Care: Life after the Children Act 1989*, London, Jessica Kingsley.

Biehal, N., Clayden, J., Stein, M. and Wade, J. (1995) *Moving on: Young People and Leaving Care Schemes*, London: Department of Health.

Department of Health. (1998) *Health Committee Second Report: Children Looked After by Local Authorities*, London, HMSO.

Department of Health. (1999) *Me, Survive, Out There?* London, HMSO.

First Key. (1996) *Standards in Leaving Care: Report of the National Working Group*. Leeds, First Key.

Morris, J. (1998) *Accessing Human Rights: Disabled children and the Children Act*, Essex, Barnardo's.

Morris, J. (1995) *Gone Missing?* London, Who Cares? Trust.

NFCA. (2000) *Rights of Passage: Young Disabled People; The Transition from Foster Care to Adult Life*, London, NFCA.

Rabiee, P., Priestley, M., Knowles, J. (2000) *Whatever Next? Young Disabled People Leaving Care*, Leeds, First Key.

Stein, M. (1997) *What Works in Leaving Care*, Essex, Barnardo's.

18. Educating Care Leavers: A Report on Research into the Aspirations and Attitudes of Care Leavers

Rebecca Berkley

They tell you at school that it doesn't matter if you don't do well your exams, and that you can always do them again another time. But when I left school I found they were wrong, and now I am having to study and work, and bring up my daughter at the same time and it's hard. They should tell you the truth: if you don't get your exams when you're at school you're nowhere.

Care leaver attending a summer school
at Southampton University, 2001.

The need to educate care leavers is one of the highest priorities that local authorities have for supporting looked after children. Education is the most effective long-term solution for tackling problems of social exclusion. It promotes independence of mind and understanding of the value of social responsibility. Education develops self-esteem by building social relations with peers and with elders and by delivering qualifications which can be converted into personal and financial rewards. Those without education are at a personal and an institutional disadvantage.

The Children (Leaving Care) Act of 2001 recognises the low levels of academic achievement demonstrated by care leavers to date. It states that local authorities have a statutory duty to support and monitor care leavers into further and higher education (FE and HE), training and employment from age 16–21 (24 if in full time education). The government has also established two targets as far as improving the educational attainment of looked after children and care leavers, namely:

- Increase to 50% by 2000–1 the proportion of children leaving care aged 16 or over with a GCSE or GNVQ qualification; and to 75% by 2002–3.

- Increase to 15% by 2003–4 the proportion of children leaving care aged 16 and over with 5 GCSEs at grade A-C (DoH 1999a).

Much of this support and guidance is to be provided by the Connexions service, a 'one stop shop' for guidance, advice and support in making decisions about life, education and career *http://www.connexions.gov.uk*. The intention is for education, training, employment, social services and local authorities to work together in supporting care leavers.

However, care leavers present a number of emotional and educational problems which can mitigate against them being successful in post compulsory education (schooling is compulsory in the UK up to the age of 16; however, qualifications leading to university entrance are normally taken at age 18). They require particular support and guidance from teachers, carers and social workers at this stage of their development.

At the University of Southampton the Dolphin Measurement Tool (DMT) (Berkley and Wheal, forthcoming) has been designed to provide a personal, social and academic profile of an individual who wishes to enter post-compulsory education but who may lack appropriate academic qualifications. The measurement tool evaluates attitudes to education, employment, physical and mental health, family and environment. It provides a diagnosis and profile of *needs*. This tool has been used to measure the needs of a sample of care leavers aged 16–21.

This chapter discusses the educational experience of care leavers, outlining reasons for the low educational attainment in many of these young people. It presents a profile of the care leavers entering post compulsory education, focusing on their attitudes and aspirations, self-image and self-esteem, communication skills and relationships with others. The material draws on the initial research findings from the DMT. The chapter concludes with a commentary on the issues facing care and educational professionals supporting care leavers into further and higher education.

The Educational Experience of Looked-after Children and Care Leavers

Many care leavers experience a dysfunctional and disrupted education, leaving them with low expectations of their potential for educational achievement. The educational achievement of looked-after children is directly related to the stability of the care environment they experience. Moving home addresses and schools is a common experience for young people with an unstable care history, and many children experience numerous and sometimes unplanned moves of home. Each move may also mean a change of school. However, research indicates that after about a year of stable care the educational attainment of looked-after children comes into line with the general population of children of the same age. Those with unsettled care histories gain few qualifications (DoH, 1999a; Garnett, 1992).

The educational attainment of care leavers is similarly directly linked to their care experience. Those who have experienced stable and supportive care when aged 16–19 are far more likely to complete education and training courses, and demonstrate the rigorous personal organisation necessary for successful academic work (Biehal et al., 1995). These students are able to develop good levels of competence in the key skills now certificated in the 14–19 curriculum (communication, application of number and information technology) as well as the wider key skills of working with others, improving own learning and performance and problem solving (*http://www.qca.org.uk/nq/ks/*). However, the educational attainment of care leavers is very low. Garnett (1992) suggests that the main reasons for low educational attainment in care leavers are social background, pre-care experiences, disrupted schooling when in care,

low expectations of carers, and a lack of continuity in care.

Vastly higher numbers of these young people have registered special education needs compared to the population as a whole. However, anecdotal evidence suggests that looked-after children and care leavers have a similar proportion of 'biological' special needs to the rest of the population: conditions such as autism, speech and hearing impairments. This suggests that most special educational needs of care leavers are 'environmental,' that is, a result of the disrupted education these young people have experienced and specifically related to poor attendance, truancy and school exclusion.

These 'environmental' special needs relate to difficulties with perception, memory, visual processing, analysing information, and applying knowledge. They are often linked to poor socialisation and behavioural difficulties. For example, a student may demonstrate difficulties with literacy, being a slow reader and having limited writing ability. This may be linked to problems with concentrating, the student may have a short attention span and be easily distracted into behaving disruptively. Dealing with these problems requires the school to provide specific educational support in developing reading and writing skills and knowledge, and to facilitate the students' development of study skills and positive behaviour through good practice in subject teaching and the pastoral care programme.

Educational research and current practice agree that students with these kinds of problems respond best to structured guidance delivered consistently by all their teachers. Students with these problems need time to improve, these are problems which take years of effective schooling to resolve. Sadly, this is exactly the kind of focused and dependable support that a looked after child with an unstable care history is likely to miss. A student with the problems mentioned above is likely to continue to be disruptive and difficult when moved into a new school, as it takes time for the student to settle into the routine required for them to progress. Assessment and record keeping of the young person may be adequate within a school, but is often patchy taken over the whole care history. Records are not always passed on when the young person moves schools and moves to new areas.

A move of school for a child in a settled family with supportive parents can be an ordeal, involving loss of friends, familiar teachers and surroundings. Usually a caring parent will smooth the way and a school's normal admissions and pastoral and peer support systems will assist the child. For the child in public care, who may have suffered abuse or harm in his or her own family, the change of school may be sudden, following an emergency placement, part-way through a school term. There may be no information about the child's circumstances given to the school; the class teacher may know nothing about what being in public care means; carers may have no record of the child's educational history.

The Educational Attainment of Care Leavers

Care leavers generally have few educational qualifications. The Department of Health presented statistics on the educational qualifications of care leavers for the first time in 2000 (DoH, 2000). Figure 1 summarises the main findings of this report. The total number of young people who left the care of local authorities in England aged 16 or over during the year ending 31 March 2000 was 6800, 3800 males and 3000 females.

The figures make for uncomfortable reading. 70% (n. 4800) of care leavers in 1999–2000 left care with no qualifications, compared to 6% of all year 11 students nationally (Joint Council for General Qualifications, ***http://www.jcgq.org. uk/***). These students leave compulsory education having failed to achieve entry level in the National Framework for Qualifications for 14–19-year-olds (Figure 2). The current UK educational system has codified the thinking and learning skills present in vocational and academic qualifications for students aged 14–19, identifying the value of using the core skills of numeracy, literacy, ICT, working with others, improving one's own performance and communication in a range of subject areas. Results from previous statistical analyses of educational attainment in care leavers presents a similar picture (Broad, 1994; DoH/SSI, 1997;

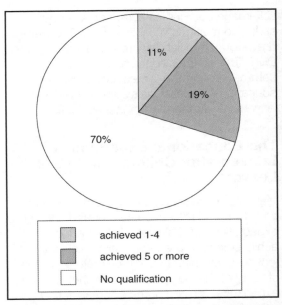

Figure 1: Percentage of care leavers with given number of GCSEs at grades A-G or GNVQs

NCB, 1992). Approximately one in a hundred care leavers go to university, compared with one in three school leavers in the general population.

The sample of care leavers represented in Figure 1 does, of course, include many of the most vulnerable of young people in society. Biehal et al. (1995) point out that lack of educational attainment does not necessarily equate with a lack of professional support, but that the problems of the individual are intense and require very detailed assistance, made harder to deliver by the young person living independently once they leave care.

More positively, in 1999-2000, 19% of care leavers achieved 5 or more GCSEs grade A-G (14% of males and 26% of females). However the distribution of figures indicates that care leavers often fail to achieve higher level passes in the core subjects of English, Mathematics, Science and Modern Foreign Languages. In 1999–2000 only 4% of young people left care with at least five GCSEs with higher grade passes (grades A-C, level 2 NVQ) (14% of males and 26% of females) compared to 48% of year 11 students nationally. The figures also indicate that females achieve higher and more numerous qualifications than males.

The legend for Figure 1 reads:

- achieved 1-4
- achieved 5 or more
- No qualification

Level of qualification	General			Vocationally-related	Occupational
5	Higher level qualifications *degrees offered by colleges and universities and diplomas of equivalent standing*				Level 5 NVQ
4					Level 4 NVQ
3 Advanced level	A level	Free standing mathematics unit level 3		Vocational A level (Advanced GNVQ)	Level 3 NVQ
2 Intermediate level	GCSE grades A–C	Free standing mathematics unit level 2		Intermediate GNVQ	Level 2 NVQ
1 Foundation level	GCSE grades D–G	Free standing mathematics unit level 1		Foundation GNVQ	Level 1 NVQ
Entry level	Certificate of (educational) achievement				

Figure 2. The National Qualifications Framework (http://www.qca.org.uk/nq/framework/)

Statistical trends indicate that in the past 20 years, young people generally have started to make the transition from education into the labour market later in life. In 1999–2000 over 70% of 16–17-year-olds were in full-time education and 11% were in employment, compared to just less than 50% in education and 33% in employment in 1984. Employment now depends on gaining FE and HE qualifications. By leaving school without significant qualifications, care leavers are unlikely to make the transition into employment, and will be left even further behind their contemporaries.

The Dolphin Measurement Tool

The DMT surveyed the attitudes and aspirations of 16–18-year-olds attending the Southampton University Widening Participation Summer School in 2001 – see the Conclusion for further information on the summer school. The sample included a significant proportion of care leavers. Analysis of the results provides a personal and social profile of the young person who wishes to enter post-compulsory education and identifies the particular fears, concerns and anxieties demonstrated by care leavers in this situation.

Academic measurement tools are legion, and provide the background of American and English selective education (Sax, 1997; APA, 1995; **http://www.collegeboard.com www.iscis.uk.net**). The majority of tests of academic aptitude are built around assessment of numeracy, literacy and verbal reasoning skills, or focus on school curriculum areas and assume prior knowledge of the school curriculum. These tests are concerned with the validity of academic knowledge and results are measured against standardised statistical analysis of a body of previous results. Whilst useful in some contexts, these results favour those who have studied in educational systems which focus on abstract and theoretical knowledge. Such testing does not allow for a representation of experience gathered outside the confines of the school curriculum (Gardner, 1993).

There is a move against summative assessments of this kind and a recognition of the value of formative assessments in classroom learning (Torrance and Pryor, 1998). Personal and social factors are a key determinant in an individual's academic achievement. It is difficult to be successful in education if a young person is at odds with themselves or the world. The Dolphin measurement tool recognises the value of experiential learning beyond the school curriculum in forming a young person's attitudes towards further and higher education.

The measurement tool comprises three parts: a questionnaire completed by the young people, evaluation of the young people's work during the summer school by the facilitators that worked with them, and observations of selected young people by the researchers. Facilitators were undergraduate and postgraduate students in the university who supervised the young people, and worked alongside them on the projects completed in each faculty. Qualitative analysis of this data allows for statistical analysis of responses of subgroups in the sample. Analysis of the quality of responses from individuals provides a rich resource of opinion and commentary from all the young people represented. Significant sub groups in the sample were gender, young people from minority ethnic backgrounds, and those without parents as next of kin.

The facilitators' reports focused on young peoples' attitudes and motivation to the work completed during the summer school, with particular reference to teamwork, independent work, their use of transferable skills and key skills, and the relationships they created during the week.

The questionnaire is in seven sections, focusing on:

1. *Views on education*, including review of working style and relationships with teachers and other students.
2. *Aspirations and attitudes to life*, including commentary on career choices in the short, medium and long term, and investigation of the young person's understanding of how they can achieve these goals.
3. *Basic skills and life skills*, asking the young person to evaluate themselves as a worker and their reactions to real-life situations of stress and crisis.
4. *Identity and the community* which focuses on the young person's self-image in the context of the world around them including investigation of their worries, views on nationality and ethnicity, crisis, and self-knowledge.

5. *Family, friends and the community*, asking students to comment on the people they have lived with and the influences these people have had on them and on future relationships.
6. *Income and housing*, in order to identify the young person's awareness of their financial needs, and their perceptions of how to manage money.
7. *Physical and mental health* in order to identify young persons' perceptions of the relevance of good physical and mental health to success in life.

Profiling Care Leavers Going into Further and Higher Education

Aspirations and attitudes to study

Analysis of the data indicates that students who live with their next-of-kin are far more likely to regard education as a means of improving their lives and achieving their long-term goals. Students who do not live with their parents demonstrate a greater antipathy towards the idea of further study, and reported more frequently that they did not believe that study would get them further in their lives. They are also much more likely to say they do not have any real ambitions for five or ten years hence, and that they do not feel that they could be successful in a job or at university.

Students who aspire to FE and HE draw on a range of sources of advice when choosing education and training courses, but the views and opinions of parents and family are consistently most influential. Parents shape a child's perceptions of work and career from early childhood, by making explicit the rewards that education provides in terms of lifestyle and opportunity. A lack of contact with parents will result in the young person seeking other role models which may not be so positive. Although the young person exerts more control over where they choose to study and the choice of subjects as they get older, parents will influence a young person's choices by suggesting particular pathways through education. A young person's perception of career fields is also built from the contracted, delegated and derived images of adult work they experience, and again parents and adults in the family are the most immediate source of images of adult life (Foskett and Helmsley-Brown, 2001).

The data indicates that students who want to study do so as they have clearly defined ambitions. Discussions with young people indicate that those who live with their parents generally regard education as a gateway to further employment, and many regard it as an essential hurdle before achieving lifestyle and career goals. Care leavers often express desires for achieving long term ambitions, but may not have a realistic perception of the self-management required to achieve them. One care leaver expressed an intention to take performing arts GNVQ in order to become a singer and dancer, but also commented that she hated the college as she found the work hard and thought the teachers too strict as she received low grades for her work. She did not apparently see the connection between her low achievement and frequent absences from college.

Self esteem and self image

Examining the correlation between students who live with their next-of-kin and self-image indicates that those who have not recently lived with their parents are generally less self-confident. In addition, males generally report that they are more confident in school or college than females. Students who do not live with their parents report worries about their looks, being overweight and not having enough friends. Having '*people talking about me behind my back*' and '*making a fool of myself in front of my friends*' is a particular concern for these students. One care leaver at the summer school was particularly anxious that other students should not find out she was living on the dole, as she thought the others would call her a 'waster.' She wanted people to know she was attending a course in ICT at college in order that she would be able to find employment.

Reports from facilitators and observation indicated that a lack of self-confidence in care leavers does not automatically translate into quiet and withdrawn behaviour. Some care leavers were reported as being noisy and difficult to manage in group work, several were described as being over sensitive to changing their ideas, and touchy about working with

people that they had not met before. This suggests that a care leavers' low self-esteem may be expressed in bravado and argument.

It is evident that the low self-esteem of students who do not live with their parents influences their behaviour in school and college. In our study 83.9% of students who lived with their parents described themselves as being confident at school compared to only 60% of students who lived without parents. Students who do not live with their parents were less likely to attend school, college or training courses regularly. These students are also less able to suggest positive strategies for organising themselves when studying, and several suggested that '*giving up*' and '*not doing it*' were ways of coping with work they found challenging. This suggests that the high incidence of truancy and low academic achievement of care leavers and looked after children in education may be, in part, due to lack of self-belief and self-worth.

Communication skills

Students who do not live with their parents also report significantly higher levels of concern over their communication skills. This may relate to specific special educational needs relating to reading and writing, as was observed in students who have experienced disrupted schooling and long periods of absence from school (more than 10% of the academic year). This group of students were very loath to deal with verbal and numerical written information, although were more prepared to manipulate information that was presented using ICT.

These students often reported concerns over contributing to discussion and communicating their viewpoints. Discussions with individual care leavers indicated that the opportunity to express their opinions was extremely important to these students. However, many of them were observed to remain taciturn in discussions and subsequently commented that they were not prepared to speak to the others in the group for fear of ridicule relating to their perceived lack of knowledge about the subject being discussed. A particular group of care leavers in one subject area entirely rejected the idea of group discussion as worthwhile, commenting that they set little store on the opinions of others, having learned that *'you have to look for number one when you are in care.'*

Further DMT results showed that students who do not live with their parents found it difficult to express themselves cogently, particularly in front of other people, and most especially in front of people that they do not know. They also described themselves as not being good at listening to instructions and finding it difficult to gather and process information. Communicating with adults appears to be particularly difficult for these students – 60% felt that teachers ignored them, compared to only 24.1% of students who lived with their parents.

Good verbal and oral communication skills are essential for educational achievement. Without the confidence and experience to use language in research and discourse these students may not be able to devise appropriate strategies for developing and using their communication skills equivalent to level four (post 14 entry) in the National Framework for Qualifications. However, observation and facilitators' reports indicated that with appropriate support and guidance, many students who reported low confidence in communication were able to make demonstrable progress during the summer school. It was gratifying to note that most care leavers were fully involved in the presentation of work and chairing discussions in the final sessions of the summer school.

Relationships with others

The responses of students who lived with their parents indicated that their views on working with others are most likely related to their character and personality. The vast majority of these students reported that they felt confident when working with others, and could decide when was the most appropriate time to seek help from others. However, students who did not live with parents consistently reported that they had difficulty relating to other people, which strongly correlated with students who lacked confidence in school and college. Only 26.7% of care leavers felt they worked well in a

team, compared to 60.3% of other students. This group also reported that they are far less likely to admit that they do not understand in school and college, partly because they are too shy to speak to a teacher about their difficulties and partly because they were not confident about speaking out in class and to their peers. Many students in this group reported negative experiences of learning in school and some cited this as the reason for their diffidence.

Many students who did not live with their parents reported anxiety about meeting and getting to know new people. For some these anxieties focused on coping with new social situations, while others were concerned about losing contact with a network of friends due to changes of address. Significantly, almost all care leavers from minority ethnic backgrounds reported a need to meet others from the same ethnic background, whereas no students from a minority ethnic background who lived with their parents reported having experienced any difficulty about meeting others from their own culture. This suggests that care leavers from minority ethnic groups feel isolated, and that there is a need among this group to network with other young people and adults from the same ethnic grouping in order to establish positive professional and social relationships.

Conclusions

Guidance and support from professionals for the care leaver in education

The transfer from compulsory education into further education normally coincides with leaving the care environment. The young person must cope with the logistics of independent living, in addition to the demands of a training or education programme. It is precisely at this point in their training and educational career when a care leaver needs specific and focused support from education and care professionals to enable them to develop the self-determination and self-organisation required to be successful in education.

Recognising success

Opportunities for the young person to be successful in the early stages of their chosen educational programme are important. They may need support in learning to be successful in personal and social aspects such as good attendance and active participation in group activities as well as in academic work. Feedback from other care leavers in education may be useful to the young person in providing an opportunity to discuss common challenges and to identify strategies for dealing with these matters.

Changing behaviour and attitudes

If a care leaver has experienced years of disaffection and disruption, then all care and education professionals must work to alter the behaviours that this will have engendered in the young person. One care leaver commented that his biggest problem at college was getting out of bed in the morning. Once he was at college he found his work interesting, but was beginning to fall behind with coursework as he was absent too frequently. In order that the young person can begin to take responsibility for their own learning, they must develop strategies for self-organisation and independent management of time and resources. The young person may need help to understand that long-term goals such as academic qualifications take time to achieve.

Flexibility in the curriculum

The care leaver must be made aware of the possibilities that are open to them in the FE and HE curriculum, and there should be close liaison between schools, colleges, the Connexions service and social workers to ensure accurate and helpful advice is available. A number of education pathways are available to students in the current framework, which enables students to combine academic and vocational qualifications with employment. The National Framework for Qualifications recognises the need to provide entry routes into levels 2, 3 and 4 for students without traditional qualifications and provides stand-alone qualifications in key skills and mathematics for such students. This may be a more attractive prospect for a care leaver than being obliged to repeat examinations. Care professionals should be aware that the qualifications framework is undergoing review, and that new developments are being introduced annually.

A new environment for learning

Care leavers need a learning environment that they find amenable. The atmosphere and ethos of an FE college with a range of students of different ages and backgrounds may well be more appropriate for the care leaver than a school.

Practical support

Care leavers must be supported in coping with the practical logistics of studying. The Action on Aftercare Consortium (AAC, 1995) comments that the Children's Act of 1989 places a duty on the local authority to promote the welfare of care leavers with support in cash and kind. It is well documented that, care leavers are obliged to manage on a combination of social security benefits, one-off payments and wages from part-time jobs. This presents considerable logistic and financial difficulties for the young person who wishes to remain in or return to education although the Leaving Care Act should provide finance for some young people in the future. Financial and emotional difficulties are often more obstructive than educational problems for care leavers. The care leaver requires practical aid in the form of financial support and the means to be able to work properly such as study facilities, a computer, a desk and stationery. They may also require help in finding child care or specialised health and disability care. The care leaver may need to study part-time, particularly if they are working.

Stability in the care leaver's home environment is essential if they are to be successful in education. Wherever possible the care leaver should be included in an after-care education programme. Thompson also notes that in the sample of care leavers she monitored in their move from compulsory to post compulsory education, those who continued into higher education had their foster places available to them at weekends and during vacation, thus providing the home support accessible to other students. Those who lived alone were very likely to leave education and training courses. Biehal et al. (1995, 68ff) tracked a sample of care leavers and reported that the majority of those in stable employment and stable education, that is full-time employment, youth training or education, retain these situations in the first 18–24 months after leaving care. Similarly, those who are in insecure positions, where they are in part-time, casual, temporary and disruptive patterns of employment and education remain in these situations, indicating that it is very hard to recover from this fixed cycle. Care leavers need the support of adults who provide a positive role model of the financial and social advantages that education can bring, and who are willing to support them through the challenges of undertaking a long-term education programme.

Pastoral support

All young people experience frustrations and disappointments during their academic career, and all require pastoral support of family, friends and teachers. It is essential that the care leaver has a readily available network of carers and professionals in easy contact when such times occur. Regular proactive monitoring and review of a care leaver's progress in education is essential and all the education and care professionals concerned must maintain close and regular contact with one other.

A lack of continuity in care and schooling and consequent lack of continuity in care providers and teachers can engender distrust between the young person and adults who are in authority. If a care leaver has undeveloped communication skills they may find it difficult to express their feelings with others, particularly teachers/tutors. The care leaver needs time to build relationships with familiar adults who they trust to advocate for their needs in education.

The higher than average incidence of special educational needs among care leavers indicates that a programme of learning support should be devised at the start of a course. The review and monitoring process should focus on the progress of the care leaver set against these targets.

Those responsible for the care leaver, including teachers and carers, must be aware of warning signs of disengagement and non-achievement in the early stages of all educational programmes. If a care leaver is returning to education, they are likely to need explicit support and guidance in developing good study habits. Evidence of poor punctuality, non-attendance, and submitting work late may be indications of the young person failing to thrive in education. Prompt action in dealing with the issues before they develop is extremely important.

It is essential to engender positive aspirations for education in the care leaver. This comes from positive self-belief built on evidence of success. This research project has indicated that care leavers often have a negative self-image of themselves as learners, often related to real or perceived low attainment in earlier school experience. The care leaver needs to be challenged to overcome these fears. Some young people are sceptical about changing their personal situation, especially if their experience is that change is destructive and damaging. The professional must challenge the young person's perceptions of schooling and education in order to puncture these views, and provide practical and pastoral support as the care leaver takes responsibility for shaping their future.

All young people need confidence, motivation and determination to succeed. For the care leaver who may be living alone, who may lack the support network of family and friends, and may be obliged to provide for themselves financially; the discipline needed to succeed seems immense. Research reiterates care leavers require 'joined up' support from carers, social workers and teachers in order to create and maintain a supportive base from which to initiate their careers. A stable home base is essential, and it must be a stable base that the young person can control if they are to develop the personal skills and experience to become an independent adult. Success at home and in work and education is mutually reinforcing.

References

Action on Aftercare Consortium. (1996) Action on AfterCare: Too Much, Too Young. The Failure of Social Policy, in *Meeting the Needs of Care Leavers*, London, Barnados.

Aldgate, J. and Statham, J. (2001) *The Children Act Now: Messages From Research*, Prepared for The Department of Health, London, DOH/HMSO.

American Psychological Association. (1995) *Standards for Educational and Psychological Testing*, Washington, APA.

Berkley, R. and Wheal, A. (Forthcoming) *The Dolphin Measurement Tool*.

Biehal, N., Clayden, J., Stein, M. and Wade, J. (1995) *Moving on: Young People and Leaving Care Schemes*, London, HMSO.

Broad, B. (1994) *Leaving Care in the 1990s: The Results of a National Survey*, Westerham, Royal Philanthropic Society.

Broad, B. (1998) *Young People Leaving Care: Life After the Children Act 1989*, London, Jessica Kingsley.

Department for Education and Employment. (2000a) *Education Protects: Guidance on The Education of Children and Young People in Public Care*, London, DfEE.

Department for Education and Employment. (2000b) *The Education of Children and Young People in Care*, London, DfEE.

Department of Health. (1999a) *The Government's Objectives for Children's Social Services*, London, DoH.

Department of Health. (1999b) *Me, Survive, out There? New Arrangements for Children Leaving Care*, London, DoH.

Department of Health. (2000) *Educational Qualifications of Care Leavers, Year Ending 31 March 2000*, London, DoH. Available at *www.doh.gov.uk/public/sb0025*

Department of Health, Social Services Inspectorate. (1997) *When Leaving Home is Also Leaving Care: An Inspection of Services for Young People Leaving Care*, London, HMSO.

First Key. (1995) *National Standards in Leaving Care: Report of The National Working Group*, Leeds, First Key.

First Key. (1996) *Standards in Leaving Care. Seventeen Standards to Assist Local Authorities to Develop Consistent Policies to Work With Young People Leaving Care*, Leeds, First Key.

First Key. (1998) *Education 'Looked After' a Training Pack for Teachers Working With Young People in Care*, Leeds, First Key.

Foskett, N. and Helmsley-Brown, J. (2001) *Choosing Futures: Young People's Decision-making in Education, Training and Careers Markets*, London, Routledge Falmer.

Gardner, H. (1993) *The Unschooled Mind: How Children Think and How Schools Should Teach Them*, London, Fontana.

Garnett, L. (1992) *Leaving Care and After*. London, National Children's Bureau.

Godek, S. (1976) *Leaving Care: A Case Study Approach to the Difficulties Children Face in Leaving Residential Care*, Social Work Papers No 2. London, Barnardo's.

Jackson, S. (2000) Promoting the Educational Achievement of Looked-after Children, in Cox, T. (Ed.) *Combating Educational Disadvantage: Meeting the Needs of Vulnerable Children*, London, Falmer Press.

Jackson, S. (Ed.) (2001) *Nobody Ever Told us School Mattered: Raising the Educational Attainment of Children in Care*, London, BAAF.

Jackson, S. and Sachdev, D. (2001) *Better Education, Better Futures: Research, Practice and the Views of Young People in Public Care*, Ilford, Barnardo's.

Marsh, P. and Peel, M (1999) *Leaving Care in Partnership: Family Involvement With Care Leavers, (Studies in Evaluating The Children Act 1989)* London, HMSO.

Mcparlin, P. (1996) *Education of Young People Looked After*, Leeds, First Key.

National Children's Bureau. (1992) *Young People Leaving Care*, London, NCB.

Office for National Statistics. (2000) *Social Focus on Young People*, London, ONS.

Sax, G. (1997) *Principles of Educational and Psychological Measurement and Evaluation* 4th edn, Washington, Wadsworth.

Torrance, H. and Pryor, J. (1998) *Investigating Formative Assessment*, Milton Keynes, OUP.

Web references

AQA (Assessment and Qualifications Alliance) *www.aqa.org.uk*

College board *http://www.collegeboard.com*

The Connexions service *http://www.connexions.gov.uk*

Edexcel *www.edexcel.org.uk*

Key Skills *http://www.qca.org.uk/nq/ks/*

Joint Council for General Qualifications *http://www.jcgq.org.uk/*

OCR (Oxford Cambridge and RSA Examinations) *www.ocr.org.uk*

National Framework for Qualifications *http://www.qca.org.uk/nq/framework/*

UK Independent Schools on the net *www.iscis.uk.net*

19. Education, Training and Employment

Linda Daniel

This chapter considers ways to improve opportunities in education, training and employment for care leavers and is based on my work as the Education and Employment Officer for a local authority leaving care team. The chapter looks at the profile and backgrounds of the young people we are trying to help; outlines the services we currently provide and the gaps in the service; then identifies the things that work and the things that don't work; and finally suggests a way to fill the existing gaps in the service

Setting the Scene

Whilst by law, education must be provided in some shape or form to all children up to the age of 16, it cannot be denied that schools allow disruptive, failing children to disappear in year 11.

Realism is a difficult concept for teenagers – as I am sure we can all remember.

This left them in the position of being legally unable to work full time and unable to move to further education, the consequence being, six months doing nothing.

Young people are indeed a most challenging group for which special resources must be found. Doing nothing is dangerous.

The cycle of non-engaging, uneducated care leavers becoming an 'underclass' in society has to be broken.

The young people are not cost effective. They rarely produce the outcomes that bring in the money!

The expectations ... that young people will behave, be on time, and complete the course, have proven to be unrealistic. The young people do not fit.

The Client Profile

Young people enter care for a variety of reasons which include:

- family breakdown
- physical or sexual abuse
- neglect
- family ill health
- homelessness
- beyond parental control
- the death of a parent
- offending behaviour (on occasions)

The highest intake is of children between the ages of ten and fifteen, a crucial time of transition from primary to secondary school and from child to teenager. Whatever the reason, these children are separated from their families. They suffer psychological damage from this experience in addition to their past experiences. This damage will continue with them and be either alleviated or compounded, dependent upon future care planning.

Whilst every child has their own individual identity, inevitably, this will be influenced by their experiences in care. Some will feel safer, some bewildered, some frightened, isolated, alienated or stigmatised. Some may have been separated from their siblings, moved to another area or to a children's home. Some will be moved from their own school and eventually to a new, unknown one. There are inevitable consequences for a child accommodated in the public care system – feelings of loss, rejection, uncertainty and having to adapt to major changes of carers and surroundings.

We also have young people with disabilities and others such as young people with:

- non-statemented learning difficulties
- undiagnosed or diagnosed health conditions
- drug and alcohol dependency
- mental health disorders
- young parents

There are others who have no educational or work ethic and no motivation. They form part of the larger disaffected and socially excluded youth in society. The age range is from 16–21. These young people are our main target and there are too many of them. It is often the case too that this group have unrealistic expectations of employment and their earning capacity.

Another group of young people are those who complete year 11 at school but achieve meagre GCSEs of below A-C grades. This may be due to lack of ability, but might be because of other circumstances e.g.:

- Placement breakdown.
- The fear of having to leave care and live independently.
- Lack of support and encouragement.
- Teenage priorities particularly social.
- Unrealistic expectations of leaving school and getting paid employment.

Leaving Care at 16 Plus

Young people are referred to the Team by their locality social workers on their sixteenth birthday. Whilst some young people remain in stable, secure foster placements or other provision and can be worked with, others are forced, or vote themselves, to make the transition towards independence. The whole process for a young person is fraught with difficulties and concerns, particularly bearing in mind the various reasons for coming into care and the reasons for underachievement, combined with the additional pressures of leaving care.

In this context, it must be acknowledged that the average age of a 'regular' young person leaving home is around 23, usually with in-built provision to return home if necessary or desirable. In addition, care leavers are teenagers with all the angst, hormonal changes, attitude, hopes and fears of any other teenager. Teenage behaviour brings conflict in any home and sadly, at this crucial time when 'parental' support and guidance is vital, what may have been a previously stable placement may break down. This may also run concurrently with disruptive behaviour or non-attendance at school. On this basis, those currently in education when they transfer to the team are monitored, supported and encouraged into sixth form, further education or training.

Some 30 young people are 'working' but at present we do not know if they will 'stick at it'. To complete the statistical profile of the group,

some 11 young people are accommodated in prisons, hospitals or are unable to work due to ill health. 11 are engaged in other short-term courses or interventions, whilst a further 11 have intermittent engagement with me. The latter group and the 28 young people who do not engage at all are of prime concern and target.

Services we Provide 16 Plus

For school leavers the authority offers resources similar to other areas. The local further education college offers a wide range of courses for all abilities, from pre-foundation for those with special needs to access to higher education. On occasions neighbouring colleges may be more suitable because of geographical location, choice of a particular course, because the young person dislikes the local college or because of conflict with peers.

For those with little direction but who are willing to be advised, we carry out a full assessment of educational and employability potential which is subsequently followed by an achievable action plan, be it college, training or work, at an agreed pace. There then ensues a search around local suitable resources. Interview skills are coached, applications completed and, if the young person requests, I will go with them to the interview for support.

Network Training Schemes, now known as Modern Apprenticeships, offer a range of courses from vehicle maintenance to retail or business skills. Other agencies offer the combination of work and training but being 18 is a key factor for access to some of these.

At the leaving care team we provide a drop-in for leisure based group work and one-to-one tuition was provided by the local college which sadly ceased due to lack of funding. We have a computer room, a small library of reference and revision books and staff who will encourage and support the few who come in to do homework or assignments. We continue to run the WOT club (Work on Tuesday) offering one-to-one careers training, employment advice and guidance. A local agency also offers an opportunity to gain a qualification in computer skills but experience has shown this works only for the more able and seriously committed young people. 'Changing Places' – the in-house work experience programme – continues to offer supported taster work placements. There is also a young mum's accredited computer course, complete with crèche, a real breakthrough! As 'extras' there are weekly one-to-one sessions with the looked after children's nurse, a drugs and alcohol counsellor, a housing surgery and pet therapy, all of which play an important holistic role in the lives of the young people.

For young people over eighteen with learning difficulties, there is a specialist local provision. But what happens to the 16–18s? For those not in education, there appears to be no such provision for them. There is then resistance from the Health Services at the age of 18 to diagnose a mental disorder other than the most extreme. There are local resources for drug and alcohol dependency but the young person must be willing to participate which similarly applies to the youth counselling service. Young parents need childcare in order to pursue education or training and currently, the provision at the local college admits only children over the age of two, which means two years doing nothing for the young mothers. Not all young mums want to do a computer course – they have other interests which cannot be realised. These are vital years for all these particularly vulnerable young people yet they are relegated to a wasteland due to lack of pertinent provision.

Gaps in the Service

During the year 2000, there were six young people, all 16 years of age, all early in the academic year and all non-attenders at school. Efforts were made to persuade the young people to return to school. However, they had no interest in returning to what had been a negative experience. This left them in the position of being legally unable to work full time, unable to move to a further education college or to training schemes which by law only accept young people of school leaving age. This has been a penalty of the school leaving age being changed for all to June. The consequence of this is that they had six months *doing nothing*.

Of the six young people, two enrolled for further education as part of their detention and training order, but did not attend. Both of these young women have since tried either work or training with work and both have been asked to leave because of attitude, behaviour and lack of soft skills. Another young woman started a training scheme and was eventually asked to leave, again due to her behaviour and erratic attendance. One young man entered a young offenders institution. Another, after several suicide attempts is now in a clinic. The remaining two have managed to avoid me for the past year! This has become an art form in itself for some. The young people do not have to see me and they know I cannot make them do anything. Therefore, I work on the basis of always trying to form a relationship early on so that when they are ready to move on in their lives they know someone is there to help.

Employment or Exploitation?

What are the needs of the job market?

Nationally, the main predicted growth areas are in the caring, business and public services sectors, of which a large number require professional qualifications or degrees. Decline is forecast in such areas as construction and building, machine and plant operatives, secretarial and clerical. NVQ2 appears to be a minimum requirement of employment.

What do employers want?

Employers expect:

- basic numeracy and literacy skills
- the ability to communicate and work with others
- basic IT skills

In addition they expect young people to exhibit soft skills, for instance:

- commitment
- punctuality
- reliability
- enthusiasm
- willingness to learn
- honesty

Whilst paper qualifications are necessary for some jobs, employers can often provide training for these if the young person has all the above attributes. Care leavers of course are not the only young people sometimes lacking in these skills but, without the basics of any work experience, lack of education, lack of social skills, lack of self-confidence, a chaotic life-style and being a stereotypical 'youth' – employment opportunities are minimal.

From the above groups of young people, some will say they wish to work but the opportunities are limited both by their expectations and by those of prospective employers. The young people have very definite ideas on work they regard as subservient, work in retail, waitressing, cleaning, refuse collection, gardening etc. They also, like many teenagers (and many adults) want a lifestyle that requires a lot of money. Young care leavers, particularly those not fostered, lack adult input which brings with it realism, the concept of deferred gratification and that there are qualities in life other than the material.

The reality is that the majority of successes in life are linked to educational success.

Some have found jobs through 'friends' in privately owned local small shops or fast food outlets. However, this has been very poorly paid and the hours very long. Needless to say, such exploitation results in short-term employment and a very bad, often first, experience in the workplace. Some have tried MacDonalds, Burger King, or agency work which has usually been packing or labouring. None has sustained this work because of the expectations of the employer around time-keeping and behaviour and because of the shock of being in the workplace where each young person becomes a very small cog in a big wheel. This contrasts painfully to what they are accustomed to. In the care system and particularly in residential placements:

Young people perceive themselves as having a lot of power, a lot of rights and they command a lot of attention! It is such a difficult transition.

Irregular employment

Another detracting factor in this irregular employment is the effect of what keeps us all motivated – an income. If a young person finds work, signs off but loses the job within days or a week, there is, often, little if any wage to be

paid. It also takes time, at least two weeks, for the benefits system to deal with their new claim. This causes a tremendous amount of stress and financial difficulty. Understandably this results in a lack of willingness to sign off in the future, based on past experience. Hands up – this is fraud but would it not be better to allow a short period of settling into employment before signing off or a faster re-instatement of benefits when employment is lost? Currently, the young person is losing in every direction. Fortunately, the Benefits Agency has said it is proposing that from April 2002, those people taking up 'short term work' will have their claim suspended rather than closed. This should address this problem.

Whatever the reasons for unemployment, after a period of time living on and off benefits and seeing others moving on in their lives, eventually, usually around the ages of eighteen and nineteen, there becomes a realisation that they are left behind. This of course compounds the feelings of rejection from employers which mirrors that experienced at school. Whilst the young people of course play a part in this rejection, what they have not had are the positive experiences that give them confidence and aspiration to better themselves. This is a void that needs to be filled before any progress is made in the job market.

All the above young people are indeed a most challenging group for which special resources must be found. Doing nothing is dangerous.

This extreme exclusion accelerates their path towards unemployment, crime, ill-health, alcohol and drug dependency, homelessness and precludes from inclusion in the community. The cost of multi-agency interventions, from social services, health, benefits and criminal justice is high and positive outcomes in terms of change, progression and re-integration into society are small in number. Some means of fast re-engagement, compensatory education and socialisation must be found and delivered in a form acceptable to the young people.

New Deal (18–24s)

If young people are not in some form of education, training or employment and are signing on for benefit they have a choice, at 18, of opting into the Government's New Deal scheme early, or waiting another six months or so, when it will be obligatory.

New Deal offers education, training, employment or voluntary work. However, experience with the hardest to engage young people is mirrored again within this framework. If we have not been able to help young people move on in their lives between the ages of 16 and 18, how is New Deal going to make it happen when their approach is far more forceful, dogmatic and punitive? Care leavers may be regarded by some organisations as a special category, for example they can apply for hardship payments if this is sanctioned, but the same processes and procedures of the New Deal programme apply to them. They have to comply with the system of regular appointments at the Job Centre, the intensive full-time course of job search, person and soft skills development etc. and of proving they are actively looking to engage in what New Deal is offering.

> The expectations of the scheme are that young people will behave, be on time, and complete the course. These expectations have proven to be unrealistic. The young people do not fit.

Sanctions are always financial. Some of the hardest to help young people of this age group have stopped claiming because of this pressure and expectation of conformity. Consequently, they have lost their accommodation due to loss of housing benefit and become homeless and 'lost'. However, one of the local New Deal providers is particularly sympathetic to some young people and, for the one or two who have entered the programme, they have been offered a good range of work experience placements, lots of support and most importantly a second chance.

Breaking the Cycle and Bridging the Gap

> The cycle of non-engaging, uneducated care leavers becoming an 'underclass' in society has to be broken.

Whilst there are agencies delivering various programmes with this aim in mind, the programmes are costly, transient and serve only the limited number on each course. Until the full effect of the new strategies and services for looked after children's life-chances and well-being shines through, we are looking at the same problems for those we work with currently and for some years to come. In reviewing what has been learned, we need to provide a new framework and style of working which offers the young people what they will respond to rather than trying to make them fit into what local resources offer – which clearly not only do not work but cause more damage and negativity.

The present Government has set targets for young people in, and leaving care. The aim is to improve the level of educational attainment for those in school and to improve the level of education, training and employment outcomes for care leavers by the time they reach 19 years of age. The Connexions service will provide advice, guidance and support for all 13–19-year-olds on a range of youth related issues, and will also share these targets.

In order to meet them, however, we need both adapted and new resources specially used for such purposes.

What works?

Outside organisations, such as the Prince's Trust, whose programmes are delivered via a residential experience, have been successful for a small number of the young people. The difficulty is that the courses are expensive. Also the locations make it necessary for participants to travel outside their territory, something many young people are suspicious of and therefore reluctant to do.

The leaving care team has found that with quality one-to-one time and good assessment, some of the young people can be persuaded to give education another try. Because we have excellent relationships with other agencies, the young people are welcomed with understanding by supportive staff. Courses, carefully chosen, are sustained by most who manage to comply with the 'rigidity' of an educational or training institution. What this means is essentially they must comply to the basics of time-keeping, behaviour and commitment to work. This has been helped by offering the young people bonus payments and lunch money for over 80 per cent attendance, as well as travel money and payments for day trips or residentials. Any problems are flagged up and dealt with by the agency involved, the leaving care team and the young person at the earliest stage to prevent breakdown.

A local college is now flexible and creative in providing what works for the individual rather than the group, but even this has limits. Two young people had to be asked to leave after exhaustive efforts had been made but the nurturing and encouraging 'hook', created by the staff at the college, enabled another young man to complete his course in the most difficult of circumstances.

The young mum's computer course is a result of a collaboration between the leaving care team, the local child and family centre and the youth service. Courses like this need to be replicated and expanded in the future. The youth service had the laptops and the expertise, the centre offered a location and crèche (for which the team pays) and the leaving care team introduced the young mums and babies. Out of the five that started the course, three saw it through to take exams at the end. Whilst the project took some organisation and negotiation, the end result is impressive. Anyone working in leaving care knows how difficult it is for any group to maintain regular attendance!

What does not work?

Modern Apprenticeships/Youth Training are a government provision for young people who leave school and want employment with training. These have not been a positive resource for the young people. A propelling factor for some new initiatives is the fact that these schemes can not accommodate the most needy young people who were, ironically, originally their target group. The reason for this is that the schemes are paid on outcomes. There is very little on offer at NVQ level 1 – where some of the young people need to begin. In addition, there is a lack of variety. Practical courses are in high demand. This applies similarly to other training agencies. Expectations are too high and having to deal with attitude, difficult behaviour, lack of social and soft skills often proves too challenging.

One of the most popular courses, painting and decorating, which is constantly being sought by the young people, and not available elsewhere in the area, was dropped some years ago.

The young people are not cost effective. They rarely produce the outcomes that bring in the money!

The construction courses attract the most male interest but, because of insurance cover, recruits need to be 18. One training provider offers a two to three year course but this is difficult to take on for a care leaver without long term vision and a stable home. It also requires a considerable time of college attendance bringing with it an expectation of conformity and basic education. However, the provider is very sympathetic and supportive of the young people. There is a construction group (linked to New Deal) that offer a six month working training scheme and a guarantee of employment on completion. This is an excellent opportunity but governed by audit and outcomes. An example of the fragility of such a placement is that of Ian.

With encouragement and a lot of support, Ian started the course albeit he was living in bed and breakfast. He initially managed his attendance well but took the occasional days off for 'sickness' which we suspect were due to seeking a supplementary income elsewhere or due to over-indulgence of drugs or alcohol. This is par for the course for many care leavers. Whilst these lapses were sympathetically viewed by the trainers, they too are accountable. The final straw came ironically when Ian was offered his quota flat, which unfortunately coincided with his social worker being on leave. This is a very stressful time for a young person and whilst the team helped him to move, the time he had to take off was the final straw for the auditors. Two weeks before completion, his traineeship was terminated. No amount of appeals could retrieve the situation. Ian understandably was devastated, as were we. He drifted into whatever intermittent casual work he could find. He subsequently lost his tenancy due to arrears. He reappeared some months later for help back into full time employment which he has since sustained.

What works for some

The WOT club, short for Work on Tuesday, is a regular Tuesday afternoon session complete with a regular careers advisor who comes to the leaving care team. Between the careers and us, young people can access private one-to-one careers guidance and job search that has engaged and significantly helped many. Unfortunately, to the less confident, the careers office is not the most welcoming of establishments, young people are reluctant to enter in to what to them is a pressurising, judgemental, middle-class environment that will make demands upon them. A quick visit to sign on is often as good as it gets. At the leaving care team, they are on their own territory and between the social workers, the advisor and the team, we manage to persuade many a young person into careers counselling. Once the initial fear is removed and relationships begin to build, inroads can be made towards action plans.

Initially, we offered an incentive of £20 if a young person attended for five sessions of guidance. Whilst at the onset this worked, the sessions for some later recruits diminished to a five minute chat, a plea of a pressing urgent appointment and a quick exit. There followed five weeks later a row over whether or not this justified the £20! Beware!

Some training and advisory schemes have proved more successful and are a natural feed from the WOT club guidance. Several of the young people have completed, or nearly completed the programme. Again this is due to staff expertise and their understanding of the young people. Young people have also been supported throughout with weekly contact (including lunch at MacDonalds!) to monitor and maintain motivation and attendance. The variety of course content initially on offer has now been substantially reduced due to college funding. These young people need short sharp boosts of interesting, rewarding activity with an educational goal.

IT, on which there is a great focus, may be the future but young people with chaotic lives and little grounding in educational etiquette struggle to sit for long periods in front of a screen. Equally, this particular activity does require minimum literacy and numeracy skills, a lack of which may have been cleverly covered up. So, rather than be shown up, many young people choose to walk out or not attend at all.

This brings us to a major problem with such schemes. The young people receive a weekly payment dependent upon attendance. These young people know that this is probably going to be problematic, they have no mum to get them up for college, be they willing or not to go! Again, I must emphasise the leniency with which absences are dealt with by the providers, but the young people fear depletion of what, in cash terms is a poverty-line existence anyway. Therefore, a course such as this is viewed as a threat rather than an opportunity. The uptake is small despite the offer of attendance and bonus incentives from us.

A works experience scheme has worked for everyone who has participated. Nobody has been asked to leave and all have completed one placement or more. However, a similar problem arises i.e. the issue of money. They operate on the basis of a three day voluntary working week for which lunch money and a weekly travel pass is provided. Any young person can take up the opportunity without benefits being affected. For those who are keen or counselled into it, by realising the benefits of work experience, increased skills and self-confidence and a reference from a local authority department, the path is smooth.

What is difficult is selling the benefits to those who see no benefit in working per se and especially for nothing when they can stay in bed for the same money!

What has worked in the past is the influence of previous participants who have standing and credibility with their peer group. It is their powers of persuasion that prove most effective. Of all those who have participated in the scheme, the majority have gone on to further education. Of the initial participants (1998–9), one is about to start an access course in social work and another has completed her first year of a nursing degree at university. All have come away with a greater sense of self-worth and self-respect. One young woman looked at her excellent reference and asked '*Is this really me?*'

Another poignantly remarked '*I can be who I like at work – nobody knows I've been in care or where I've come from'*. Even so, there remains a group of young people who are unwilling or unsuitable even for this nurturing environment.

Why do Children in Care Under-achieve?

- Lack of continuity in schooling, due to numerous moves of school and homes.
- Periods of time out of school whilst new places are found or due to truancy, exclusion prior to or after coming into care.
- Lack of continuity of carers, teachers and peer groups – constant moves make relationships difficult to form and impossible to sustain.
- The historical focus of general welfare/crisis management taking precedence over education in placement planning.
- Lack of ability to rely on and trust adults.
- Lack of confidence and self-esteem because of previous and current experiences, which preclude full participation in school.
- Lack of advocacy and support from carers, teachers and social workers in the educational arena, which is often due to lower expectations and the undervaluing of education.
- Lack of quick response to implement compensatory education where disruption has occurred.

In terms of care placements, young people with stable foster homes generally achieve far better academically than those placed in other provision and are far more likely to go on to further education and some on to higher education. The leaving care team is now an important component in the training for foster carers, the objectives of which are:

- To emphasise how important and effective this high quality care and support is in the long term for young people.
- To emphasise the value of education.
- To open dialogue with the individual carers around working together with the leaving care team.

Young people who are fostered also reap the benefits of friends outside of care who do well at school and are more likely to have outside interests. Having support and encouragement around education, extending the placement until further education is completed and negotiating returns home during university vacations all culminate in the young person feeling safe, supported and cared for – as all children should be.

The consensus among teachers in the field is that *non-authoritarian, learning centred approaches* work the best for young people in, leaving and who have left care. Other suggestions are:

- *Activities* should be targeted initially towards what the young person feels they need.
- *Ease them back into school gently but quickly*. Past experience confirms that young people respond better on their *own territory* rather than within mainstream institutions. A 'hook' is needed, be it a safe, comfortable place to be, a meal, money, some leisure activity (of which they are sorely starved) a trip out. Whatever it takes to engage.
- The location and staff must be right.
- A 'drop in' at the leaving care team, run by the youth service, failed because it was in a place associated with social workers, conflict and a statutory or financial obligation to be there – rather than a voluntary desire. The fact that the weekly programme offered everything from making CDs, videoing, narrow-boat trips, mountain biking, bowling did not impress the young people one iota. Successful groups are usually those run at locations away from statutory locations and away from social workers.
- The provision of full-time alternative education must be offered to excluded children in care with reintegration being the main aim.
- Interagency work brings together a wealth of knowledge, skills and experience which when *consolidated* becomes an effective catalyst for change. Bringing these agencies to the young people works.
- Aspirations, must be as high as for all other children.

So what are the key factors to helping the young people and the workers to bridge the gap in provision?

- Stability of accommodation or placement.

- Fast intervention to avoid periods of non-engagement and inactivity.
- Relationships with the young people built on trust and honesty.
- The right environment where young people are comfortable, can develop and learn.
- Skilled multi-disciplined, inter-agency workers.
- Working one-to-one or in small groups
- Mentoring.
- Flexible provision to meet their needs.
- Learning activities that are fun.
- Practical independence skills – budgeting, cooking, first aid, how to decorate, change a plug, plumb in a washing machine etc.
- Services that will address their other needs ranging from offending behaviour, substance abuse, physical and mental health issues, homelessness, pregnancy, anger management, isolation.
- Self-esteem and confidence building, soft skills.
- Raising the profile and demystifying the public perception of 'young people in care'.
- Networking with local employers to provide a wide range of work experience with or without the possibility of employment.
- Reward achievements, however small.

It would appear that what works best for care leavers is a separate drop-in centre which serves the needs of this range of young people *immediately*, whilst linking in all the various agencies that are working with them at any one time. The service should provide formal activities in the morning, predominantly educational support which would include basic skills, IT, social skills and vocational support, plus benefits advice, health care, therapy, and counselling, together with assessments and sessions with personal advisors. In the afternoon or evening, more informal, leisure based activities led by the youth service such as digi-music, drama, leisure pursuits and mentoring, all of which would culminate in a residential week or weekend away. This scheme is wide in its remit and may be expensive in cost but offers a way to re-engage the target group before they opt out, become disengaged and later join the unemployment, young parent or criminal statistics.

The Wilderness

Without early intervention, probably fifty per cent of the young people will become part of the cohort of the unemployed, developing a life-long dependency on benefits or entering into the 'alternative' labour market or into crime. That is why the early years, between 16 and 18, are so important if positive changes are to be made. At 18, bad habits have settled in.

Conclusion

The last two years have been illuminating, disillusioning, inspiring and disappointing.

The greatest impact and learning has come from the young people who have spelt out, in both words and actions, what does and does not work for them in terms of education and training and how the employment market can reject or exploit them.

Funding will always be an issue. However, what I have learned, or really been taught, is that other options can be created albeit from fragmented local resources and from the tremendous goodwill of other agencies and the community at large. Whilst the solution to helping these young people on the road to sustainable employment has remained elusive, networking with local agencies and research has now highlighted the things that do work. This cannot be ignored.

The services we provide have to be set within a multicultural framework, and must allow for mistakes if we are to meet the needs of these diverse, challenging and chaotic young people. It is they who are important in all of this. We must listen to them, be flexible, maintain both our, and their, motivation, respond quickly and keep the door open at all times.

References

Benefits Agency. (2000) *Cashflow Newsletter of the Hounslow Welfare Benefits and Money Advice Unit*. May, London, Benefits Agency.

Centre for Economic and Social Inclusion. (2001) *Working Brief Issue 125*, June, London, Centre for Economic and Social Inclusion.

Department of Education. (2000) *Education of Young People in Public Care: Guidance*, Department of Education and Employment.

First Key. (2001) *Keynotes, issue 24*, Feb, Leeds, First Key.

NACRO and the Audit Commission. (1997) *A New '3 R' for Young Offenders*, NACRO.

Save the Children. (1995) *Keynote 7, UK and European Programmes*, Save the Children Information Section.

Wheal, A. (1999) *The RHP Companion to Foster Care*, Lyme Regis, Russell House Publishing.

Wilson, J. L. (2001) *Connexions Consultation: Research Amongst Young People*, 2nd edn, London, Marketry.

Note:
A new booklet which is free to all local authorities and published by The Who Cares? Trust and Department of Health is entitled: *Employability: Building Futures for Young People in and Leaving Care*.

For further information contact: The Who Cares? Trust, Kemp House, 152/160 City Road, London ECIV 2NP

20. Financial Arrangements for Care Leavers: Developing a Service

John Short

The aim of this chapter is to provide information on systems that need to be developed in order to meet the new financial arrangements set out in the Children (Leaving Care) Act 2000. This chapter is based on a paper that was produced for Enfield Social Services and reflects their circumstances and goals. However, it may be adapted to suit other local authorities who wish to introduce a fair and equitable scheme for care leavers. Appendix 1 and 2 provides information on who is affected by the Act and Appendix 3 provides a suggested list of what might be purchased from the Setting Up Home Allowance.

I would like to acknowledge and thank Enfield Social Services who have given me permission to use the paper as the basis for this chapter.

Introduction and Background

The establishment of financial protocols is particularly pressing in the light of the need to implement the Children (Leaving Care) Act 2000 from 1st October 2001. Young people, carers and staff must be provided with clear information about the types of financial support available and, how they can be accessed.

The Act introduces new financial arrangements for care leavers and makes clear that the responsible authority will normally be the young person's primary source of income. Access to Job Seeker's Allowance, Income Support and Housing Benefit for the majority of 16 and 17-year-olds who cease to be 'looked after' is removed.

This new income role for social services and social work departments will mean that they must provide allowances that cover maintenance, accommodation and other expenses such as travel and leisure costs.

Each young person will have a different set of needs and different capacity to manage a budget. Some may have sources of income of their own, such as employment. This means that in each case the responsible authority will have to agree with the young person a personal support package and how it is to be managed. The details of this will be recorded in the young person's pathway plan.

The table at the end of this report provides further information about the different groups of care leavers covered by the Children (Leaving Care) Act 2000 and their legal entitlements.

Categories of Care Leavers

In order to establish equitable and consistent financial systems local authorities should consider the adoption of a framework that recognises four broad categories of care leaving young people, aged 16 plus.

Category 1

Eligible 'looked after' young people from age 16 to the end of school year eleven.

Category 2

Eligible young people who have completed year eleven at school and remain in a social services/social work departments' placement, i.e. 16 and 17-year-old 'looked after' young people subject to Section 20 and Section 31 of the Children Act 1989.

Category 3

Relevant young people age 16 and 17 who move into a semi-independent or independent placement and were previously 'looked after' under section 20 of the Children Act 1989. Eligible young people who move into a semi-independent or independent placement but remain 'looked after' and eligible by virtue of being subject to Section 31 of the Children Act 1989.

Category 4

Former Relevant young people age 18 to 21 and in certain circumstances up to the of age 24.

Entitlements

Category 1

This category of young people remains subject to current financial arrangements that are applicable to 'looked after' children.

Category 2

This category of young people covers those who remain 'looked after' in a social services/social work departments placement and are preparing for independence.

The transition at the end of year eleven, from school to employment, training or further education marks a significant milestone in moving towards independence. This provides a key opportunity to establish a set of incentives, allowances and a positive financial framework. The allowances should be consistent across all residential units and, where possible, create parity with agency and foster placements. These should be in line with training allowance and benefit rates.

Where possible allowances should be paid through bank accounts, with foster carers, residential workers and personal advisors providing assistance with budgeting and money management as set out in the young person's pathway plan. Clarity on what items the allowance is to cover and the proportion allocated to each item would contribute to the development of budgeting skills.

Category 3

This category of young people who previously could claim Job Seekers Allowance, or Income Support are no longer entitled to these benefits until they reach age 18 with a few exceptions. In effect, this creates parity with young people subject to a Section 31 Care Order who were unable to claim benefits until the age of 18, even if they were living independently.

Social services and social work departments now have the primary income maintenance role for this category of young people.

The Children (Leaving Care) Act 2000 is clear that social services/social work departments must provide a minimum income standard to this group that covers their accommodation and maintenance costs.

A minimum standard must cover:

- housing costs
- a personal allowance (in line with benefit rates, currently £42 per week)

Additionally the guidance on the Act states that a number of items and areas should be considered a priority for funding. These include, but should not be restricted to:

- travel costs e.g., for education
- educational materials/special equipment
- other educational costs
- costs associated with special needs (such as a disability or pregnancy)
- childcare costs
- clothing
- contact with family or other significant relationships
- cultural/religious needs
- counselling or therapeutic needs
- hobbies/holidays

Information on locally agreed priorities should be available to all interested parties and should be explained clearly to the young people themselves.

The Act places a duty on local authorities to establish a financial framework to encourage young people into education, training and employment; this may necessitate in social services/social work departments establishing a set of financial incentives. Several authorities now provide an extra amount for young people who remain on a traineeship. A number of other authorities provide a bonus for young people who remain on a traineeship for ten weeks, 20 weeks etc.

It is important to explore and develop procedures for young people who are working, providing incentives for low wage earners and a system of contributions for those earning over a given threshold. A sliding scale of incentives that is linked to young people's wages or, a system of bonuses could be introduced. In addition, it would be appropriate to develop a system whereby young people who are earning well could make a small financial contribution towards their placement costs or forfeit their personal allowances. Any contributions that young people provide should always be undertaken from the principle of preparing for independence and becoming used to budgeting for rent or bills.

Category 4

The responsible authority does not have the primary income support role for this group. However the local authority now has a duty, rather than a power as previously, to provide assistance in kind or cash in respect of former relevant children.

These duties include:

- Providing general assistance.
- Providing assistance with expenses associated with employment.
- Providing assistance with expenses associated with education and training.
- Providing vacation accommodation (or the funds to secure it) to care leavers in higher education or on a residential further education course that requires them to live away from home as agreed in the pathway plan.

Further categories

Additionally, young people who do not meet the Children (Leaving Care) Act 2000 eligibility criteria, but have been 'looked after' for a period on or after their 16th birthday are termed 'Qualifying Children and Young People'. This group are entitled to the general powers and duties associated with Section 24 of the Children Act 1989 and:

- Assistance with education and training up to age 24.
- Vacation accommodation if attending higher education or residential further education courses.

Financial Allowances for Relevant Young People

Education, training and employment incentives

As previously stated a set of financial incentives and protocols should be established in order to encourage young people into, and remaining in, education, training or employment. A £10 per week allowance should be seen as a baseline and could be used to reward young people for positive activities related to education, training or employment. This could be paid on a five weekly basis to ensure that young people remain on a traineeship, or in education and would be dependent on satisfactory attendance

and monitoring. The allowance could be paid in cash and would help to enable young people who are living independently to be economically viable. Alternatively, where young people are attending an education course the incentive could be provided in the form of book tokens etc. Consultation with the young person should be undertaken to ascertain their preference.

Where young people undertake a traineeship the training provider will provide an allowance. If social services or social work departments provide an incentive of say £10 per week and the young person remains on the traineeship, social services or social work departments will make a saving as in any circumstance social services or social work departments must provide a minimum income per week regardless of whether the young person is in education, training or employment.

To ensure that incentives are fair and do not cease when the young person reaches their 18th birthday a sliding scale of reductions would need to be adopted, or payments should cease when a pre-determined income is achieved.

Other education costs

Costs associated with education, training and employment is a priority area in both the Quality Protects framework and the Children (Leaving Care) Act 2000. All costs should therefore be linked into the young person's assessment of need and linked into the pathway plan. Allowances should be in line with those associated with acting as a 'reasonable parent'. A schedule of items and allowances should be developed that covers specific grants for books, course equipment etc.

Travel

The provision of free travel passes for the local area would have many benefits and should be provided to all Eligible, Relevant and Former Relevant young people, at least until the age of nineteen. These would have benefits in promoting:

- Access to education, training and employment.
- Maintaining and promoting family and social networks.

- Encouraging access to leisure services.
- Enabling young people to access leaving care support and drop-in services.
- Enabling access to community based support services in the London area.

Clothing

It is important to ensure that young people who are moving to independence are fully provided with the clothes they need for general living, educational needs, training needs and employment needs. From the point of independence until the young person's 18th birthday a clothing allowance could be provided in a variety of ways:

- A weekly, monthly or half yearly allowance.
- Developing a system to ensure that each young person has adequate clothing for general living and their educational, training and employment needs.
- The provision of emergency clothing grants for crisis situations.

Birthday and Christmas allowances

Social services or social work departments should decide whether they will provide these allowances and at what age they should cease.

Leisure, hobby and other needs

Social services or social work departments should decide on leisure allowances and priorities. These could be linked to free leisure passes or activities undertaken with a personal advisor aimed at extending social and community links.

Social services/social work departments should, with few exceptions, fund all items related to the following areas, or ensure that young people gain access to their assessed need:

- maternity allowances and child care costs
- counselling or therapeutic needs
- special needs
- health needs

Emergency payments

Emergency payments should be provided to alleviate a particular crisis or where a young

person has no other immediate access to cash payments.

These should link to an immediate assessment of need and be provided on a one off basis. Where appropriate, the young person's personal advisor should then undertake work on addressing the issue that caused the crisis. Where payments are requested on a regular basis they will need to be linked to long-term work on budgeting and money management. Emergency payments could be provided in the form of food parcels and/or by providing credit on utility accounts.

The above issues in the main apply to Relevant young people up to the age of 18. With the exception of the setting up home allowances and deposits, the majority of issues in the following section will apply to Former Relevant young people.

Allowances for Former Relevant Young People

Setting up home allowance

As a minimum standard each young person should be allotted a reasonable sum to be used over a period of time as they move from a semi-independent option to an independent one. For example, certain items should be purchased on moving into a semi-independent accommodation and further items purchased on moving into permanent accommodation. This amount represents an approximate minimum required to equip a studio, or one bedroom flat with mainly second-hand items. Young people should always be given practical assistance in deciding what they need and in purchasing items. Personal advisors or carers should always purchase items with young people. Receipts and copies of receipts should be retained so that expenditure can be accounted for, VAT can be reclaimed and, if necessary, faulty goods can be returned.

As good corporate parents social services or social work departments should provide all young people with their initial television licence when they become independent, paid for out of their allotted home allowance. Personal advisors should help with the budgeting for future licences by encouraging the purchasing of television licence stamps for example.

In order to ensure that all young people are treated fairly and equitably an agreed set of items should be established. The items acquired by each young person should reflect their different needs and preferences and their type of accommodation i.e. supported lodgings, hostel or unfurnished flat. The financial allowance should be available in cash form and spent by the personal advisor or leaving care worker or carer, in conjunction with the young person. This would enable the young person to have more choice on how their money is spent and make the process easier for the personal advisor or carer. The key principal being, that young people are provided with all the items necessary for independent living. See Appendix 3 for a list of setting up home items.

Young people from age fifteen, their families and where appropriate, carers should be encouraged to acquire over a period of time, those items that are necessary for independent living. Where young people have bought their own items they should not subsequently lose out by receiving a lower allowance but be able to use this to buy a small number of new items rather than numerous second-hand ones.

In addition to receiving the setting up home allowance, young people who move into the private sector will often need to pay a deposit and rent in advance. This should not be paid out of, or counted as part of their allotted setting up home allowance. Care leavers are exempt from the Single Room Rent Restriction up to age 22 and can therefore claim higher levels of housing benefit. Before young people move into the private sector a Pre-Tenancy Determination must be undertaken to ensure that Housing Benefit will cover the level of rent.

Higher education protocol

The Act requires the development of a specific higher education financial protocol. The protocol should provide clarity with regard to:

- The levels of financial support available during term time for university students.
- The level of support available during the Christmas, Easter and Summer vacations.
- The level of support available to foster carers if they are able to offer their previously

fostered young people the opportunity to return to them during vacations.
- Support to enable young people to apply for:
  - University access funds
  - Student loans
  - Tuition fee exemption

Further education protocol

The Act is less prescriptive in relation to the support to be provided to young people in further education. The support to this group of young people should link to the duty to provide general assistance with education, training and employment. The Act specifies a duty to provide vacation accommodation for those young people attending residential further education courses.

General allowances and payments

Social services/social work departments should produce a written schedule of general allowances and payments that are available to Former Relevant young people. The schedule should also define the circumstances that will trigger payments.

Emergency payments

Social services/social work departments should specify the level and circumstances that will trigger emergency payments to Former Relevant young people.

Systems of Payment and Verification

As part of preparation for independence, it may be appropriate to consider encouraging all young people to open a bank account by the time they leave school, or by the end of year eleven. Allowances should be paid into the bank account and personal advisors should provide help and support with managing the account and budgeting. Accounts without credit facilities should be encouraged.

Where young people have difficulty budgeting and have chaotic life styles it will be necessary to develop systems to provide payments in cash. In such circumstances personal advisors may need to give guidance and assistance to ensure that young people are able to manage their finances.

Assistance should always be given when purchasing large items and when young people need support with managing money.

A crucial process that must be established is to ensure that all 'looked after' young people are in receipt of their National Insurance number by their 16th birthday. There must be a standardised procedure whereby social services/social work departments apply to the New Registrations Department (form CA 353 OU) for each young person's number when they reach age 15 and ten months.

It is important that procedures and forms are developed to monitor and audit payments to young people.

It is vital that procedures are developed with the benefits agencies to verify care leavers' eligibility for benefits. These will need to commence at least two months before a young person's eighteenth birthday in order that claims are operating by that date. Social services/social work departments will need to continue to provide allowances until payments from the benefits agencies are established (see attached letter).

Payments made under Section 17 and Section 24 of the Children Act 1989 and Section 23C of the Children (Leaving Care) Act 2000 are not counted as income when calculating benefit entitlement.

Personal advisors will need to complete the appropriate form in order to ensure Relevant, and where appropriate Former Relevant young people can access dental treatment, free prescriptions etc.

Information on Financial Arrangements

To ensure that all new financial procedures and protocols are adopted and understood, a programme of dissemination should be undertaken to include all social services/social work departments staff, carers and staff in partner agencies. User-friendly leaflets, information and a guide to financial allowances should be produced to inform young people of their rights, choices and new developments.

It is important to provide information to young people from the age of fifteen in order to be fully informed of their future options and rights.

Information provided at this stage should avoid disputes when the young person reaches age 16, as they will be more aware of their rights and responsibilities.

A dispute procedure must be developed in relation to the financial arrangements that contain a 14 day informal resolution period.

As a result of training courses I have provided on the new Act for numerous authorities and, through listening to concerns at regional leaving care forums and meetings, it is apparent that the degree of financial support remains a key issue.

Whilst each area needs to reflect local circumstances and, therefore, set its own priority funding items (as defined in the Act) and levels of financial support, the degree of variability remains immense. For example, the level of the leaving care grant/setting up home allowance varies between less than £500 to more than £1400 across neighbouring authorities in the South East. Additionally, there is little clarity regarding what the allowance covers, such as whether it is for television licences, deposits and rent in advance or, solely for furniture and household items. From work I have previously undertaken I estimate that at the present time, the minimum amount required in establishing a new home is £1000 plus. Even this sum would not allow for flexibility where a young person is allocated accommodation that requires carpets, curtain rails, a cooker and other essential items.

In addition, many authorities have developed examples of good practice in relation to supporting young people attending higher and further education courses, and are providing good financial packages. However, these authorities report that as numbers rise each year, and as young people will remain on courses for several years, budget pressures will increase and the level of support to individual young people may have to be scaled down.

Conclusion

The information provided in this chapter is intended for guidance only and, does not provide an exhaustive list of issues that need to be addressed when developing financial arrangements for care leavers. The provision of clear information for staff, carers and young people about the arrangements is vital. This information is necessary in order that assessments and a young person's plans can reflect levels of support and services that they can expect. Such information may influence potential and future opportunities for the care leaver.

Appendix 1: Who is Affected?

Eligible children	Children aged 16 and 17 who have been looked after for at least 13 weeks since the age of 14 and who are still looked-after.
Relevant children	Children aged 16 and 17 who have been looked after for at least 13 weeks and who have left care.
Former relevant children	Young people aged 18-21 who have been either *eligible* or *relevant children*, or both. If at the age of 21 the young person is still being helped by his responsible authority with education or training, he remains a *former relevant child* to the end of the agreed programme of education or training even if that takes him past the age of 21.
Qualifying children and young people over 16	Section 24 (1): Any young person aged under 21 (under 24 if in education or training) who ceases to be looked after or accommodated in a variety of other settings, or privately fostered, after the age of 16.
Responsible authority	Section 23A (4): The council which last looked after the child or young person.

Appendix 2: Who Gets What?

Eligible children	• All the provisions of the looked-after system. • Personal adviser Part II Schedule 2 paragraph 19c. • Needs assessment Part II Schedule 2 paragraph 19B(4). • Pathway Plan Part II Schedule 2 paragraph 19B(4) and (5).
Relevant children	• Personal adviser Section 23B(3). • Pathway Plan Section 23B(3) and (4). • Accommodation and maintenance Section 23B(8). • Assistance to achieve the goals (eg educational goals) agreed and set out in the Pathway Plan Section 23B(8). • The responsible authority must keep in touch Section 23B(11).
Former relevant children	• The responsible authority must keep in touch Section 23C(2). • Personal adviser Section 23C(3). • Assistance with employment Section 23C(4)(a). • Assistance in general Section 23C(4)c. • Vacation accommodation for higher education or residential further education if needed Section 23C(9).
Qualifying children and young people over 16	• The same benefits as under section 24 before amendment Section 24A and 24B. In addition, • The responsible authority must keep in touch as they think appropriate in order to discharge their functions under sections 24A and 24B Section 24(4). • Care leavers are entitled to assistance with education and training up to the age of 24 Section 24B(3). • Care leavers are entitled to vacation accommodation for Higher Education courses or residential Further Education courses if necessary Section 24B(5).

Appendix 3: Setting up Home Allowance

Suggested list of basic equipment

Furniture

bed	settee	table and chairs
chest of drawers	shelving	television
coffee table	stereo system	wardrobe

Kitchen and household

alarm clock	iron	toaster
cleaning equipment (mop, bucket etc.)	ironing board	vacuum cleaner
cooker	kettle	washer
crockery	kitchen equipment (bowl, drainer etc.)	television licence
cutlery	paint and wallpaper	contents insurance
fridge	pans	

Linen and soft furnishings

carpets	duvet	pillows
curtain tracks	duvet covers × 2	sheets × 2
curtains	lamp shades	towels

21. The Role of the Connexions Service

The Connexions Strategy Team

This chapter aims to demonstrate and discuss the role Connexions can play in improving the lives and aspirations of young people, particularly those that are at high risk of social exclusion. Of course, one such group of young people are care leavers. Initially, it is helpful to discuss the aims and key principles behind the Connexions service, and the role of the personal advisor.

What is Connexions?

The Connexions Service is intended to bring together the range of services working with young people to ensure all 13–19-year-olds in England are provided with integrated information, advice, guidance and access to personal development. It aims to help young people engage in learning, make a smooth transition to adult and working life and achieve their full potential. The support offered to young people will vary according to their needs, but will aim to respond to early signs of social exclusion and prevent escalation of adverse circumstances.

How is Connexions organised?

Connexions Partnerships are responsible for providing the service. The partnerships share boundaries with the 47 local Learning and Skills Councils, and will be responsible for planning the service while delivery will be organised by local management committees, covering the same areas as local authorities. In this way, the particular needs of an area can be targeted by those with intimate knowledge of the problems young people face in the locality.

In September 2001, we extended the Connexions service to three new areas. This is in addition to the 12 areas where partnerships were established in April 2001 (For a full area list of the Connexions Partnerships, see Annex A). The service will be available nationally by 2003. Connexions Direct was also launched in September 2001, piloting a phone and Internet based service in the North East to help provide an alternative route for young people to get the support and guidance they require.

How can Connexions make a difference?

Connexions Partnerships are multi-agency bodies comprising a range of partners such as local education authorities (LEAs), careers services, youth offending teams (YOTs), social services departments (SSDs), health bodies and voluntary sector agencies. Partnerships will need to develop a strategy, and policies for collaborative working across these agencies, so that the identified needs of the young people are addressed.

Young people will be given access to a personal advisor. The personal advisor will be able to offer support and guidance to the young person as a single point of contact, brokering specialist support as required. By developing the service across organisational boundaries, with the focus on the young person, Connexions will help to develop consistency in the support young people receive, based on a shared understanding of their needs, and will help to strengthen the links between agencies.

The Connexions Key Principles

- **Raising aspirations** – setting high expectations of every individual.
- **Meeting individual need** – and overcoming barriers to learning.
- **Taking account of the views of young people** – individually and collectively.
- **Inclusion** – keeping young people in mainstream education and training and preventing them moving to the margins of their community.
- **Partnership** – agencies collaborating to achieve more for young people, parents and communities than agencies working in isolation.

- **Community involvement and neighbourhood renewal** – through involvement of community mentors and through personal advisors brokering access to local welfare, health, arts, sport and guidance networks.
- **Extending opportunity and equality of opportunity** – raising participation and achievement levels for all young people, influencing the availability, suitability and quality of provision and raising awareness of opportunities.
- **Evidence based practice** – ensuring that new interventions are based on rigorous research and evaluation into what works.

The Role of the Connexions Personal Advisor

The Connexions personal advisor will be central to the Connexions Service. All young people will have access to a personal advisor whose aim will be to ensure that the needs of individual young people are met so that they are able and motivated to engage in education, training and work opportunities to achieve their full potential.

The personal advisor's role may include any or all of the following elements (also see Figure 1):

- Engaging with young people to identify and address their needs, offering information, advice and guidance on learning and career options and personal development opportunities, with a view to raising the aspirations of each young person.
- Utilising and supporting education and training institutions and employees in meeting the needs of young people.
- Working with a network of voluntary, statutory and community agencies, and commercial bodies to ensure a coherent approach to support for the young person.
- Working with parents, carers and families to support young people.
- Managing information effectively to facilitate the process of meeting the needs of young people.
- Reviewing and reflecting upon their own professional practice to achieve continuous improvement.

Where will these Personal Advisors Come from?

The work of the Connexions personal advisor can be split into direct work with young people and brokerage of services. The balance between direct work and brokerage will depend on both the skills and knowledge of the personal advisor and the needs of the particular young person. Hence, **Connexions personal advisors may come from many different backgrounds or participating agencies**. Personal advisors may be directly employed by the Connexions Service, seconded to the service, or remain within their existing professional context, working under a Partnership Agreement with the Connexions Service. A Connexions personal advisor will be identified for each young person taking into account the views of the young person and the skills and background the advisor will require to best address the young person's needs and circumstances.

In this way, many staff in existing agencies will be able to operate as personal advisors, offering a coherent, rounded service to young people under the Connexions 'umbrella', whilst still being employed by the same organisation.

Those attending the 'Understanding Connexions' and 'Diploma for Connexions personal advisors' training courses have been found to have backgrounds including the careers service, youth service, probation service, social services and the police. Many Connexions partnerships are involving young people in the recruitment of personal advisors to ensure that the prospective personal advisors are sufficiently skilled to meet a young person's needs.

What will Happen to the Careers Service?

As the Connexions Service rolls out, it will take over from careers service companies providing careers information, education and guidance to young people. Information and guidance on learning and career options is central to Connexions. This must deal with choice of Key Stage 4 options, including vocational and academic pathways, the implications of

Brokerage

School/college/trainer provider

- Sharing evidence based practice
- Securing improved responses to young people - enhanced resources for young people
- Contributing to SEN/gifted and talented/curriculum/work experience practice/personal social and health education/careers education/citizenship

Planning and working with other agencies

- Working to appropriate protocols
- Advocacy

Informal and community networks

- Enabling access to community resources
- Securing participation in personal development programmes - leisure/arts/sport
- Promoting involvement in volunteering and peer mentoring
- Developing access to community mentor

Direct Work

Assessment

- Responding to self-referrals and professional referrals
- Comprehensive information gathering
- Using connections assessment framework
- Anticipating likely level of need - information/support and guidance/specialist referral

Personal adviser

Planning and intervention

- Engaging young people
- Working to agree the nature of the key issues
- Negotiating/determining a plan for change
- Individual and group work
- Information, advice, guidance
- Referral to other connections services

Review

- Tracking young people
- Monitoring progress against plans
- Refining plans
- Gathering outcome information (including feedback from young people and parents/carers)
- Reviewing outcomes to inform evidence-based practice
- Ensuring appropriate management information

Planning and working with parents/carers

- Encouraging parental involvement in school/college
- Mediating/home visits
- Signposting

Figure 1. The role and functions of the personal adviser

disapplication of the curriculum, post-16 choices, and higher education (HE) or further learning, including better ways to help young people to gain skills and qualifications by the age of 19. Work should be tailored to individual need, building on the lessons of work experience and development activities, and using careers information materials, group discussions, one-to-one interviews and ongoing support from a Connexions personal advisor as appropriate. Many parents, colleges, training providers, employers, schools and young people themselves seek improved guidance in the face of a rapidly changing jobs and learning market. Connexions will provide this.

What is the Relationship Between Connexions and the Youth Service?

The relationship between the Connexions Service and the youth service is fundamental to the success of Connexions and in making a real difference to young people's lives either on a one-to-one basis or through group activities. The youth service, both statutory and voluntary sector, already perform a range of valuable support functions for young people, and often undertake excellent outreach and personal advisor work. They will make an important contribution to the wider work of the Connexions Service. As part of their contribution to the Service, local authorities will be expected to plan, manage and deliver all their 13–19 youth work as part of a joint working agreement between the youth service and the Connexions Partnership. But, when devoting resources to the Connexions Service, it will also be important that local authorities preserve the wider work of youth services in their areas, and that these activities are integrated with the Connexions Service. Such work includes centre based and residential activities with groups of young people, and that provided by voluntary organisations with local authority funding – for instance motivation and outward bound work. The Connexions Service will have an important role in ensuring that all youth service activity is effectively co-ordinated, coherent, and that gaps in provision are filled.

Connexions Funding and Resources

The Connexions Service is funded from three sources:

- National grant from the Connexions Service National Unit. This includes the current Careers Service and New Start budgets, and the additional funding which has been made available in the Government Spending Review 2000. This amounts to £320m in 2001–02 and £420m in 2002–03.
- Existing resources that are devoted to youth support and guidance activities at local level. For example, we expect Connexions Partnerships to bring together relevant aspects of the work of local authority youth services, education welfare services, youth offending teams and quality protects (particularly services to care leavers). We expect their business plans to set out the contribution that each can make to delivery. Funding for these services will therefore form part of the overall resources that are available at a local level. Partners are not necessarily expected to transfer staff or money to the Connexions Partnership, unless they agree that it would be helpful to do so. Rather, they are asked to identify the work that they do that will *also* help to deliver the goals of the Connexions Service, and to make sure that this is co-ordinated effectively to ensure that young people receive a seamless service.
- Regional European Social Fund money.

What Connexions will Offer Young People

Every young person aged 13–19 can expect help from the service with the aim of ensuring a smooth transition to adulthood and help them reach their full potential, delivered primarily through a personal advisor. The service will be fully inclusive but differentiated according to the varying needs of young people, and will take account of how these needs may change over time.

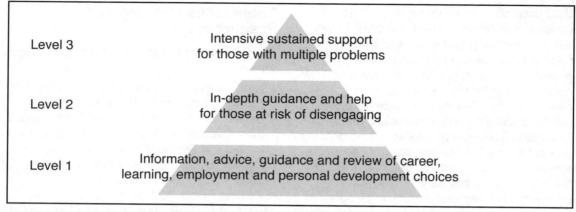

Figure 2. Broad levels of personal adviser intervention

There will be three broad levels of service according to young people's need:

1. All young people will receive information, advice and guidance on careers, learning, personal development and other issues and opportunities.
2. Those people at risk of disengaging from learning will receive more in-depth one-to-one support along with a full assessment of their needs. The personal advisor will develop an action plan with the young person to address the underlying factors, such as problems at home and school, and ensure their continued engagement in learning.
3. For those facing multiple problems, such as drug, mental health or housing problems, the role of the personal advisor will be to broker access to specialist support as necessary and ensure a co-ordinated approach to supporting the young person across agencies so that the young person receives the more intensive support they need.

Connexions Partnerships have particular responsibilities in the area of assessment and planning for young people with learning difficulties or disabilities, which includes special educational needs (SEN). These responsibilities will be discharged through the personal advisor. For young people with statements of special educational needs, the Connexions personal advisor will have an important role in the development and implementation of Transition Plans governed by the SEN Code of Practice.

The Connexions Service will also be required to arrange assessment for those with learning difficulties and/or disabilities in the last year of compulsory schooling who intend to continue learning. To build on this, the Connexions Service will, in partnership with local agencies, continue to support this group of young people up to their 25th birthday if they are not ready to access the adult services provided locally. Full guidance on Connexions and young people with learning disabilities can be found on the Connexions website at *www.connexions.gov.uk*

Access to the Connexions Service

The Connexions Service will have a strong base in schools and further education colleges. However, the Connexions Service must be available to every young person, including those who are not in education, employment or training. To address this, the Connexions Service will have outreach and drop-in centres.

Access to the service will be by a variety of routes:

- **Self-referral** – for example in school or college, at or Connexions centres, via training providers, through the youth service and other informal settings, over the phone or in time over the web (Connexions Direct).
- **Parental or carer referral** – parents or carers may well make the initial contact with Connexions, having been informed about the service by the school or college or by publicity.

- **Professional referral** – *either*:
  - –Referral where a young person is in formal or informal learning, and where the school/college/training provider/youth worker will have to make a judgement about who is referred to Connexions.

  or

  - –Referral where a young person is not in learning. Such a young person should always be considered a priority client and may be referred by any agency that is in contact with the young person (including health services, YOTs etc.).

As we have discussed, the key behind the success of Connexions is *partnership*. Single agencies cannot provide a seamless service for all young people themselves. But by working closely at *all stages* (planning, implementation and evaluation) with a Connexions Partnership, agencies and their staff can be confident that the young people in their local area are being supported throughout the transition from adolescence to adulthood and are being provided with the opportunity to fulfil their potential. By bringing together all these resources and skills, Connexions will make a difference.

Connexions and Social Services

We have issued a series of guidance notes that set out principles of joint working between Connexions and important partners. Of particular interest to the reader may be '*Working Together – Connexions and Social Services*'; see this document for further details about this vital relationship, which we have outlined in the following section (For details of how to obtain these guidance notes, see Annex B).

Connexions Partnerships will need to work closely with existing services to ensure that the young person receives a coherent service. The way to do this will differ according to the young person's views, local circumstances and provision, but there are some principles that underpin successful, joined-up working:

- The Connexions Service should not duplicate or replace the work of existing agencies, but should build on, and work closely with, existing services to ensure that resources are used to best effect, and there is more

cohesive service planning and delivery for 13–19-year-olds, both as a group and for individuals.

- The most appropriate worker should be identified to lead the young person's case management and ensure that the roles of different agencies are clearly agreed and followed (thus in effect acting as the young person's Connexions personal advisor), drawing on all the resources available through different routes. Where a child's name has been placed on the child protection register or the child is looked after, the social services department will have lead responsibility for implementing and reviewing the child's plan. There are a number of issues that should be considered when deciding on the respective roles of individuals working with a young person. These include:
  - –The views and wishes of the young person.
  - –Any transition points in the young person's life so that the worker assigned to the young person will be able to provide consistency during these transitions.
  - –Clear identification by all workers of the relevant statutory responsibilities and who is fulfilling which roles, including the case management and referrals to other agencies.
  - –The relative skills and experience of the individual workers.

- The number of other professionals working directly with the young person should be rationalised, to avoid confusion or duplication from the young person's point of view and to stop them being passed between agencies unnecessarily. For example, by a personal advisor getting advice from a specialist colleague where appropriate, rather than automatically making a referral. Where specialist intervention is required, the personal advisor will need to ensure clearly differentiated roles are agreed between workers. Awareness and understanding of one another's roles should be developed between support workers, for example, through joint training, meetings, secondments, exchanges or using shared/adjoining premises.

- Young people receive continuity and consistency of support and professional boundaries do not impair the support the young person receives. Referrals to specialist advice and key transitions should be managed in as supportive a way as possible.

- Information about young people needs to be managed and shared (with the young person's consent) and a dialogue maintained, to ensure that repeat assessment of the young person is avoided and an overview of their needs is maintained over time and across agencies, ensuring that the young person does not fall through gaps. It is essential to seek the young person's consent to share information, except where sharing information may place the young person at an increased risk of significant harm, in which case information may be shared without the young person's consent. In addition to seeking consent from young people it may also sometimes be necessary to seek the consent of parents or others.

- There should be co-ordinated, complementary accountability and quality assurance arrangements to ensure each young person can be sure they will receive all of the support they need.

Young Person's Advisor and Connexions

The Children (Leaving Care) Act 2000 requires the responsible authority to arrange for each 'eligible', 'relevant' and 'former relevant' child to have a personal advisor. The appointment of a personal advisor to these young people is therefore a statutory requirement. This emphasises the importance of the role and reflects the belief that young people living in and leaving care should be able to identify someone as committed to their well-being and development on a long-term basis. The local authority can either provide these services themselves or subcontract them, for example, to a voluntary organisation or to Connexions.

As the role of the young person's advisor, appointed by the local authority for the purposes of the Children (Leaving Care) Act, will be very similar to that of the Connexions personal advisor, it is expected that the young person's advisor will normally also act as the young person's Connexions personal advisor.

Whoever takes on the role of the young person's advisor will need a thorough understanding of the new legislation and the powers and duties of local authorities to young people under these circumstances, as well as being familiar with the Connexions Service. For the introductory years (i.e. up to March 2004) of the Children (Leaving Care) Act 2000, local authorities will receive a specific grant ring-fenced for implementation of the Act, including provision of young persons' advisors. Authorities can add to their ring-fenced grant from other resources available to them. The local authority will be able to make decisions locally on how best to use its leaving care grant to provide the young person's advisor service in the light of local circumstances, the composition of the local Connexions partnership, and the needs of the individual young people.

A case scenario for a Young Person's Advisor becoming the Connexions personal advisor is set out later.

If the Connexions personal advisor understands the requirements and workings of the care system and the Children Act, they would be well placed to continue to advise the young person. They could therefore fulfil the role of the young person's advisor as well as Connexions personal advisor, with the work of the young person's advisor being subcontracted to Connexions. In this situation the Connexions personal advisor will need to be in close contact with the leaving care team to receive support and supervision over the preparation and implementation of the pathway plan. In addition, arrangements will need to be put in place for a possible transition at the young person's 20th birthday, as the young person moves out of the Connexions Service remit, but will still be entitled to support under the Children (Leaving Care) Act 2000, unless the work is subcontracted to the Connexions Service. In this case the Connexions personal advisor could continue to act as the young person's advisor until the young person reaches the age of 21, or for longer if they remain in an agreed programme of education past this age.

The pathway plan prepared by the young person's advisor fulfils the function of the young person's personal action plan under the

Connexions Assessment, Planning, Implementation and Review (APIR) guidelines. Further assessment and planning by a Connexions personal advisor would be unnecessary.

Conclusions

- Full and effective partnership is vital in order to provide a full support service to young people leaving care. Connexions will put in place integrated needs mapping, service planning and delivery structures for all 13–19-year-olds.
- Connexions will ensure that young people are allocated a personal advisor without duplication of effort. For care leavers, their young person's advisor appointed by the local authority under the Children (Leaving Care) Act 2000 will usually be their Connexions personal advisor. However, in this, as in all contexts, the young person's views, their relationships with existing workers, their needs and the specialist skills of the potential advisors will be considered when appointing the individual personal advisor.
- The support network developed by the Connexions partnership will make it easier for care workers to supply young people with all the information and support they need.

Case Scenario – Natalie

Background

Natalie has been in care since she was a small child, is completely estranged from her family and subject to a care order. She is approaching her 16th birthday and has been living in a local authority children's home for a year since her last foster placement broke down. Natalie was excluded from school at around the time that her foster placement broke down.

Current situation

Natalie was reintroduced into school in a new secondary school about 6 months ago at the end of the last academic year and has settled well. She is in Year 10 due to the amount of school time she has missed. Natalie has been in

contact with her Connexions personal advisor at school and has begun to trust him.

Issues

- Natalie feels she is ready to live alone, but residential staff are concerned about her ability to cope in independent living at such a young age.
- When she reaches 16 Natalie will be an eligible child under the Children (Leaving Care) Act 2000 and the local authority which has been looking after her will have a duty to provide her with a young person's advisor and a pathway plan.
- There are concerns about Natalie's health needs – she has recently started going out with an older boy and may be sexually active.
- Natalie could leave school at the end of the academic year, but staff at the children's home are keen that she should complete year 11.

Process followed

Natalie's social worker convenes a review of her care plan as Natalie is approaching 16 and her responsible authority has a specialist leaving care team which deals with all cases of young people aged 16 and over. This review begins the process of the statutory needs assessment that will form the basis of her pathway plan from her 16th birthday. The review will deal with the question of who is to be Natalie's young person's advisor under the Children (Leaving Care) Act. The review is attended by Natalie's Connexions personal advisor, a social worker from the leaving care team, and staff from the children's home.

Outcomes of the review meeting

The school Connexions personal advisor does not have the understanding of the requirements of the Children Act and the local procedures for planning for young people who are looked after and is therefore not able to take on the role of the young person's advisor. Therefore at the meeting it is agreed with Natalie that her responsible local authority will appoint a young person's advisor. The young person's advisor will work with her to draw up her pathway plan (drawing on her existing care plan and incorporating her personal education plan) and on independent living skills drawing on the Connexions Service at school to help address her education and training needs. Natalie's young person's advisor will also be able to broker access for her to other services, particularly health services.

Annex A – Areas covered by Connexions Partnerships

The Connexions Service has been piloted in different forms around the country. Twelve Phase 1 areas (listed below) began delivering the service in April 2001.

- The Black Country
- Cheshire and Warrington
- Coventry and Warwickshire
- Cumbria
- Devon & Cornwall
- Lincolnshire & Rutland
- London North
- London South
- Milton Keynes, Oxfordshire and Buckinghamshire
- Shropshire, Telford and the Wrekin
- South Yorkshire
- West of England

Three further Phase 1 areas started to deliver the service in September 2001. The remaining 32 Partnerships will begin Phase 2 delivery by 2003.

- Suffolk
- Greater Merseyside
- Humber

Annex B – Connexions publications

Further copies of Connexions publications can be obtained from DfES publications. Please quote the relevant reference number when ordering.

'Working together – Connexions and Social Services' – CXSS

'Working together – Connexions and Teenage Pregnancy' – CXTP

'Working together – Connexions and Youth Justice Services' – CXYJ

'Working together – Connexions and Homelessness Agencies' – CXHA

N.B. A summary definition of terms used in the Children (Leaving Care) Act 2000 are contained in Section 1, Chapter 2.

Section 4 – Conclusions

Ann Wheal

The aim of this chapter is to highlight some of the recurring themes from the book and to look at ways to ensure that in the future

> ... *aftercare is not afterthought* ...
> John Pinkerton, Chapter 4.

There should be a service that will meet the needs of all young people who leave, or have left, the care service regardless of their race, creed, disability, sexual orientation or political status which will enable them to take their rightful place as active citizens in society. However, equally important, and some would say more important, is the preparation young people receive before they leave the care system, in other words, for aftercare to be effective, throughcare work must be excellent.

From the original concept of this book, the idea has always been to find ways to help care leavers to live happy and fulfilled lives and for them to become full players in the society in which they live. In order to do this they must, as with other young people, be involved in the decisions that affect them, both whilst in care and when they leave care.

In 2001 the University of Southampton ran a fully residential 6-day Summer School for young people from inner city areas who might not normally go to university. The aim of the summer school is to give these young people a taster of university life and to let them see what is possible for them.

Following a pilot scheme, the University offered in 2001, additional places at the Summer School for care leavers to provide them with the same opportunities as other young people. Within these places, facilities and accommodation were available for anyone with a disability. We arranged funding so money was not an issue. Eventually 35 places were unfilled. The vast majority of the care leavers who attended had a wonderful time, the few who did not enjoy the taster, soon realised that university was not for them – an equally important experience.

> ... *for ... it was a life changing experience.*
> Leaving care worker.

> *I felt I could walk along the road and hold my head up high.*
> Care leaver.

> *if it takes me until I'm 40, I'm going to get to university. I don't want to be just another statistic – an unemployed single parent.*
> Care leaver.

> *Thank you for helping me. I feel so much more confident now.*
> Care leaver.

Confidential records were kept by the University administrators on all care leavers. Access to this information was available on a 'need to know' basis only, so that the care leavers were treated as 'summer school student' rather than as care leavers. In the event, this information was needed on only two occasions during the six days of the summer school. However, many care leavers chose to tell their groups of their status. As one colleague noted:

> ... *they (care leavers) seem to bring with them a lot of baggage about being a care leaver. It is almost as though they are used to being treated differently from other young people so expect it, which is a pity.*
> University lecturer.

So what is the relevance of the summer school information?

The relevance is, that all the different agencies are meant to be working together and there is much debate in the book about this 'joined-up' approach. However, in the case of the summer school, for example, the different agencies all thought it was the other agency's job to help the young person to apply for the summer school when in fact no-one was doing it. This meant that 35 places were lost to other young people who might have attended and benefited from the experience. Ciaran Kelly in his mental health chapter notes that for inter-agency working to be effective it must be clear as to who is doing what, for whom, how and by when. Incidentally, there was also a direct correlation between the amount of benefit the care leaver enjoyed from their time at the summer school and the amount of preparation they were given before attending. The importance of effective inter-agency working and the need for preparation in all aspects of a care leaver's life is imperative.

Another example of the 'baggage' mentioned in the above quotation, but in reverse, was a young person who was absolutely furious that the Head of her college had called her in and said that she didn't have to take part in a fund raising event if she didn't want. The Head had assumed that as she was a care leaver she might not be able to afford it or want to do it.

These two examples beg the question, 'Do people need to know about the care experience of the people concerned?' Should they know? What difference does it make? Why did many young people at the summer school choose to tell everyone? Did they feel it necessary or were they so used to doing it that they thought nothing of it? I am sure it wasn't told as an excuse, or a reason for not being as good as other young people and especially not to try to get better treatment. Asylum seekers, young people with special needs, young offenders are other examples of labels that stick and make the care leaving experience doubly difficult for the young people concerned. Clearly there is a need for a far reaching debate around the whole question of labelling and how to avoid the stigma of having been in care.

I can be who I like at work. No-body knows I've been in care or where I've come from.
                                        Care leaver.

Confidentiality is another area that causes young people a good deal of concern and where clear national guidelines should be produced and followed once a serious debate has occurred which must include young people.

In Chapter 11 Keir Parsons notes that under the new Act local authorities are required to provide accommodation during the vacation if a care leaver is studying in higher education. In reality this is fraught with difficulties. For example, one young person had a flat in his local area. When he went to university he was undecided as to whether to give up the flat or not. If he gave it up he had nowhere to store his possessions and would have had nowhere to go for the vacations. If he kept it on it was empty for most of the time and might have been broken in to, become damp or been vandalised. He would also have had to continue paying the rent. As one leaving care team manager said:

... this part of the Act has clearly not been thought through. In reality in this area (inner city) we haven't had any care leavers move away to go to college or university. It's not that they don't want to go, it's because they don't want to have to give up their flat, especially if they have worked hard to make it a home and they certainly don't want to live in a B & B during the holidays.

... a point confirmed by Mohamed in the Introduction.

On the question of higher education, Mark Ellis, again in the introduction, discusses the successes of the care leavers with whom he has worked. However, John Short (Chapter 20) gives a note of caution about allowances for higher education and notes the wide variables in the amount of allowances paid across the country. He points out that even the local authorities who are paying a fair allowance to a young person who is studying for a degree may have difficulty in continuing with the same rate of allowance if the numbers increase in the future as expected.

Another point on payment is the practise of paying young people a sum of money in order to get them to attend college. Anyone who has any knowledge of motivational theories will know that motivation by financial reward only works for a limited amount of time. These payments do not appear to have any relationship to success at college or learning new skills. At present, it seems that going to college is being used as a way of keeping a young person off the streets and out of trouble rather than encouraging them to improve their education.

John Pinkerton (Chapter 4) sets out a suggested framework looking at the idea of a *care career* with its focus on the components of *time periods and key decisions*. He suggests that this would provide a structure to help in the production of comparable, detailed descriptions of practice that could usefully be considered against criteria based on global best practice. These might be:

- Measurement around the assessment, planning, implementation and review process.
- Relevant informal and formal support networks.
- Material and psycho social needs being addressed.
- Young people being actively involved and consulted throughout.

This notion would seem to have merit for all care leavers. The dictionary definition of 'career' is 'progress through life' that implies on-going decisions. At the start of a care career, a system should be in place that would look at all aspects of a young person's life, including moving from a safe environment, into independence. The following is a simple example using the suggested headings above around a wish to become an electrician after leaving school. It could be equally used for 'moving on' planning, choosing where to live or seeking sexual health advice amongst others. In fact this system could be used in any care planning, for young people in care, leaving care and for those who have left care. It is about knowing where to go, when, what will be needed, who will help or guide them, and what happens if things go wrong. It should also provide a realistic time frame. All of this could be completed on an easy to use form that could then make evaluation and monitoring a very simple task as there would be yardsticks by which measurement could be made.

'I want to be an electrician' – example
Assessment, planning, implementation and review

In order to become an electrician it will be necessary to:

- Find out what qualifications are necessary plus details of the schemes; by which date must these be achieved; when must the application be submitted. Timing for this would be before choices of subjects are made i.e. at the end of year 9 (**assessment**).
- Having established that five GSCEs are necessary, including Maths and English there is a need to work towards these (**planning**).
- Apply (with help if desired) at appropriate time for modern apprenticeship and take aptitude tests and have a medical examination.
- If successful, read agreement and get a relevant adult to read it, both to explain any points and to check that it is a reasonable agreement. Sign and return to employer. The agreement should include rates of pay, hours worked, holidays, conditions of service etc.
- (If unsuccessful discuss other options with appropriate adults).
- Obtain tools, equipment, books and clothing.
- Register on college course.
- Start work (**implementation**).
- Receive regular reviews/appraisals of progress plus advice on areas of weaknesses or for improvement – from employer, training organisation and or college tutor and make plan for changes (**reviews**).

Relevant information and formal networks

In this example, the young person would, of course, have been consulted, although the idea of being an electrician may have been suggested to them or they may have known someone who was doing the job. However, the actual decision must be theirs. All young people at this time will need help to find out information. They will also need to receive help to change their plan if they are unlikely to obtain the appropriate grades in their exams. This means that carers, social workers or leaving care teams should attend parents evenings, show an interest in progress and help them with their homework and help and support them with decisions, as most parents would.

Informal networks throughout this process might be school pals, previous carers, relevant adults, other apprentices, college chums plus other care leavers who know the difficulties of being on your own and living independently and who wish to share their experiences in order to help others.

Formal networks would be teacher, Connexions or personal advisor, training group representative, company person responsible for apprentices, college tutor, all of whom may or may not know that the young person is in, or leaving care. The young person should be consulted around the decision to 'tell' or not. All the above people would be the same regardless of circumstances. If a young person lived at home the parents or other family members would be involved but in the case of the care leaver then any or all of the following might additionally be involved – social worker, carer, leaving care team, mentor, advocate. All of these should work together to ensure that the young person knows where they can go for advice, information, support and help if things go wrong.

Everyone needs to have a caring relationship which is why stability of placement is so important to young people in care. They need someone who might go with them to an interview or even to the doctors; someone to encourage them in their education and other aspirations. They also need relationships with people outside the care system. Someone who will 'hear' what they have to say, understand their concerns and be there when needed. As Kathy McAuley says in her chapter:

> ... We therefore need to be pro-active in putting in place preventative strategies that offer genuine opportunities to looked after children/care leavers to develop positive and consistent relationships with adults; access to a range of stimulating and nurturing activities and receive support, encouragement and high expectations for the maximisation of their potential and their educational achievements.

Moira Walker in Chapter 1 highlights other people's work in this area – Gilligan, 2000, Johnson, 2000, Marsh, 1999 as well as her own work (Walker et al., 2002).

Two PhD statistics students analysed the results of the measurement tool mentioned in Chapter 17. One asked the question (about care leavers) '... so they really don't have parents?' They then both agreed how awful it would be, they couldn't bear thinking about it. One said 'I don't know how they cope – I ring my mother all the time, just for a chat and always if I have a problem. Who do they ring?'. Who do they ring? We can only conjecture as to what it is like not to have someone emotionally close to call or to visit. The importance of support networks and someone who has the time and the interest, who is at the end of a telephone line, cannot be overemphasised.

Material and psycho social needs being addressed

Material needs around leaving care are accommodation; setting up home; allowances; practical skills, not just cooking, budgeting and other personal household tasks. It is also around keeping work tools appropriately, caring for working clothes or knowing what to wear; respecting books and equipment – yet how does a young person learn these skills if kitchens or book cases are kept locked for example, as evidenced in a local children's home.

It is also important that young people learn about relationships, making and keeping friends, stickability if things go wrong, anger management, time-keeping and appropriate work behaviour – often the cause of placement breakdowns as well. A very hard lesson for many care leavers to learn when they start work, as Linda Daniel notes in her chapter:

> ... they become a very small cog in a big wheel. This contrasts painfully to what they are accustomed to. In the care system and particularly in residential placements, young people perceive themselves as having a lot of power, a lot of rights and they command a lot of attention! It is such a difficult transition.

Enjoying leisure and social activities is a very important part of leaving care, not only for meeting new people and learning new skills, but a way of learning and seeing how others behave in different circumstances and also having somewhere to go when feelings of loneliness occur (and they will).

> I think the most difficult thing is having to cook and eat all by myself, I don't think I have ever eaten alone before. And even if I have learnt how to prepare basic meals I am a very bad cook and when you have to eat it by yourself.
> Michael, young asylum seeker.

Care leavers also must have the confidence and skills to visit their GP, the sexual health or mental health clinic for example *and* to explain what is wrong or what help they need. They often have the practical knowledge but not the emotional and social skills to go with it. These are not skills that can easily be learnt in a short space of time. Staff at the Caldecott Foundation have realised this and since the end of 1999 have included preparation and planning for adulthood from the point of admission. The Caldecott Foundation may be different from main stream leaving care work, but, all the evidence from young people suggests that preparation for leaving care left to the last minute does not work.

Young people actively involved and consulted throughout

In our example above, the young person chose their career, chose their training programme within the choices available, knew how to go about achieving their goal. The support networks were also in place to endeavour to ensure success.

This example is around individual involvement relating to discussions that affect a young person's life. The other type of involvement, at a strategic level, is where young people wish to be involved in designing the services to which they have access. The second type of involvement will only work if young people feel involved at an individual level.

The First Key chapter challenges the difference in perception between consultation and involvement so clear definitions must be made and agreed. First Key also emphasise the importance of concentrating on outcomes rather than outputs otherwise young people will be disillusioned.

A point of caution here regarding consultation/involvement/participation at strategic level. We all know that some young people are naturally articulate, confident and have strong opinions. Others, with training, can become equally vociferous. We must beware of allowing these young people to be the only ones whose opinions or advice are considered. If we do, other young people will become disinterested as their voice is not being heard and the others will be in constant demand to speak at conferences, advise government ministers, attend meetings or run groups. Although this may be the easy option, it may give these young people an unrealistic view of themselves especially when later they have to get on with the rest of their life. We must also beware of tokenism in the consultation process.

There is, as never before, the opportunity to help those leaving care and those who have left care. The Leaving Care Act has put the framework in place, the Quality Protects finance should enable this to happen and the MAPS should monitor success. We have the National Care Standards Commission and a new General Social Care Council which has been set up in relation to the qualifications and training of those working in the field. We also have research that tells us where the gaps in provision are and how these might be addressed and resources targeted. Clearly there is no better time:

- To involve young people in the decisions that affect them now and in the future.
- To ensure young people are prepared physically, emotionally and practically as far as is possible long before it is time to leave the care system.
- To have support networks in place to help them.
- To provide them with information so that they know what to do and where to go if things go wrong.

However, we must be sure that the UN End of Year report commenting on '*the time it takes for political consensus on children to be translated into effective action*', does not apply to work around the Leaving Care Act and that the full implementation occurs without delay. Most importantly, we must also remember the words of Omri Shalom in Chapter 5:

> *...no two young people are going to have exactly the same circumstances, so their needs will be different, and need to be met in their individual case.*

Useful Information

British Agencies for Adoption and Fostering (BAAF) promotes public understanding of adoption and fostering; develops high standards of practice amongst child care and other professionals; provides high quality training tailored to meet specific needs; acts as an independent voice in the field of child care to inform and influence policy-makers.

Connexions Service is delivered by local Connexions partnerships who provide a modern, multi-disciplinary service to help all young people make the best start in life, reach their full potential and make a successful transition to adult and working life.

Coram Leaving Care Service (CLCS) provides accommodation, aftercare, mentoring, education and group-work services for young people in or leaving care. It has particular expertise in delivering services for pregnant young women and young mothers, has pioneered the Boys2MEN group-work project for young black men and fathers in the care system and is developing a parenting support mentoring service.

First Key is the national leaving care advisory service. It seeks to improve the lifechances of young people in and leaving care through providing services to those who themselves provide services to young people. In addition to its consultancy, training, research and project work it works closely with policy makers and politicians to advise on issues concerning care leavers.

Fostering Network (previously NFCA) has taken the lead in raising standards for the 40,000 UK young people in foster care. It is committed to seeing that their concerns are given a voice and ensuring services are developed to meet their needs. The services it provides include dedicated workers for young people, advice, mediation, information, consultancy as well as an extensive training and publications programmes.

NCH Action for Children helps those children who need it the most reach their full potential. Through some 55 projects NCH provides support to vulnerable young people and those leaving care and offers a range of services designed to enable them to make a successful transition from care to independence.

National Voice exists to make a positive change for young people in and leaving care by giving them a collective voice supported by regional forums. The aim is to support existing groups in local authorities and, to enable young people to set up their own groups who can then influence government decisions and campaign to improve the public perception of young people in and leaving care.

The Prince's Trust aims to help young people, who would not otherwise have the opportunity, to succeed. It offers a wide variety of awards and provides support, encouragement and financial assistance to enable disadvantaged young people to achieve their goals.

Voices from Care offers training, advocacy, befriending, support and advice on leaving care, benefits, housing, drugs and rights. It was set up by, and for, young people who are, or have been, looked after in Wales. All the advice and support workers have personally experienced the care system themselves as children or young people.

Voice of the Child in Care (VCC) exists to: empower young people to speak out for improvement to the quality of their lives by providing information, advice and advocacy; raising awareness of children's rights; campaigning for changes in law, policy and practice; supporting the active participation of young people; delivering high quality services; ensuring equality of opportunity and anti-discriminatory practice; and providing a link for people and agencies who aspire to good childcare practice.

Index